FARRIERY
A Complete Illustrated Guide

*A proper mode of shoeing is certainly
of more importance than the treatment of any
disease, or perhaps of all the diseases
incident to horses. The foot is a part that
we are particularly required to preserve in
health; and if this art be judiciously
employed, the foot will not be more liable
to disease than any other region.*

EDWARD COLEMAN, 1765-1839

FARRIERY

A COMPLETE ILLUSTRATED GUIDE

JOHN HICKMAN M.A., F.R.C.V.S.
Reader in Animal Surgery, University of Cambridge

J. A. ALLEN : LONDON & NEW YORK

Hickman, John
    Farriery.
    1. Horseshoeing
    I. Title
682'.1'0941   SF907   77-30059

ISBN 0-85131-228-4

Library of Congress Cat. No. 77-30059

Published in Great Britain in 1977 by
J. A. Allen & Company Limited,
1 Lower Grosvenor Place,
Buckingham Palace Road,
London SW1W 0EL
and in the United States of America in 1977 by
Sporting Books Center, Inc.,
Canaan,
N.Y. 12029.

Line drawings by John Christiansen.

Book production by Bill Ireson.

Typeset in 11/12pt Monotype Ehrhardt by
HBM Typesetting Limited, Chorley, Lancs.
Printed and bound in Great Britain by
Redwood Burn Limited,
Trowbridge, Wilts., and Esher, Surrey.

Foreword

THE Worshipful Company of Farriers has a statutory duty to maintain a high standard of competence within its craft and places the onus for the discharge of this duty on its Craft Committee. As Chairman of that body I find this book extremely welcome and most timely. For a long while the need for just such an authoritative manual has been apparent to instructor and apprentice alike. Here we have a straight-forward well-illustrated description of the recommended techniques for the preparation of the foot and for the making, fitting and nailing on of the shoe, combined with a lucid explanation of the anatomical and physiological factors that must be kept continually in mind if shoeing is to be a blessing in helping to preserve the foot and the action of the horse, rather than a curse because of the chronic locomotor disabilities likely to result from the constant repetition of unsatisfactory shoeing practices; to say nothing of the acute suffering that can be caused by an untutored hand clumsily driving a nail into the sensitive part of the foot.

The apparent simplicity of the shoeing operation can be deceptive. It is true that it is not too difficult to learn to tack a ready-made shoe on to the hoof: in the days of horsed cavalry this elementary skill was expected of a trained cavalryman in case a shoe should be cast when his troop was operating away from base; but this was regarded merely as a form of first-aid and, in the interest of the soundness of the horse and the safety of the rider, a farrier was called on to reshoe the animal at the first opportunity.

In fact, as the author plainly shows, the farrier is a skilled craftsman, capable of shoeing all types of feet, whether normal or defective; of making shoes to suit all types of work and working conditions; and of devising corrective measures to compensate for faulty limb action when this is causing brushing, over-reaching and other injuries.

In order to attain these standards of craftsmanship, first a four-year apprenticeship is served under a master-farrier; this period of practical experience is interspersed with special training courses at approved schools of farriery and culminates with a formal written and practical examination which entitles the successful candidate to register under the Farriers (Registration) Act and so become licenced to practice the trade. Then, with further experience and training, the registered farrier may become, through examination, an Associate of the Farriers Company of London; and finally he may aspire to the highest qualification, namely the Fellowship of the Worshipful Company of Farriers.

Some years ago, this ancient Company, dating back to the 14th century, had reason to fear that its useful days might be numbered because the trade was slowly dying through lack of new recruits to replace the older men in its ranks; and this despite the obvious need to provide a service for the half-million or so horses and ponies of the United Kingdom. To halt the disastrous decline, an apprentice scheme was introduced and, thankfully, is producing the desired result. It would indeed have been tragic if farriery had become a lost art, not only because of its practical value today but also because its roots plung very deeply into history. Lt.-Colonel Hickman deserves particular thanks for bringing out the latter point in a fascinating and erudite chapter dealing with the origin of this still-essential craft which has been practiced with little change in its basic techniques since the beginning of the Christian era.

Brigadier J. Clabby, C.B.E., M.R.C.V.S.

Dedicated to my wife Beryl
and to
Celia, Gaynor and David

Contents

Acknowledgements

I WISH to thank the Committee of the Home of Rest for Horses, Aylesbury, Bucks. for a most generous grant to cover the cost of the line drawings so ably executed by John Christiansen of Fen Drayton, Cambs. I am indebted to him for the care and precision with which he has drawn the anatomical illustrations, the horseshoes and diagrams for Figs. 2 (after Megnin), 4, 5 and 6 (after Fleming), 7–10, 11–28, 31–37, 39–42, 43–67, 71–83, 86–106, 167–185, 205, 215, 216–219, 221, 222, 237, 254, 255, 280, 284–287, 290–295, 297–300, 302–306, 308–312, 314–317, 320, 328, 331, 333, 336 and 337. Also I must thank Farrier Sergeant Major D. Symons, R.A.V.C. of the School of Farriery, Royal Army Veterinary Corps Training Centre, Melton Mowbray, Leics. for many helpful suggestions and for demonstrating and arranging the subjects for the photographs to illustrate making a shoe, the practice of shoeing and immobilising a sandcrack with a horseshoe nail. The photographs of these procedures are due to the skill of Mr. P. Lancaster for Figs. 107–163, 186–204, 206–214, 216, 223–227, 235, 236, 238–253, 265–273 and 321–327, and of Mr. H. D. Williamson for Figs. 228–234.

For other photographs my thanks are due to the Curator, Museum of Archaeology and Ethnology, University of Cambridge for Fig. 1, to Miss Mary M. Hurrell, Department of Archaeology of the Museum of Antiquities of the University, and the Society of Antiquities, of Newcastle-upon-Tyne for use of the drawing in Fig. 3 [a], to Mr. A. Clark of the Museum of London for the drawing in Fig. 3 [b], to Mr. P. Price for Figs. 259, 260 and 262, to Mrs. J. Patten for Figs. 288 and 289, 330 and 332, and to Mr. G. Owen for Figs. 256–258, 261, 263, 264, 301 and 307.

Messrs. William Allday and Company, Alcosa Works, Stourport-on-Severn, Worcs. kindly supplied the photograph for Fig. 69 and the blocks for Figs. 68 and 70 and Parweld Ltd. of Stourport-on-Severn, Worcs. the photographs for Figs. 274–279 illustrating the use of horseshoe borium.

I wish to thank "Mordax" studs of Iver, Bucks. for lending the shoes and studs which are illustrated in Figs. 258–264, and Chas. Gray and Company Ltd. and A. J. Pledger and Company Ltd. of Stamford, Lincs. for the loan of various shoes, and Day, Son and Hewitt Ltd. of Bradford for samples of the Aintree Hoof Cushion.

I am most grateful to Brigadier John Clabby for his Foreword and to Charles Mitchell for checking the manuscript and finally I must express my thanks to the publishers, J. A. Allen and Company Limited and to Mr. Ireson for their help and co-operation.

JOHN HICKMAN

Preface

PRIMARILY this book is written for farriers and in particular for apprentice farriers, but it is hoped it will serve as a useful book of reference for veterinary surgeons and veterinary students alike, and indeed for all who are interested in the horse and its welfare.

Every attempt has been made to make the book both interesting and readable whilst presenting the subject matter in a simple, concise and logical manner most helpful to the reader, and at the same time maintaining a balance between theory and practice.

The anatomy and physiology of the foot has been dealt with in some detail as a basic understanding of these sciences is essential if the horse's foot is to be protected and preserved, and a rational approach to shoeing adopted.

Only the methods of shoeing as practised in the United Kingdom have been included with the emphasis placed on the practice and theory of the farrier's daily tasks such as dressing the foot, making a shoe, fitting a shoe and nailing it on. For a better understanding of the problems associated with these tasks an introduction to the conformation and gait of the horse has been given.

The use of special shoes has not been neglected, but whether the shoe is required for a defective foot, to prevent injuries due to abnormalities of gait or to assist in the treatment of a disease or injury, the underlying condition has been explained. Accordingly, the type of shoe recommended is based on an understanding of the condition and of its effect on both structure and function.

The best way of learning a craft is to assist or watch an expert. In consequence special attention has been given to illustrating the text with line drawings and photographs which it is hoped will contribute to ease of understanding and appreciation of the subject matter.

To provide the material for this book all the best known authors on farriery have been consulted and the information collated, and it is inevitable in a book of this type that some of the illustrations are similar to some previously published. The works of the authors consulted have been set out in a bibliography for persons wishing to pursue the subject further.

The anatomical terminology of *Anatomy of the Domestic Animals* by Sisson and Grossman has been used throughout the text except where common usage demands or it is more appropriate. Also, an explanation of some of the more technical words is included in a short glossary, which it is hoped will, should the necessity arise, provide for a better understanding of some of the passages.

With the introduction of the Farriers (Registration) Act 1975 it is hoped many young men will be attracted to the trade and the information set out in this book will assist them in attaining their aims and thereby play its part in promoting the welfare of the horse.

CHAPTER ONE

Introduction and history of horseshoeing

Section I: INTRODUCTION

WHEN the horse was living in its natural environment its hooves provided adequate protection for the underlying sensitive structures of the foot. As soon as man used the horse to carry loads or pull vehicles he must have observed that during certain seasons of the year, when working on hard and rough surfaces, the hooves wore away more quickly than they were renewed, exposing the sensitive structures which resulted in pain and lameness.

For the successful use of the horse, its comfort and welfare some method had to be devised to prevent the horn from being worn away. This necessity depends to a great extent on the quality and hardness of the horn which varies with the climate and the soil. In hot, dry climates the horn is hard and horses can be worked to a considerable extent without shoes, whereas a wet climate is conducive to soft horn which soon wears away.

The first protection employed was probably sandals of woven grass for horses that went lame on the line of march. This was followed by leather sandals, attached by thongs, which were later strengthened by metal plates or studs.

With the passage of time the idea of protecting the foot with a plate of metal, nailed to the wall, was developed and soon it must have been discovered that it could be modified to secure a firm foothold or alleviate some types of lameness.

Without adequate defence of its hooves a horse cannot perform the work expected of it, and to keep a horse at work its feet must be kept in a healthy and efficient state. Indeed, for a horse to be an economical proposition it must remain 100% locomotor efficient. To this end its feet must be prevented from breaking and wearing away without any interference with normal function. This is attained by the farrier fixing a shoe to the foot without damaging or mutilating it. But it must be remembered that the foot is a living and growing structure and if protected normal wear cannot occur and so at each shoeing the foot has to be reduced to its normal proportions. Thus the preparation of the horse's foot, and the fitting of a shoe, must be based on a sound knowledge of the anatomy and function of the foot.

Section II: HISTORY

The period covered by the early history of horseshoeing is quite arbitrary, but it is convenient to consider that it extends from the first methods adopted to protect the horse's foot until the fall of the Roman Empire, when the fitting of a rim of iron to the hoof with nails was practised.

Many factors have to be taken into account to determine when man first adopted measures to protect the feet of horses and which eventually led to the introduction of horse shoes. After the Iron Age the main migration of horses was from Turkistan, over the Caucasian Mountains to Asia, and by 2000 BC they were established in the Middle East. The Assyrians (2000 BC) are credited with having the first blacksmiths, and by 1400 BC iron was being used by the Hittites. As a result of wars with their neighbours this knowledge, and their craftsmen, spread to Mesopotamia and thence to Egypt, the Aegean, and then along the Bronze Age trade routes to

Italy, reaching central Europe by 700 BC and Britain not earlier than 400 BC.

Account has also to be taken of which race or tribe first recognised the strength, speed, endurance and adaptability of the horse and domesticated it for civil and military purposes. Even so, the environment must have played an important rôle. The heat and dryness of the Middle East countries is conducive to very hard hooves which are capable of withstanding severe wear, whereas the damp and cold of northern Europe results in soft hooves which rapidly wear away when the horse is put to work.

Therefore horseshoeing, as we understand it, could not have commenced before the domestication of the horse coupled with a knowledge of working in iron and suitable climatic conditions.

The Ancient Greeks. It is generally assumed that the Ancient Greeks shod their horses, but a study of their sculptures and writings tends to disprove this supposition. Some of the passages from Homer (*circa* 1200–850 BC) have led to the belief that he was familiar with metallic foot defences. He describes the horses that drew Neptune's car as "brazen-footed" or "brass-hoofed" but also he uses the same word to describe the voice of Achilles which is translated as "brazen-voiced". Although brass was in common use in the days of Homer, surely he used the word metaphorically to indicate strength. The poet Tryphidorus states that iron was put on the hooves of the Trojan horse to make its resemblance more complete, but it should not be lost sight of that he lived in the 5th and 6th century AD when horseshoeing was an established practice.

Xenophon (430–354 BC) the Greek general and author wrote extensive treatises on cavalry training. When selecting horses he emphasised the importance of examining the feet and stated "If he has not good feet there is no profit in him as a war-horse". He described a good foot as being "thick not thin, high and with hollow hooves and hard to be fit for service".

Presumably horses with flat feet were not unknown to him, and because he had had experience of their propensity for becoming footsore he emphasised the importance of the concavity or vaulting of the sole which he considered must be preserved. To this end he recommended that not only should stable floors be embedded with round stones but also when a horse was taken outside for grooming it should be stood on a bed of stones. These measures by spreading the feet were thought to preserve and strengthen them. Undoubtedly if horseshoes had been in use Xenophon would not have found it necessary to emphasise and describe these methods of preserving the hooves, in such detail.

It is interesting to note that the army of Alexander the Great (356–323 BC) on its march through Asia was often impeded because the horses wore down their feet, became lame and had to be abandoned.

The Greeks portrayed detail with great accuracy and true representation in their sculptures. In the frieze of the Parthenon (447–438 BC) 110 horses are depicted and not one has shoes. Indeed, the perfect shape of their feet indicates that none of them had ever been shod.

In view of these observations, coupled with the fact that the dry climate of Greece is conducive to hard and durable hooves and that no Greek author writing on military science, animals or agriculture has mentioned shoeing, it is reasonable to conclude that fixing a rim of iron with nails to the feet of horses was not known or practised by the Ancient Greeks.

The Romans. The Romans were not an equestrian nation and their armies, until a late date, depended on their infantry. Indeed, the Ancient Greeks surpassed the Romans in their use and management of horses and much in the Roman literature concerning them appears to have been borrowed from the Greeks.

The Roman authors Varro (116–25 BC) and Virgil (70–19 BC) like their Greek counterparts, stressed the importance of selecting horses with hard hooves. Columella (40 AD) in his works on veterinary medicine not only advised selecting horses for purchase with hard, upright and hollow hooves, but also recommended that when foals were weaned they should be pastured on mountains and other inhospitable places to harden their hooves so as to resist wear and enable them to undertake long journeys.

Suetonius (70–140 AD) writing on the extravagances of the Emperor Nero (37–68 AD) states that he never travelled with fewer than 4000 four-wheeled chariots, drawn by mules shod with silver. Poppaea, his wife, not to be outdone, ordered her favourite mules to be shod with gold. This story is often used to support a case for the Romans shoeing their horses, but it cannot be accepted on its face value. Silver and gold apart from other considerations are soft metals and would be most unsuitable for horseshoes. The most probable explanation is that the hooves were silvered or gilded or the mules' fetlocks were adorned with silver or gold trappings.

To control inflation, the Emperor Diocletian (245–318 AD) issued an edict fixing maximum wages and included those to be paid to the mulomedicus, the sick animal attendant, for clipping, grooming and trimming the hooves of horses and mules. If shoeing was in vogue it certainly would have been included. This view is supported by the writings of Vegitus Renatus

Flavius (circa 375 AD) who in a military treatise enumerates everything pertaining to an army forge but makes no mention of staff to shoe horses or of any farriery tools. This is further supported by the works of Vegitus Renatus Publius (450–510 AD) on veterinary medicine. He gives detailed instructions for keeping horses' hooves hard and for trimming them, but makes no mention of shoeing or accidents associated with it.

The Romans, especially their sculptors, were very exacting in everything relating to the horse, and so it is not without significance that Trajans Column (circa 130 AD) depicts no shod horses and none of the equestrian statues from Pompeii have shoes.

Although the Roman authors consistently draw attention to the necessity for hard hooves and methods to conserve them, they make no mention of actually shoeing horses. But it is obvious from their writings that various forms of hoof protection, when necessary, were provided. The word soleae is used in association with footwear for horses and was probably a a temporary contrivance such as a leather boot. Soleae sparteae were, in all probability, boots made from plaited rope – like materials or woven twigs as used for basket making. It is assumed

Fig. 1. A typical Hipposandal, found at Arrington Bridge, near Cambridge.

they were used, because of their temporary nature, only in emergencies for footsore horses on the line of march or for retaining dressings. But it is not without interest that in Japan, up until the 19th century, shoes for horses were made from plaited rice straw, and on long journeys a supply was carried or was purchased in the villages en route.

Soleae ferreae is generally translated as indicating an iron shoe. Towards the end of the Roman Empire this may well have been true as the art of protecting horses' feet with iron shoes was practised. But before the Romans made contact with the Gauls and Celts the term probably indicated a leather type of boot with metal studded soles similar to the Roman sandal. Such boots could easily be carried and either used for footsore horses or put on as a true protective measure when the terrain warranted it.

Hipposandals. There are several varieties of hipposandals, but basically they consist of iron plates with raised side pieces having a hook in front with another behind (*Fig. 1*). They are of considerable interest because their true purpose is doubtful although it is generally accepted they were shoes for horses, retained with cords or straps. They are made of good quality iron, are of first class workmanship and the under surface is grooved as if to make it non-slip. Considerable time and a large amount of iron is required to forge them.

There is no evidence of them before Roman times, but they have been found wherever the Romans settled from Italy to Britain. Horse skeletons have been excavated with hipposandals in actual contact with the bones of the hoof. In spite of this it has been suggested they were used to keep foot dressings in place, as stirrups, skid pans and even for holding wax candles. But surely, in some way, they must have been associated with the horse, and the most commonly accepted theory is that they were the fore-runner of the nailed on shoe.

Hipposandals could not have been a very practical form of footwear as it would have been difficult for a horse to travel any distance in them, or at speed, and they are too small to have been used as snow shoes or for working on marshy ground.

Romano-Gallic and Romano-British Period. The custom of burying the horse with its master is a very ancient one and horseshoes found in ancient graves have provided evidence to show that the Gauls and the Celts were probably the first people to protect their horses' feet by nailing a rim of iron to their hooves.

The dating of horse shoes is not easy because iron oxidises rapidly and soon disintegrates. But sufficient horseshoes and horseshoe nails have been found in securely stratified and dated deposits, and in Celtic barrows throughout northern Europe, to indicate that they were in use in Britain, most probably before the Roman invasion and certainly during the occupation. These Iron Age people had arrived in Britain by 450 BC. They were advanced workers in iron, making ploughs and weapons, and used horses extensively for riding and for drawing their chariots. The wet and damp climate was conducive to soft hooves and these people soon would have appreciated the advantages to be gained by nailing a rim of iron to their horses' hooves to preserve and prevent them from becoming footsore.

Fig. 2. A typical Celtic horseshoe.

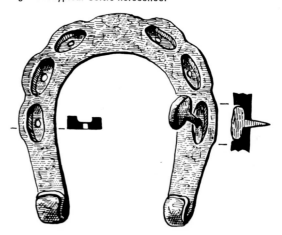

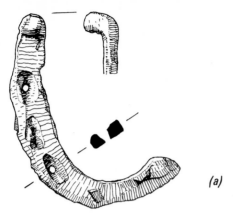

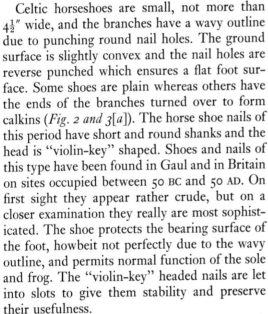

(a)

(b)

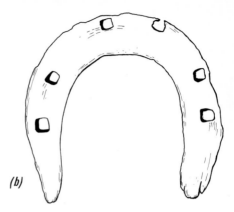

Fig. 3. (a) A typical specimen of a Celtic or Romano-British horseshoe (found at Brough, Westmorland in 1847) which is characterised by its wavy outline, countersinks to take the "violin-key" headed nails and the end of the branch turned over to form a calkin; *(b)* A plain Roman horseshoe with square nail holes found in the Roman gravel layers of the Thames foreshore.

Celtic horseshoes are small, not more than $4\frac{1}{2}''$ wide, and the branches have a wavy outline due to punching round nail holes. The ground surface is slightly convex and the nail holes are reverse punched which ensures a flat foot surface. Some shoes are plain whereas others have the ends of the branches turned over to form calkins (*Fig. 2 and 3[a]*). The horse shoe nails of this period have short and round shanks and the head is "violin-key" shaped. Shoes and nails of this type have been found in Gaul and in Britain on sites occupied between 50 BC and 50 AD. On first sight they appear rather crude, but on a closer examination they really are most sophisticated. The shoe protects the bearing surface of the foot, howbeit not perfectly due to the wavy outline, and permits normal function of the sole and frog. The "violin-key" headed nails are let into slots to give them stability and preserve their usefulness.

Shoes of the classic Celtic variety for both horses and mules with the "violin-headed" nails in position have been found on Roman sites in London. It is not possible to say whether these shoes were made by Roman or British craftsmen, but it is interesting to reflect on how long it was before the defects of a shoe with a wavy outline

and retained by nails with round shanks were overcome. A plain horseshoe with square nail holes has been found in the Roman gravel layers of the Thames foreshore, which is a securely stratified and dated deposit of the 1st and 2nd centuries (*Fig. 3 [b]*).

Taking everything into consideration, it is reasonable to assume that the most ancient people to nail iron shoes to their horses' feet were the Gauls and the Celts, and that the Romans were not acquainted with this art until they assumed their culture. By the time the Roman legions left Britain, Roman ingenuity combined with British craftsmanship had overcome the defects of the Celtic shoe retained by "violin-key" nails and had been replaced by plain shoes retained by square nails.

The Middle Ages (5th to 15th century). Following the departure of the Romans from the shores of Britain and until the arrival of the Normans there appears to have been little change in the pattern of horseshoes. If anything they tend to have been a little heavier and broader than those of the Romano-British period (*Fig. 4*).

The Norman knights brought many horses to England and without doubt attached great

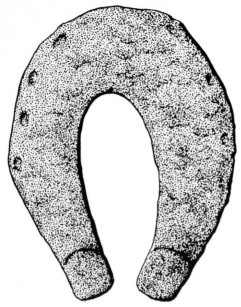

Fig. 4. A typical horseshoe of the Middle Ages. A wide webbed shoe with "fine" nail holes.

importance to shoeing as they were accompanied by their farriers. This influx of farriers must have had considerable influence on the art in Britain. William the Conqueror fully recognised the importance of farriery as instanced by his appointment of Henry de Farrariis to be in control of his farriers and by his giving, to Simon St. Liz, the town of Northampton and the whole hundred of Falkley, to provide shoes for his horses.

It would appear that during the 13th and 14th centuries it was not the general practice to shoe horses and they were shod only during frosty weather to prevent slipping and when their feet were exposed to excessive wear, such as on a long journey. However, examination of farm accounts of this period reveals that many farm horses were shod and by calculating the number of shoes made from a given weight of iron it is indicated that they were shod with little more than tips.

When Edward II took his army to France in 1359, forges for making horse shoes were included in the equipment; probably the first field forges to be taken by a British army on

active service. During the 15th century quantities of horseshoes were imported into Scotland from Flanders and it is of interest that they were large and fullered.

Although during the Middle Ages there were no notable advances in the art of farriery, its importance did not pass unrecognised. Indeed, it can be said that the establishment of the trade in England was instituted in 1356 by the Mayor of the City of London. In that year he summoned the farriers because "many offences and dangers" were being committed by people who kept forges in the city and resulted in the loss of many horses. This was followed by the establishment of the Fellowships of "Marshalls of the City of London" and the appointment of wardens with powers to govern the trade.

16th and 17th centuries. During these centuries works on horseshoeing appeared in Italy and France. The most important was a complete treatise by Caesar Fiaschi comprising 35 chapters. It was a very remarkable and advanced work for the period which soon was translated into French and published in Paris in 1564. The author describes 20 varieties of shoes including bar and bevelled shoes, a shoe with an extended toe piece and an expansion shoe with the branches hinged at the toe. In addition, details on paring the feet and the form of nails, calkins and tips are described.

Towards the end of the 16th century Carlo Ruini, a senator of Bologna published an extensive work on the anatomy and diseases of the horse. He drew attention to the evils of paring the sole, opening up the heels and shoeing with high calkins. He recommended that contracted feet should be treated by fitting a shoe with thin heels to allow the posterior part of the hoof to come in contact with the ground. But the most important contributions to the art of farriery during this period are to be found in the publications of the Frenchman Jacques Labessie de Solleysel which were translated into many languages, including English. The author attempts to put the art on a scientific basis. He pointed out that the shoe should fit the foot and the sole should not be pared or the heels opened up. He advised the use of thin small nails and recognised that nails get a better hold at the toe than at the heels because of the thicker wall. He condemned high calkins and recommended the shoe should be as light as possible.

In England at this time the only work of note on farriery was by Thomas Blundevil but there is little doubt his views were greatly influenced by the Italian and French authors. Unfortunately he did not accept much of the sound advice to be found in these publications and made the error of recommending excessive paring and rasping of the feet. On the other hand, Andrew Snape, farrier to Charles II, rendered the art a great service by drawing particular attention to the structure of the foot in his *Anatomy of the Horse*.

There can be little doubt that during the 16th and 17th centuries the methods of farriery practised, and the standards attained, varied considerably throughout the country and any advances made were in no small measure due to Italian and French influence. But the importance of farriery was gaining official recognition and a further stage in the establishment of farriery as an approved trade was taken by the City of London. The Fellowship, established in 1356, was incorporated by a Charter of Charles II and in 1692 the Farriers Company was established by the court of aldermen as a livery company.

Establishment of the Veterinary Schools (18th and 19th centuries). With the establishment of the veterinary schools it was to be expected that enlightened knowledge of the anatomy and function of the horse's foot would be acquired and applied to the problems of shoeing. Towards the end of the 18th century and during the first half of the 19th century, many treatises were published on farriery but attention will be drawn only to those which had an important influence, for good or bad, on the art. This was an era of experimentation and also of dogmatism which often led to the perpetuation of harmful practices based on drawing incorrect conclusions. In consequence, many years were to pass before the practice of farriery based on sound scientific anatomical and physiological principles was accepted.

In France, the views of Etienne Guillaume Lafosse contributed greatly to establishing farriery as a science. He based his opinions on a study of the anatomy and function of the foot which he related to its natural wear. He pointed out that only the wall is worn away and as the function of the frog is to prevent slipping, it, together with the sole should not be pared. As a result of his observations he was able to show that many of the methods of shoeing in vogue were harmful in that they did not conserve the foot but contributed to injury, and in consequence he suggested alternative rational methods. He recommended a shoe with flat foot and ground surfaces, with thin heels and that calkins should only be fitted to prevent slipping. Although his publications contained much good and sound advice, this was slow to be accepted.

The person who had the most profound and lasting influence on shoeing in France during this period was the renowned veterinary surgeon Claude Bougelet. He considered the foot should be maintained as found in nature and recommended a shoe based on his observations of the mechanics of the limb. The shoe he recommended was slightly curved in length, wider

Fig. 5. Bougelet's horseshoe. The shoe has a flat foot and ground surface. The toe is turned up equal to the thickness of the shoe and the heels to half the thickness of the shoe.

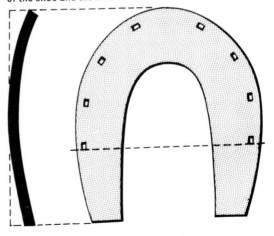

at the toe than at the heels and with regularly placed nail holes (*Fig. 5*). This shoe has remained in general use in France, with few modifications, well into the 20th century.

In England at this time three notable works were published on the anatomy of the horse's foot and shoeing. Jeremiah Bridges, condemned heavy shoes and excessive paring of the foot. Also, he had some novel ideas to counter contracted feet which included shoes with sloping clips on the inside of the heels to force them outwards. His practice of making five cuts or scissures on the outside of the hoof down to the quick is, presumably, the forerunner of what today is known as "grooving the heels". William Osmer's contribution was based on the teachings of Lafosse. He emphasised the undesirable practices of paring the sole and frog and of opening up the heels and pointed out that shoes with short heels, if left on for too long, would press on the sole and result in corns. Without doubt, of the three, James Clark, Farrier to His Majesty for Scotland, deserves the most credit. He had an enlightened approach to shoeing and developed a practical shoe based on sound principles. He recommended a shoe which resembled the natural tread and shape of the foot. A concave fullered shoe with a flat

Fig. 6. Clark's horseshoe. A concave fullered shoe, slightly seated out and with a wider web at the toe than at the heels.

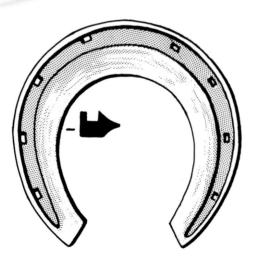

foot surface slightly seated out to take pressure off the sole (*Fig. 6*). It was broad at the toe, with narrower heels to allow the frog freedom and was retained with only eight to ten nails instead of the popular 16 to 18.

Although the recommendations of these practical men had gone a long way towards establishing a satisfactory form of shoe, based on scientific principles deduced from a sound knowledge of the anatomy and function of the foot, many years were to pass before they were generally accepted and put into practice. When the Veterinary College was founded in London in 1791, the era of scientific investigations was just beginning. In consequence, one would have thought the existing knowledge of the anatomy of the horse's foot coupled with practical and scientifically orientated investigations into its precise function would soon have led to the art of farriery being established as a science based on sound principles. This was not to be. The horse owning public and the farriers must have been not only confused but exasperated by the diverse views expressed and so ardently held by many eminent veterinary surgeons. Professor Edward Coleman, Principal of the London Veterinary College and his pupil Bracy Clark were no exceptions.

Coleman was a medical man. He failed to appreciate the significance of the anatomy of the horse's foot in relation to function and in consequence made a number of incorrect deductions. He held an exaggerated idea of the importance of the elasticity and expansion of the foot and of frog and heel pressure. To this end he recommended the sole be scooped out until it responded to thumb pressure and to ensure frog pressure he introduced numerous artificial pads.

Bracy Clark adopted the views of Coleman but was obsessed with the descent of the sole and lateral distension of the foot. He tried to prove that shoes were unnecessary and when it became obvious they would have to be used to protect horses' feet, he introduced several nailless shoes which, needless to say, met with no practical success. In his view the unyielding rim of iron attached to the horse's hoof was responsible for

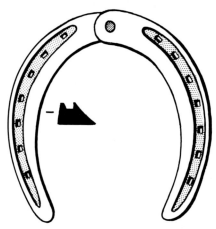

Fig. 7. A typical hinged expansion shoe. This type of shoe fails to allow expansion of the foot because its branches are nailed to the non-expanding toe.

most diseases of the foot and to overcome this he turned his attention to developing a hinged shoe not dissimilar to the one illustrated by Caesar Fiaschi in 1564 (*Fig. 7*). This, likewise, met with no success as he failed to appreciate that the branches of the shoe were nailed to the non-expanding toe of the foot. He agreed with Coleman that the sole should not come into contact with the ground and held similar views on the frog.

There is little doubt that the incorrect deductions of these two men concerning the part played by the expansion of the foot and the descent of the sole in the normal functioning of the foot, and the practices they advocated to assist these functions, had an unfortunate influence on the practice of farriery which contributed to the all too common "contracted foot" syndrome.

The military authorities adopted a practical approach to shoeing and by 1778 a regimental pattern shoe had been introduced into the cavalry and any farrier found guilty of making one of another pattern was liable to receive corporal punishment. This shoe was introduced by the tenth Earl of Pembroke and was based on the shoe recommended by James Clark of Edinburgh, from whom he had received instruction. The *Rules and Regulations for the Cavalry* laid

down in 1795 included instructions for shoeing horses. A standard pattern shoe with flat foot and ground surfaces was introduced and the sole, frog and bars were not to be pared. Also, instructions were given regarding the care of the feet when horses were turned out to grass, which stated that the toes were to be kept short and the edge of the wall rasped round.

In 1820 Joseph Goodwin, veterinary surgeon to George IV, published details of a new type of shoe which had a concave ground surface to secure a good foothold and a foot surface inclined from the inner to the outer edge to encourage expansion of the foot and thereby prevent contraction (*Fig. 8*). This shoe only met with limited approval and proved difficult to make and fit.

William Youatt, writing in the middle of the 19th century, stated that the frog supported weight and assisted expansion of the foot and that reducing it in size and raising it off the ground was conducive to contraction of the foot. In spite of this appreciation he considered the frog required only occasional contact and pressure with the ground and, therefore, should be kept trimmed level with the shoe. He, like many of his colleagues, was obsessed with the descent of the sole and recommended it should be pared down until it yielded under pressure and a

Fig. 8. Goodwin's horseshoe. A concave shoe with a sloped foot surface to encourage expansion of the foot.

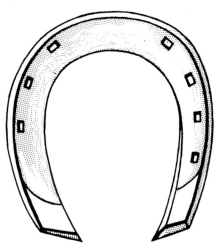

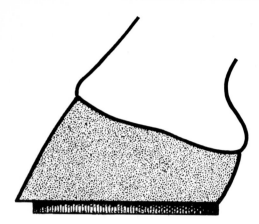

Fig. 9. Charlier system of shoeing. A strip of horn is cut away to form a groove round the wall and into which a thin shoe is embedded.

seated-out shoe should be fitted to allow its descent.

The cult of the descent of the sole and its mutilation was slow to disappear and some farriers continued to scoop it out well into the 20th century. But for all practical purposes it can be said that the end of irrational conclusions being drawn from a knowledge of the anatomy and function of the foot and applied to farriery, rapidly came to a close with Sir Frederick Fitz-wygram's *Notes on Shoeing Horses* which was published in 1863. This was an admirable work based on a rational and common sense approach to preserve the integrity and form of the hoof and to conserve the sole and frog. He recommended a shoe similar to Goodwin's but with a flat foot surface and slightly rolled toe. Although an excellent shoe, based on sound principles, it was not generally accepted and used because it was difficult to make and fit.

In 1865 M. Charlier, a veterinary surgeon practising in Paris, introduced preplantar shoeing which is generally referred to as the "Charlier System". His method of embedding a thin rim of iron into the wall, which is phsyiologically acceptable, received wide and popular support. A groove is cut in the wall using a special guarded knife which regulates its width and depth and enables a perfect fit to be obtained (*Fig. 9*). The foot is not easy to prepare for a Charlier shoe and fitting and nailing it on is not without difficulties. The union between the sole and the wall is weakened by the groove, the

weight bearing is not distributed evenly over the wall and edge of the sole but is taken entirely by the wall. Of necessity the shoe has to be thin, which soon wears and spreads and leads to it being trodden on or injuring the opposite leg. In consequence, a short Charlier shoe was adopted (*Fig. 10*), which for all practical purposes only serves the purpose of a tip. The Charlier shoe did not meet with the claims made for it, and after extensive trials was rejected.

By the end of the 19th century, publications by such eminent veterinary surgeons as George Fleming, John A. W. Dollar and William Hunting had established farriery both as an art and a science based on a sound scientific understanding of the anatomy and physiology of the foot. The correct deductions from this knowledge led to a rim of iron being correctly fitted to the hoof so as to protect it and at the same time to conserve its natural functions.

In 1889 the Worshipful Company of Farriers resolved to establish an organisation "for the promotion of skilled farriery and the registration of farriers in London and throughout the country". In 1890–91 they brought into operation a scheme for the examination and registration of shoeing smiths. At first farriers had only to meet the requirements of a short theoretical examination to be enrolled, but this was soon put to rights and the value of the Company's Certificate of Registered Shoeing Smith, following a practical and oral examination, received the recognition which was its due. The higher qualifications of Associate and Fellow of the Company were introduced in 1907 and 1923 respectively.

In addition, other organisations were interested in encouraging apprenticeships and raising the standard of the trade. The National Master Farriers and Blacksmiths and Agricultural Engineers Association introduced an apprentice scheme, the Berkshire County Council, for example, instituted a travelling farriery school and the Agricultural Societies deserve much credit for making farriery competitions a feature of their shows.

Section III: THE FUTURE

It is often said that the heyday of the horse is past. True, the horse is no longer indispensable to agriculture or the military and the transport system of the country is no longer dependent on it. But the horse still makes an important contribution to the economy of the country, in particular through the Thoroughbred industry. In addition, the horse continues to play an essential part in sport, entertainment and in a great variety of recreational pursuits. These include hunting, racing, polo, eventing, show jumping and the many activities encouraged by the riding, driving and pony clubs which flourish throughout the country.

After the First World War there was a steady decline in the horse population and it gradually disappeared from our roads and farms. At the end of the Second World War, due to rapid mechanisation throughout all walks of life, the number of horses dwindled to such an extent that many feared the days of the horse were over. In consequence, the demand for farriers declined and the future for the trade was indeed black as the majority of farriers still practising were beyond middle age and the prospects were such that it was not being taken up by the younger generation.

Fortunately the Worshipful Company of Farriers did not take such a gloomy view. They foresaw the country returning to normality and an increasing prosperity which inevitably would lead to a resurgence of the horse population. There can be little doubt that during this period, when the trade was in the doldrums, the introduction by the Company of their apprenticeship scheme saved the day as it enabled a small cadre of trained farriers to be maintained.

Farriery is both an art and a science and it is essential that persons practising the trade should learn the art based on sound scientific principles.

Fig. 10. A short or modified Charlier shoe. It was introduced to overcome the disadvantages of a full-length shoe, but only serves the purpose of a tip.

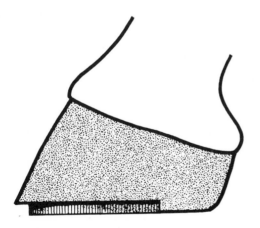

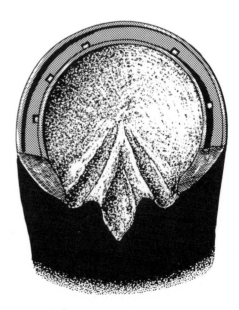

To ensure and maintain proper standards within the trade and to prevent unnecessary suffering and cruelty to horses arising from them being shod by unskilled persons, the Farriers (Registration) Act 1975 was introduced.

The Act, by prohibiting the shoeing of horses, including ponies, mules, donkeys or other equine animals, by unqualified persons primarily protects the horse but also is of great benefit to the trade as it provides for the training of farriers. These advantages impose certain responsibilities, especially on the Worshipful Company of Farriers who are required to maintain a standard of competence and conduct and to promote and encourage the art and science of farriery.

The passing of this Act will go a long way towards raising the status of the farrier, thereby educating the public in a more enlightened appreciation of his skills. This, it is hoped, will lead to the farrier's advice on shoeing and the care of horses' feet being more readily accepted and result in immense benefit to the horse and its owner.

CHAPTER TWO

The anatomy of the
front and hind
legs

ANATOMY is the branch of biological science which deals with the form and structure of the body.

Section I: OSTEOLOGY.

The study of the bones is termed osteology. The term skeleton is applied to the framework of bones and cartilage which provides a rigid supporting structure and protective framework for the body (*Fig. 11*). Without the support of the bones the animal would collapse and without their protection vital organs such as the heart, lungs and abdominal viscera would be vulnerable to injury.

Bones are complex living structures which, in addition to serving as supporting columns, act as levers concerned with movement. Also they are mineral reservoirs for calcium and phosphorus and manufacture both red and white blood cells.

CLASSES OF BONE

Bones are of all shapes and sizes but it is customary to divide them according to their general shape into four classes.

Long bone. A long bone is defined as one which is greater in length than breadth and possesses a medullary (marrow) cavity for example, the humerus, radius, femur and tibia. The central or cylindrical part is termed the shaft (diaphysis) and the two ends which are covered with articular cartilage are called the extremities.

Short bone. Short bones are comparatively small in size and cubical in form. They are found in the knee (carpus) and hock (tarsus) joints and play an important part in serving to distribute weight and pressure and thus reduce the risk of injury from concussion.

Flat bone. A flat bone is expanded in two directions and hence is more or less plate-like. These bones, such as the scapula, provide a large surface for the attachment of muscles and afford protection to the underlying organs.

Irregular bone. This class includes bones of an irregular shape, such as the bones of the vertebral column (backbone).

PHYSICAL PROPERTIES OF BONE

Fresh dead bone is yellowish-white in colour, but when exposed in the living body is tinged bluish-pink due to the blood contained in the vessels of the bone. It is very hard and resistant to pressure, having a compressive strength of some 20,000 lbs. per square inch.

COMPOSITION OF BONE

Dry fat-free, adult equine bone consists of 45.7% organic (animal) and 54.3% inorganic (mineral matter). The organic matter consists of a mixture of protein and carbohydrate which is the source of gelatin when bones are boiled out. The hardness of bone is due to the inorganic matter which is comprised mainly of calcium, 28.6%, and phosphates 12.9% with traces of magnesium, sodium and other elements.

If the mineral matter is removed by immersing a bone in a 5% solution of hydrochloric acid, the bone retains its original shape but is rendered

31

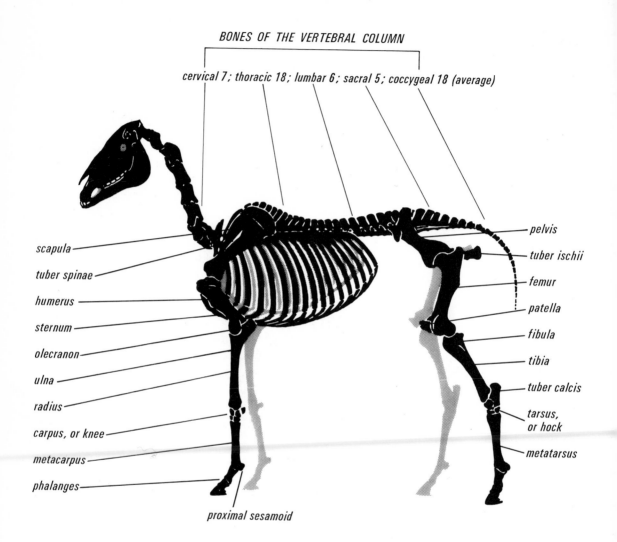

BONES OF THE VERTEBRAL COLUMN

cervical 7; thoracic 18; lumbar 6; sacral 5; coccygeal 18 (average)

scapula

tuber spinae

humerus

sternum

olecranon

ulna

radius

carpus, or knee

metacarpus

phalanges

proximal sesamoid

pelvis

tuber ischii

femur

patella

fibula

tibia

tuber calcis

tarsus, or hock

metatarsus

Fig. 11. Skeleton of the horse. The skeleton comprises
205 bones:

Vertebral column (back bone) – 54
Ribs   – 36
Sternum   – 1
Skull   – 34
Front limb   – 40
Hind limb   – 40

soft and pliable. Conversely, if the inorganic matter is removed the bone becomes brittle and is easily broken.

STRUCTURE OF BONE

A section through a bone shows that two varieties of tissue enter into its composition (*Fig. 12*). An outer shell of dense hard material or compact bone, within which is a more loosely arranged spongy substance called cancellous bone.

Compact bone is dense and hard. It differs in thickness to conform with the stresses to which the bone is subjected. In long bones it is generally thicker towards the middle of the shaft and thins out towards the extremities. In the large metacarpal bone of the front leg, for example, it is thicker anteriorly than posteriorly and also thicker medially than laterally, which corresponds to the stresses of weight bearing.

Cancellous bone is light and porous in appearance. It consists of intersecting delicate bone plates and spicules. The spaces between the plates are filled with marrow.

Periostium is the thin membrane which invests the outer surface of bone except where it is covered by articular cartilage or where tendons are attached. It consists of two layers. A dense outer protective fibrous layer and an inner cellular or osteogenic layer. This inner layer contains an abundance of cells, especially in young growing bone, which are concerned with the formation of new bone and are termed *osteoblasts.*

Endostium is the thin fibrous membrane which lines the medullary cavity.

Bone marrow is the substance which occupies the interstices of the cancellous bone and the medullary cavity of long bones. There are two varieties. Red marrow a blood-forming substance which is found only in young animals and

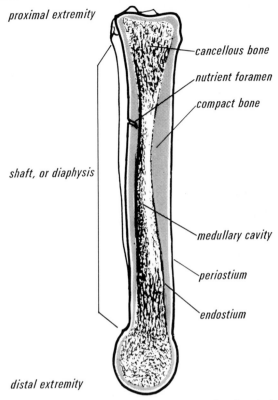

proximal extremity

cancellous bone

nutrient foramen

compact bone

shaft, or diaphysis

medullary cavity

periostium

endostium

distal extremity

Fig. 12. Large metacarpal bone, saggital section. A typical long bone.

is gradually replaced in the medullary cavity by *yellow marrow* which is composed principally of fat cells.

BLOOD VESSELS AND NERVES OF BONE

Arteries. Two sets of arteries are recognised – periosteal and medullary. The *periosteal arteries* ramify in the periostium and give off small branches which pass through minute openings on the surface to enter the compact bone. In the larger bones and especially the long bones, the shaft is penetrated by the so-called nutrient foramen (*Fig. 12*) through which the *medullary* or nutrient artery passes to ramify in the bone marrow.

Veins. Near the articular surfaces are found numerous openings which give exit to veins returning blood from the cancellous bone.

Fig. 13. Large metacarpal bone (cannon bone) and small metacarpal bones (splint bones).

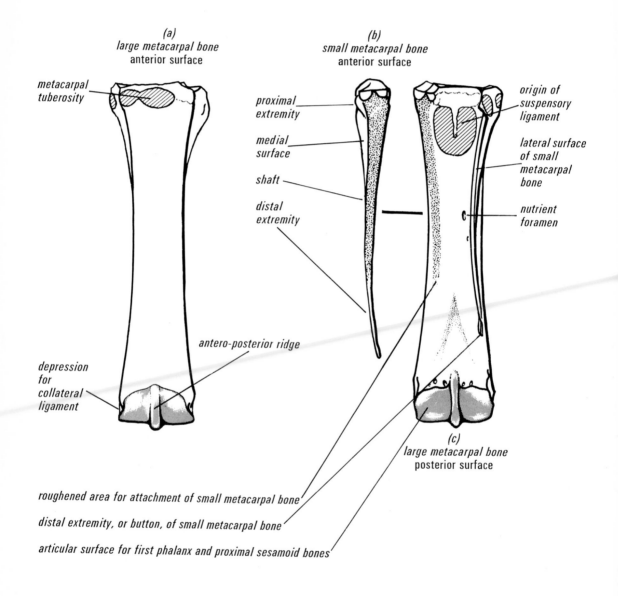

(a)
large metacarpal bone
anterior surface

(b)
small metacarpal bone
anterior surface

metacarpal
tuberosity

*proximal
extremity*

*origin of
suspensory
ligament*

*medial
surface*

*lateral surface
of small
metacarpal
bone*

shaft

*distal
extremity*

*nutrient
foramen*

antero-posterior ridge

*depression
for
collateral
ligament*

(c)
large metacarpal bone
posterior surface

roughened area for attachment of small metacarpal bone

distal extremity, or button, of small metacarpal bone

articular surface for first phalanx and proximal sesamoid bones

Nerves. Nerves accompany the blood vessels in the compact and cancellous bone and in the marrow cavity.

BONES BELOW THE KNEE
AND THE HOCK JOINT:
(The Metacarpal bones)

In the typical mammalian hand five metacarpal bones are present, one for each digit as is the case of the front foot of a dog. In the horse three metacarpal bones are present and of these only the third or *large metacarpal bone* (*cannon bone*) (*Fig. 13* [*a*]) is fully developed and carries a digit. The other two, the second and fourth or *small metacarpal bones* (splint bones) (*Fig. 13* [*b*] *and* [*c*]) are small slender bones, unprovided with digits and placed on each side of the large metacarpal bone.

THE LARGE METACARPAL BONE
(Cannon bone)

This is a typical long bone and occupies a nearly vertical position between the carpus (knee) above and the first phalanx (os suffraginis-long pastern) below. The shaft is slender yet it is one of the strongest bones in the skeleton. The great weight it has to support is compensated for by the amount of compact bone which is especially thick anteriorly and medially.

The Anterior Surface (*Fig. 13* [*a*]) is smooth, rounded from side to side and nearly straight in its length.

The Posterior Surface (*Fig. 13* [*c*]) is comparatively flat from side to side and commencing just above the middle of the bone on either side, is a roughened area for the attachment of the small metacarpal bones. These bones form a wide channel for the suspensory ligament. Towards the junction of the upper and middle thirds is the nutrient foramen for the transmission of the nutrient artery.

The proximal (*upper*) *extremity* has an articular surface adapted for the distal row of carpal bones. On the antero-medial aspect of this extremity is a roughened projecting surface, the metacarpal tuberosity, for the insertion of the tendon of the extensor carpi radialis.

The distal (*lower*) *extremity* has an articular surface for the first phalanx and the proximal sesamoid bones. A ridge running anteroposteriorly divides it into two articulations, the medial one being slightly the larger. On either side is a small depression for the attachment of the collateral ligaments of the fetlock joint.

THE SMALL METACARPAL BONES
(Splint bones)

These are the second and fourth metacarpal bones (*Fig. 13* [*b*] *and* [*c*]). They are situated on each side of the posterior surface of the large metacarpal bone. They have no medullary cavity and are described as possessing a shaft and two extremities.

The shaft is a three-sided slender rod of bone which tapers to its distal extremity and is slightly curved in its length.

The anterior or attached surface is comparatively flat and rough except towards its distal extremity. The greater part of this surface is attached to the posterior aspect of the large metacarpal bone by an interosseous ligament which in horses past middle age becomes totally or in part ossified.

The lateral surface is smooth and round and the *medial surface* which is smooth and concave from edge to edge helps to form the channel for the suspensory ligament.

The proximal extremity or head is relatively large. The articular surface, in the case of the medial bone, has two facets which support the second (trapezoid) and third (os magnum) carpal bones, whereas the lateral bone has a single facet and supports the fourth (unciform) carpal bone. The anterior aspect of the proximal extremity of both bones has two small facets for articulation with the large metacarpal bone and its lateral aspect is rough for tendinous and ligamentous attachments.

The distal extremity comprises a small nodule, frequently termed the "button" of the splint bone. It stands out a short distance from the posterior surface of the large metacarpal bone and is easily palpated as a slightly movable process.

Fig. 14. Cross section of *(a)* the large metacarpal and *(b)* the large metatarsal bone.
Note that the large metatarsal bone is more cylindrical.

(a)

(b)

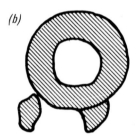

The small metacarpal bones vary in length, thickness and curvature, and the medial one is generally the larger of the two both in length and volume. The curvature is very variable and in some cases the distal extremity is a definite projection.

THE METATARSAL BONES

The three metatarsal bones of the hind leg have the same general arrangement as the metacarpal bones of the front leg, but they are directed slightly more obliquely downwards and forwards.

THE LARGE METATARSAL BONE

In form it closely resembles the large metacarpal bone, but it is longer by about one sixth and in a medium-sized horse the difference is between 2″ and 2½″. The shaft is more cylind-

rical (*Fig. 14*), narrowest towards its middle and has slightly expanded extremities.

The shaft on its proximal and lateral surface shows a shallow groove which runs obliquely downwards and marks the course of the great metatarsal artery. The medial surface shows a similar but fainter groove for the metatarsal vein. On the posterior surface the nutrient foramen, which is sometimes double, is placed relatively higher than on the metacarpal bone.

The proximal extremity is correspondingly much wider antero-posteriorly than that of the metacarpal bone (*Fig. 15*). Its articular surface is slightly concave and has a large non-articular depression. On the anterior surface and slightly to the medial side is a rough ridge for the insertion of the peroneus tertius muscle (flexor metatarsi).

The distal extremity only differs from the large metacarpal bone in that it is larger both in its transverse and antero-posterior diameter.

THE PROXIMAL SESAMOID BONES

There are two proximal sesamoid bones in each leg. They are placed on the posterior surface of the distal extremity of the large metacarpal bone (*Figs. 16 and 18*) and are closely attached to the first phalanx by ligaments. Their function is to afford increased leverage to the flexors of the digit.

Each sesamoid bone has the form of a three-sided pyramid.

The anterior or articular surface conforms to the posterior aspect of the distal articular surface of the larger metacarpal bone.

The posterior surface in life is covered by cartilage and with the posterior surface of the opposite sesamoid bone forms a smooth groove for the passage of the deep digital flexor tendon.

The abaxial surface is the narrowest of the three surfaces and gives attachment to the

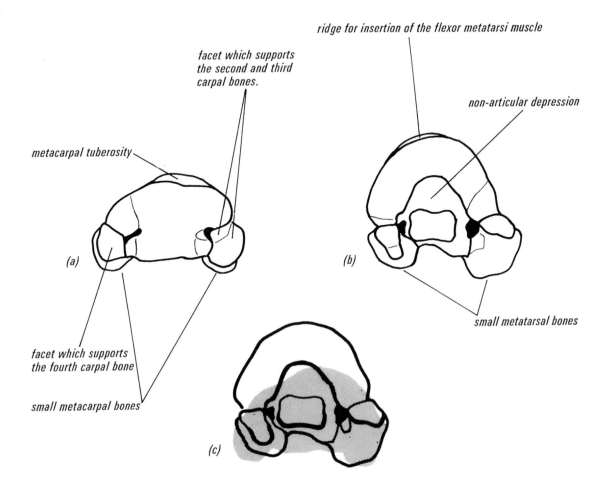

ridge for insertion of the flexor metatarsi muscle

facet which supports
the second and third
carpal bones.

non-articular depression

metacarpal tuberosity

(a)

(b)

facet which supports
the fourth carpal bone

small metacarpal bones

small metatarsal bones

(c)

Fig. 15. Diagram of *(a)* the articular surface of the proximal
extremity of the metacarpal bone and *(b)* of the proximal
extremity of the metatarsal bone.

When the articular surfaces of these two bones are
superimposed *(c)* it will be noted that the articular surface
of the metatarsal bone is wider antero-posteriorly and
possesses a larger non-articular depression.

collateral sesamoidean ligaments, the collateral ligaments of the fetlock joint and part of the suspensory ligament.

The apex of the pyramid is rounded and *the base* affords attachment for the inferior sesamoidean ligaments.

The proximal sesamoid bones of the hind leg are slightly smaller, except in thickness, than those of the front leg.

THE DIGIT

The digit of the horse comprises three main bones, called the phalanges, and a sesamoid bone, the navicular (*Figs. 16, 17 and 18*).

THE FIRST PHALANX
(*os suffraginis – long pastern*)

The first phalanx is a long bone situated between the large metacarpal bone and the second phalanx. It occupies an oblique position being directed downwards and forwards at an angle of about 55° with the horizontal plane. When the slope of this bone is excessive undue strain is thrown on the tendons and ligaments at the back of the leg, and if it is nearly upright then practically the whole weight of the horse is thrown on this bone. It consists of a shaft and two extremities.

The shaft is wider and thicker proximally than distally. The *anterior* surface is smooth and slightly rounded from side to side. The *posterior* surface is flattened with a rough triangular shaped area for the attachment of the middle sesamoidean ligament. The *borders* or medial and lateral surfaces have at their centre a roughened area or eminence for the attachment of ligaments, and a shallow groove which in life accommodates a branch of the digital artery.

The proximal extremity has an articular surface moulded to the distal extremity of the large metacarpal bone. It is separated into two shallow articular cavities by a deep groove running antero-posteriorly. The medial cavity is

slightly the larger. On each side is a tuberosity or buttress-like projection for attachment of ligaments, and at the middle of the anterior edge is a slight elevation for the attachment of the lateral digital extensor tendon.

The distal extremity is smaller, and the articular surface is divided into two condyles by a shallow, ill-defined groove running antero-posteriorly, the medial area being slightly the larger. At either side of the distal extremity is a depression surmounted by a small tubercle to which the collateral ligament of the pastern joint is attached.

The first phalanx of the hind leg is a little shorter, wider proximally and narrower distally, than the corresponding bone of the front leg.

THE SECOND PHALANX
(*os coronae – short pastern*)

The second phalanx is a short bone and does not possess a medullary cavity. It is situated between the first and third phalanges and is placed obliquely in the digit corresponding with that of the first phalanx. It may be described as possessing two extremities and two surfaces.

The proximal extremity is articular and moulded on the distal extremity of the first phalanx. It is separated into two shallow cavities divided by a low ridge running antero-posteriorly, the medial cavity being slightly the larger. The middle of the anterior border is roughened for the attachment of the common digital extensor tendon. The posterior border has a thick overhanging and smooth transverse prominence which in life is covered with a complementary plate of fibro-cartilage over which the deep digital flexor tendon passes.

On either side of the border is an eminence for the attachment of the collateral ligament and the superficial digital flexor tendon.

The distal extremity articulates with the third phalanx and navicular bone to form the terminal

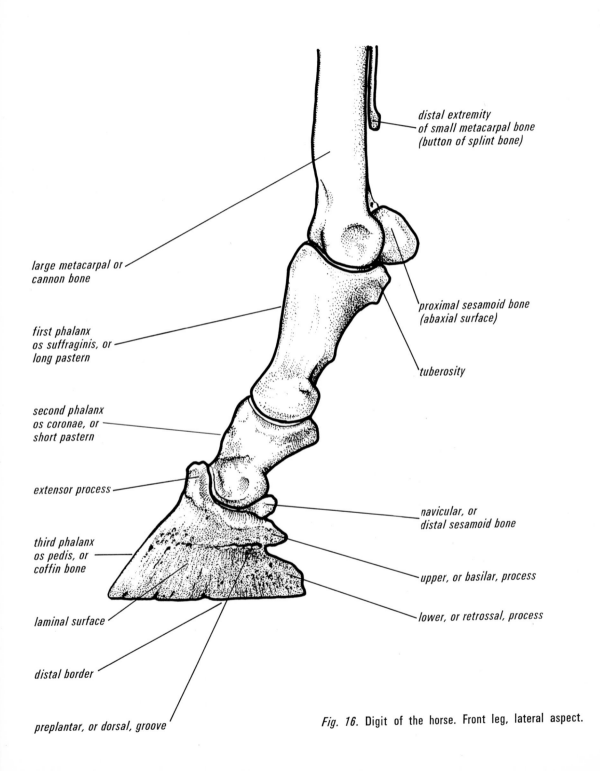

large metacarpal or
cannon bone

first phalanx
os suffraginis, or
long pastern

second phalanx
os coronae, or
short pastern

extensor process

third phalanx
os pedis, or
coffin bone

laminal surface

distal border

preplantar, or dorsal, groove

distal extremity
of small metacarpal bone
(button of splint bone)

proximal sesamoid bone
(abaxial surface)

tuberosity

navicular, or
distal sesamoid bone

upper, or basilar, process

lower, or retrossal, process

Fig. 16. Digit of the horse. Front leg, lateral aspect.

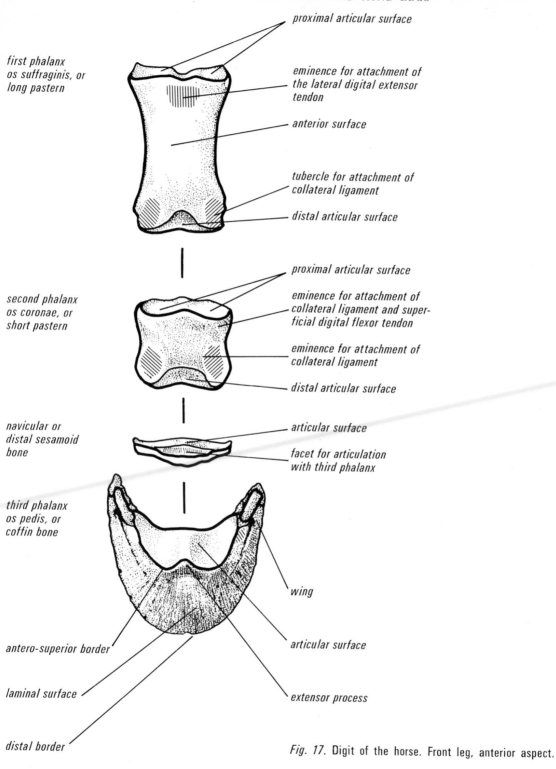

first phalanx
os suffraginis, or
long pastern

proximal articular surface

eminence for attachment of
the lateral digital extensor
tendon

anterior surface

tubercle for attachment of
collateral ligament

distal articular surface

second phalanx
os coronae, or
short pastern

proximal articular surface

eminence for attachment of
collateral ligament and superficial digital flexor tendon

eminence for attachment of
collateral ligament

distal articular surface

navicular or
distal sesamoid
bone

articular surface

facet for articulation
with third phalanx

third phalanx
os pedis, or
coffin bone

wing

antero-superior border

articular surface

laminal surface

extensor process

distal border

Fig. 17. Digit of the horse. Front leg, anterior aspect.

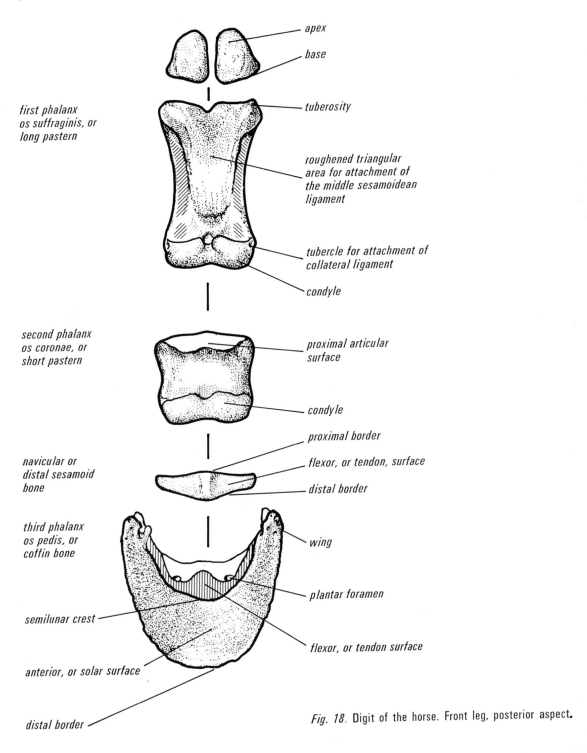

proximal sesamoid bones

apex

base

first phalanx
os suffraginis, or
long pastern

tuberosity

roughened triangular
area for attachment of
the middle sesamoidean
ligament

tubercle for attachment of
collateral ligament

condyle

second phalanx
os coronae, or
short pastern

proximal articular
surface

condyle

navicular or
distal sesamoid
bone

proximal border

flexor, or tendon, surface

distal border

third phalanx
os pedis, or
coffin bone

wing

plantar foramen

semilunar crest

flexor, or tendon surface

anterior, or solar surface

distal border

Fig. 18. Digit of the horse. Front leg, posterior aspect.

joint of the digit. It resembles in form the lower extremity of the first phalanx but is rather more extensive in the antero-posterior direction.

The anterior surface is slightly depressed and wider in its transverse diameter.

The posterior surface is comparatively smooth with a number of foramina for the passage of blood-vessels.

The second phalanx of the hind leg is narrower and slightly longer than the corresponding bone of the front leg.

THE THIRD PHALANX
(os pedis – coffin bone)

This bone is entirely enclosed within the hoof. to which it has some resemblance in shape. It is composed of very compact bone and is denser than any other bone in the skeleton, with the exception of the petrous temporal bone which contains the inner ear. It is a short bone and can be described as possessing three surfaces, and two wings (*Figs. 16, 17 and 18*).

The laminal or anterior surface slopes down-wards and forwards at an angle of between 45° and 50° to the ground. Laterally the height gradually diminishes and the slope becomes steeper especially on the medial aspect. Its surface somewhat resembles pumice stone and is perforated by numerous foraminae of various sizes. On either side is a groove, the *preplantar or dorsal groove*, which runs forward from the wings and terminates anteriorly in one of the large foraminae. The distal border is convex, thin and irregularly notched, with often a particularly wide and deep notch in front. In life this surface is covered by sensitive laminae which dovetail with the horny laminae of the wall of the hoof.

The articular or dorsal surface is moulded on the distal articular surface of the second phalanx and is divided into two shallow cavities by an ill-defined ridge running antero-poster-iorly. Along the posterior edge is a transversely elongated flattened area which articulates with the navicular bone. The antero-superior border which separates the articular and laminal surfaces has a central eminence, the *extensor or pyramidal process* for the insertion of the com-mon digital extensor (extensor pedis) tendon. On either side is a small pit for the insertion of the collateral ligaments.

The ventral surface is divided into two un-equal parts by a curved line, the semilunar crest. *The anterior or solar surface*, which is the

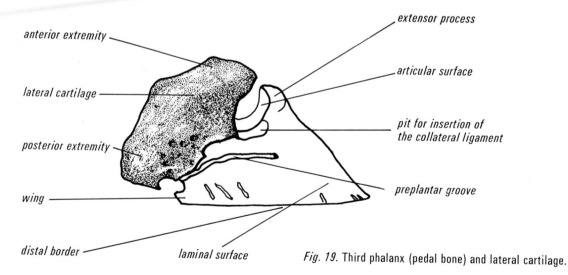

anterior extremity

lateral cartilage

posterior extremity

wing

distal border

laminal surface

extensor process

articular surface

pit for insertion of the collateral ligament

preplantar groove

Fig. 19. Third phalanx (pedal bone) and lateral cartilage.

larger area, is smooth, crescentric in shape and slightly vaulted.

The posterior surface which is related to the deep digital flexor tendon is termed the *flexor or tendon surface*. On each side of this surface is a large plantar foramen which transmits respectively the terminal branches of the medial and lateral digital arteries into the semilunar sinus in the centre of the bone where they anastomose. Between the large plantar foraminae and the semilunar crest is the rough tendinous surface for the insertion of the deep digital flexor tendon.

The wings (*lateral angles*) are directed posteriorly on either side, and the medial one is usually the shorter. Each is divided by a notch into an upper (basilar) or lower (retrossal) process. In old horses these processes are generally joined by a bridge of bone converting the notch into a foramen. The proximal borders of these wings support the lateral cartilages of the foot.

The lateral cartilages of the third phalanx are rhomboid curved plates attached to the upper borders of the wings (*Fig. 19*). They are large and extend sufficiently above the coronet to be palpable. They contain and support the digital cushion and, being elastic, permit some expansion of the posterior part of the foot. With age they lose their elasticity and if converted into bone constitute the condition called "Side-bone disease."

The third phalanx of the hind leg is more pointed at the toe and the ventral surface is more concave or vaulted.

THE NAVICULAR OR DISTAL SESAMOID BONE

This is a small shuttle-shaped bone, situated behind the articulation of the second and third phalanges.

The articular surface, which has a central eminence, articulates with the distal articular surface of the second phalanx. The *flexor or tendon surface* resembles an articular surface but is more extensive and not so smooth. In life it is covered by fibro-cartilage and the deep digital flexor tendon passes over it.

The proximal border is wide and grooved in its middle. *The distal border* has anteriorly a transversely elongated facet which articulates with the third phalanx, and behind this is a grooved portion perforated by numerous foramina. *The extremities* are blunt pointed.

The navicular bone of the hind leg is shorter and narrower.

Section II: ARTHROLOGY

A joint or articulation is formed by the union of two or more bones or cartilage and their study is termed *arthrology*. It is customary to describe joints in three groups, fibrous, cartilaginous and synovial. The most important and largest group is that of the synovial or diarthrodial joints (*Fig. 20*). These have a joint cavity and a joint capsule and are characterised by their great freedom of movement. If the joint is formed by two articular surfaces it is called a *simple joint*, but if formed by several articular surfaces, as in the formation of the carpus (knee), then it is called a *composite joint*.

The articular surfaces vary in form and are composed of dense compact bone.

The articular cartilage forms a covering over the articular surface of the bones. It is very smooth and thickest in those joints subject to most pressure and friction. Its function is to diminish concussion and reduce friction.

The joint capsule in its simplest form is a tube, the ends of which are attached around the margins of the articulating surfaces. It is

0

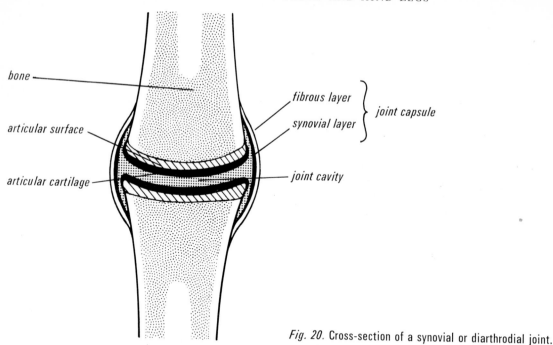

bone

articular surface

articular cartilage

fibrous layer
synovial layer
} joint capsule

joint cavity

Fig. 20. Cross-section of a synovial or diarthrodial joint.

composed of two layers. An outer *fibrous layer* which is attached around the margins of the articular surface to which is attached the inner or *synovial layer*. This is a thin membrane which lines the joint cavity and secretes synovia or joint oil. *Synovia* is a glairy, straw-coloured fluid which lubricates the joint.

Ligaments are strong bands of fibrous tissue which bind bones together. They are classified according to their position. Those which form part of the fibrous layer of the joint capsule are called *periarticular* ligaments, those within the joint cavity *intra-articular* ligaments and those situated at the sides of a joint are called *collateral* ligaments. Ligaments which connect directly opposed surfaces of bone such as a small metacarpal to the larger metacarpal bone are called interosseous ligaments.

THE FETLOCK JOINT
(*Metacarpo–phalangeal articulation*)

The bones that enter into the formation of this joint are the large metacarpal, first phalanx

and proximal sesamoids. The movements of the joint are flexion and extension but when flexed slight abduction, adduction and rotation are possible. With the horse in the standing position the angle formed by the metacarpal bone and first phalanx in front of the fetlock joint is about 140° whereas in the hind leg it is about 145°.

The two sesamoid bones are united by the *intersesamoidean ligament* which in essence is a mass of fibrocartilage filling the space between them. It extends above the level of the sesamoid bones and its posterior surface forms a smooth groove for the passage of the tendon of the deep digital flexor.

The formation of the fetlock joint is studied by examining, firstly, the attachment of the sesamoid bones to the first phalanx and, secondly, the attachment of the conjoined sesamoid bones and first phalanx to the distal extremity of the large metacarpal bone.

Attachment of the sesamoid bones to the first phalanx. The sesamoid bones are attached to the

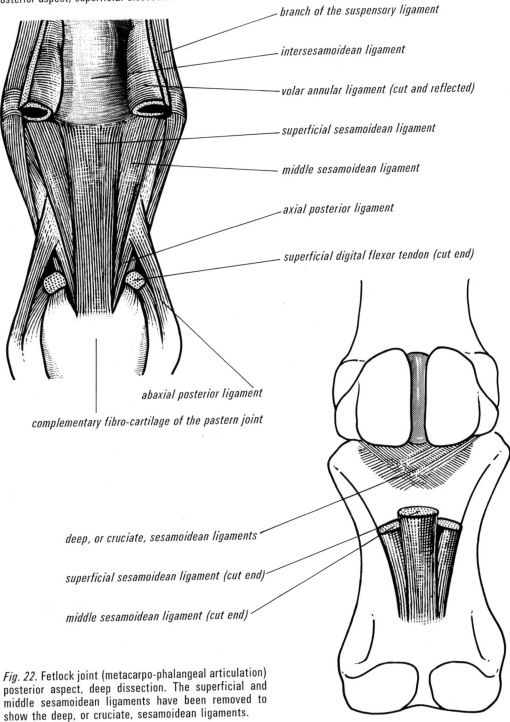

Fig. 21. Fetlock joint (metacarpo-phalangeal articulation) posterior aspect, superficial dissection.

branch of the suspensory ligament

intersesamoidean ligament

volar annular ligament (cut and reflected)

superficial sesamoidean ligament

middle sesamoidean ligament

axial posterior ligament

superficial digital flexor tendon (cut end)

abaxial posterior ligament

complementary fibro-cartilage of the pastern joint

deep, or cruciate, sesamoidean ligaments

superficial sesamoidean ligament (cut end)

middle sesamoidean ligament (cut end)

Fig. 22. Fetlock joint (metacarpo-phalangeal articulation) posterior aspect, deep dissection. The superficial and middle sesamoidean ligaments have been removed to show the deep, or cruciate, sesamoidean ligaments.

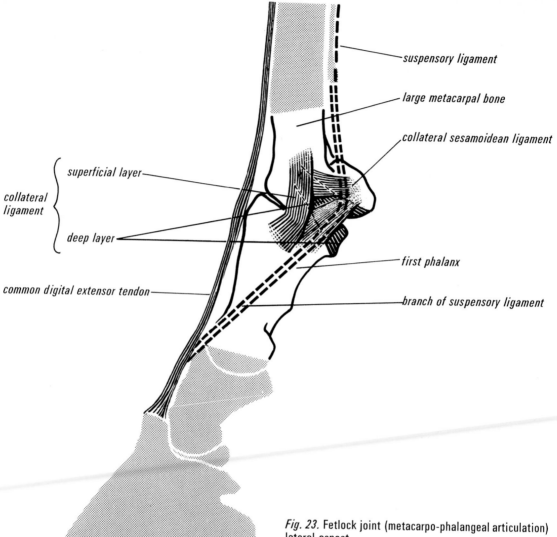

collateral ligament { superficial layer
collateral ligament { deep layer

common digital extensor tendon

suspensory ligament

large metacarpal bone

collateral sesamoidean ligament

first phalanx

branch of suspensory ligament

Fig. 23. Fetlock joint (metacarpo-phalangeal articulation) lateral aspect.

first phalanx by the distal or inferior sesamoidean ligaments, the collateral sesamoidean ligaments and the suspensory ligament.

A. *The distal or inferior sesamoidean ligaments* are three in number (*Figs. 21 and 22*).

(i) The superficial sesamoidean ligament is riband-like and attached proximally to the base of the sesamoid bones and distally to

the complementary fibro-cartilage of the second phalanx.

(ii) The middle sesamoidean ligament is triangular with thick margins and a thin central portion. It is attached to the base of the sesamoid bones and the triangular area on the posterior surface of the first phalanx.

(iii) The deep or cruciate ligament consists of

two layers of fibres which arise from the base of the sesamoid bones, and cross each other to be inserted on to the posterior proximal extremity of the first phalanx.

B. *The collateral sesamoidean ligaments*, lateral and medial (*Fig. 23*), arise on the abaxial surface of each sesamoid bone and divide into two branches which unite the corresponding side of each sesamoid bone to the distal extremity of the large metacarpal bone and the proximal extremity of the first phalanx.

C. *The suspensory ligament*. The principal function of this ligament is to support the fetlock joint by controlling excessive extension when weight is borne by the limb. It originates from the distal row of carpal bones and the roughened area at the posterior and proximal extremity of the large metacarpal bone (*Fig. 13 [c]*). It has the form of a wide thick riband, lies in the groove formed by the three metacarpal bones and at the distal extremity of the large metacarpal bone the ligament bifurcates. The branches diverge to gain the abaxial surface of the corresponding sesamoid bone to which a considerable part of each branch is attached. The remainder, as a flat narrow band, passes obliquely downwards and forwards to the anterior surface of the first phalanx where it joins the tendon of the common digital extensor.

Attachment of the conjoined sesamoid bones and first phalanx to the large metacarpal bone. The proximal extremity of the first phalanx with attached sesamoid bones is joined to the distal extremity of the large metacarpal bone by the collateral ligaments of the fetlock joint supported by the attachment of a branch of the collateral sesamoidean ligament (*Fig. 23*).

The collateral ligaments of the fetlock joint, are divided into two layers.

(i) *the superficial layer* which passes vertically from the distal extremity of the large metacarpal bone to the roughened area on the

corresponding aspect of the first phalanx and

(ii) *the deep layer* which originates beneath the superficial layer in the pit at the distal extremity of the large metacarpal bone and passes obliquely downwards and backwards to be attached to the abaxial surface of the sesamoid bone and proximal extremity of the first phalanx.

The joint capsule of the fetlock joint is attached around the articular margins. It is thickened in front, and here a bursa is interposed between it and the tendon of the common digital extensor. Posteriorly it forms a pouch which extends upwards between the large metacarpal bone and suspensory ligament. Distension of this pouch is called an *articular windgall*.

THE PASTERN JOINT
(Proximal interphalangeal articulation)

The joint is formed between the distal extremity of the first and the proximal extremity of the second phalanx (*Fig. 24*). The posterior articular surface is extended by a *complementary plate of fibro-cartilage*. Anteriorly it supports the joint capsule and posteriorly it is part of the anterior boundary of the digital synovial sheath, through which the tendon of the deep digital flexor passes.

The joint possesses two collateral ligaments and two pairs of posterior ligaments. When the horse is in the normal standing position the joint is extended with the first and second phalanges at the same angle. Joint movements are limited to flexion and extension. When flexed slight lateral and medial movement and rotation can be produced by manipulation.

The collateral ligaments are short strong bands which are attached proximally to the sides of the distal extremity of the first phalanx and distally to the sides of the proximal extremity of the second phalanx.

Some of the anterior fibres are prolonged downwards and backwards to form part of the

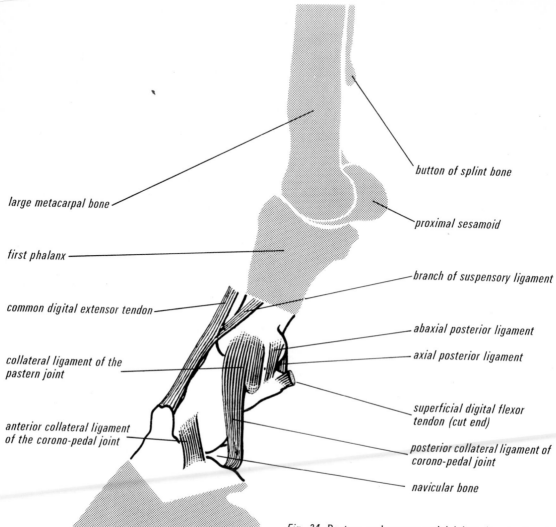

large metacarpal bone

first phalanx

common digital extensor tendon

collateral ligament of the
pastern joint

anterior collateral ligament
of the corono-pedal joint

button of splint bone

proximal sesamoid

branch of suspensory ligament

abaxial posterior ligament

axial posterior ligament

superficial digital flexor
tendon (cut end)

posterior collateral ligament of
corono-pedal joint

navicular bone

Fig. 24. Pastern and corono-pedal joints (proximal and distal inter-phalangeal articulations) lateral aspect.

posterior collateral ligament of the corono-pedal joint.

The posterior ligaments consist of two pairs. The abaxial pair pass from the postero-lateral aspect of the first phalanx to the complementary fibro-cartilage, whereas the axial pair, which are shorter, pass from the posterior aspect of the first phalanx to the complementary fibro-cartilage.

The joint capsule blends anteriorly with the

tendon of the common digital extensor and on each side with the collateral ligament.

Posteriorly it extends proximally to form a small pouch.

THE CORONO-PEDAL JOINT
(Distal interphalangeal articulation)

This joint is formed by the junction of the second and third phalanges and the navicular bone (*Fig. 24*). The distal articular surface is formed by the combined articular surfaces of the third phalanx and the navicular bone. The navicular bone is firmly united to the third phalanx by the *interosseous ligament* which is composed of short fibres that pass from its distal border to the tendinous surface of the third phalanx.

The united third phalanx and navicular bone is connected to the first and second phalanx by two pairs of ligaments, the anterior and posterior collateral ligaments.

The anterior collateral ligaments, medial and lateral, pass from the side of the second phalanx to the pit at the side of the extensor process of the third phalanx.

The posterior collateral ligaments, medial and lateral, are in part a continuation of the anterior fibres of the collateral ligament of the pastern joint. Each passes downwards and backwards to terminate chiefly on the extremity of the navicular bone, but detaches a branch to the wing of the third phalanx and the axial surface of the lateral cartilage.

The joint capsule is supported anteriorly by the expanded tendon of the common digital extensor and at the sides by the collateral ligaments. Posteriorly it extends proximally forming a considerable pouch, and on each side is a small pouch which lies close to the lateral cartilage.

The normal movements of this joint are extension and flexion, but when flexed slight lateral movement and some rotation is possible.

The fetlock joint, suspensory ligament, pastern joint and corono-pedal joint of a front leg resemble in the closest manner the corresponding joints and ligaments of a hind leg.

Section III: MYOLOGY

Myology is the study of muscles and their accessory structures. Muscles make up between 40% and 45% of the total body weight and by contraction produce the movements of various organs and parts of the body. Also, they are great liberators of energy in the body and the energy is used to perform mechanical work and to heat the body. There are three varieties of muscle.

Visceral or smooth muscles which are involuntary in that they are independent of the central nervous system and display constant rhythmic contractions. They are made up of longitudinally fibrillated spindle-shaped fibres, are present in such structures as the lungs, stomach, intestine and bladder and even in sleep do not rest.

Skeletal or striated muscles which are voluntary in that they are directly under the control of the central nervous system and remain at rest until stimulated to contract. A typical skeletal muscle is a mass of fleshy tissue which is made up of longitudinally fibrillated fibres with transverse markings which end in a fibrous cord or *tendon* and by which the muscle is attached to a bone. When the muscle contracts it becomes shorter and thickened, acts on the bones to which it is attached and results in movement of the limb.

Heart muscle is characterised by its syncytial network of fibres which are cross striped. Heart muscle like visceral muscle is involuntary in that it is independent of the central nervous system and maintains a continual rhythmic contraction and relaxation of the heart.

THE MUSCLES OF THE FOREARM

The forearm is covered on three sides by muscles leaving the medial aspect of the radius subcutaneous. The extensors of the carpus and digit lie on the anterior and lateral aspect while the flexors are located on the posterior aspect (*Fig. 25*).

EXTENSORS OF THE DIGIT

Common digital extensor (extensor pedis). This muscle arises from the distal extremity of the humerus and proximal extremity of the radius. Its tendon passes downwards over the anterior

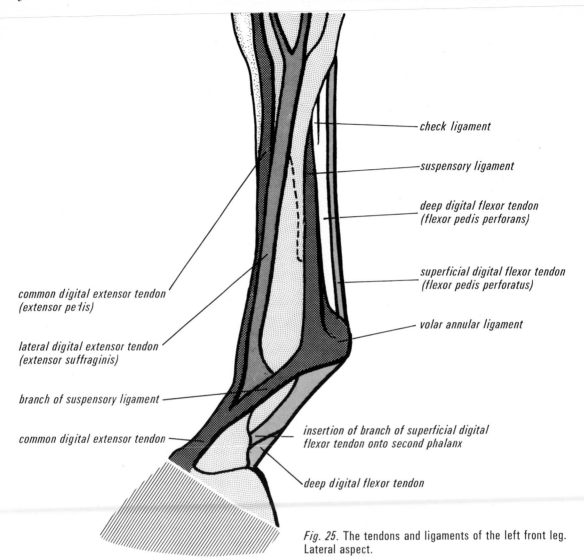

check ligament

suspensory ligament

deep digital flexor tendon
(flexor pedis perforans)

superficial digital flexor tendon
(flexor pedis perforatus)

volar annular ligament

common digital extensor tendon
(extensor pe tis)

lateral digital extensor tendon
(extensor suffraginis)

branch of suspensory ligament

common digital extensor tendon

insertion of branch of superficial digital
flexor tendon onto second phalanx

deep digital flexor tendon

Fig. 25. The tendons and ligaments of the left front leg.
Lateral aspect.

surface of the large metacarpal bone and of the fetlock joint. A little below the middle of the first phalanx it is joined by the branches of the suspensory ligament, which greatly increase its width. It then passes over the pastern joint and the second phalanx to be inserted on to the extensor process of the third phalanx. At the fetlock joint a congenital bursa is interposed between it and the joint capsule.

Lateral digital extensor (extensor suffraginis). This muscle arises from the lateral and proximal aspect of the radius.

Its tendon passes downwards on the antero-lateral surface of the large metacarpal bone. It passes over the anterior aspect of the fetlock joint to be inserted on the eminence on the proximal aspect of the anterior surface of the first phalanx.

FLEXORS OF THE DIGIT

Superficial digital flexor (flexor pedis perforatus). This muscle arises from the distal extremity of the humerus and posterior surface of the radius. Its tendon passes down the posterior aspect of the metacarpus on the deep digital flexor tendon (flexor pedis perforans). At the fetlock joint it widens, still covering the deep digital flexor tendon, and here both tendons are supported and retained by the volar annular ligament as they pass over the intersesamoidean ligament. Towards the distal extremity of the first phalanx the tendon divides, to form a ring which permits the passage of the deep digital flexor tendon, and is inserted on the eminence on either side of the proximal extremity of the second phalanx.

Deep digital flexor (flexor pedis perforans). This muscle arises from the distal extremity of the humerus, the olecranon and posterior surface of the radius. Its tendon in its passage down the metacarpus lies between the superficial digital flexor tendon and the suspensory ligament. Towards the middle of the metacarpus it is joined by a strong fibrous band, *the check or subcarpal ligament* which is a direct continuation of the posterior ligaments of the carpus.

The tendon descends over the intersesamoidean ligament, passes through the opening formed by the division of the superficial digital flexor tendon, and then continues over the flexor surface of the navicular bone to be inserted on the flexor surface of the third phalanx.

> In the hindleg the tendons of the extensor and flexor muscles, and the suspensory and check ligaments have the same distribution below the hock joint as the corresponding structures of the front leg.

SYNOVIAL BURSA

A synovial bursa is a closed sac lined by a synovial membrane and containing synovia (*Fig. 26*). It is usually present or develops in areas subject to pressure or friction such as where a

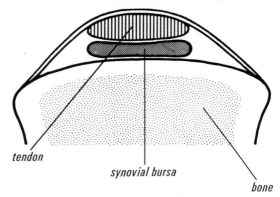

Fig. 26. Cross-section of a synovial bursa.

tendon passes over a bony projection. There are two varieties of bursae.

Congenital or deep bursae which are present at birth and situated between tendon and bone or between tendons.

Acquired or superficial bursae are generally situated between the skin and a bony prominence and develop after birth. A typical example is the development of a capped elbow following slight but repeated injury.

SYNOVIAL SHEATH

A synovial sheath is a sac containing synovia which is folded around a tendon (*Fig. 27*). The function of a synovial sheath is to prevent friction and protect a tendon as it passes through a canal. A synovial sheath has two layers. An

Fig. 27. Cross-section of a synovial sheath.

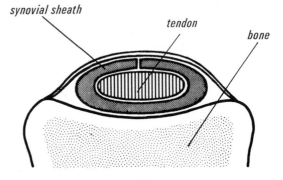

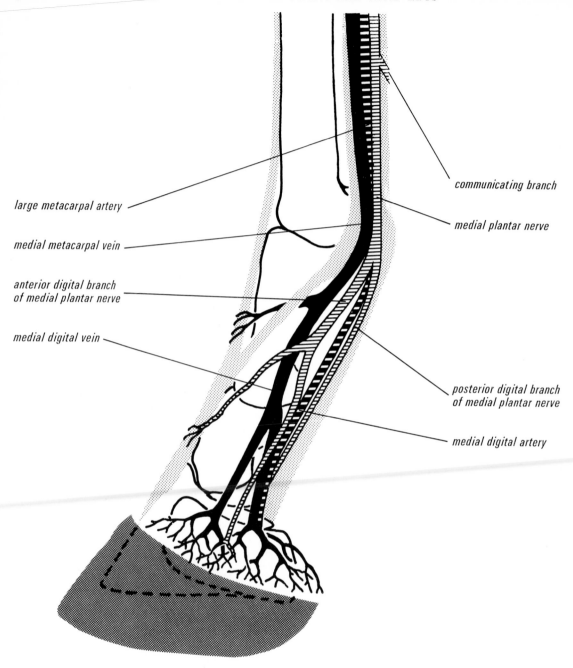

large metacarpal artery

medial metacarpal vein

anterior digital branch
of medial plantar nerve

medial digital vein

communicating branch

medial plantar nerve

posterior digital branch
of medial plantar nerve

medial digital artery

Fig. 28. Arteries, veins and nerves, front leg and foot.
Medial aspect.

inner layer which is adherent to the tendon and the outer which lines the canal in which the tendon lies.

The *carpal synovial sheath* commences 3″ to 4″ above the posterior aspect of the carpus and extends downwards to the middle of the metacarpus.

The *digital synovial sheath* commences 2″ to 3″ above the posterior aspect of the fetlock joint and extends downwards to the middle of the second phalanx.

As the tendons of the superficial and deep digital flexors descend the front limb they are enveloped in the carpal synovial sheath as they pass through the carpal canal and in the digital synovial sheath as they transverse the inter-sesamoidean ligament between the proximal sesamoid bones. Distension of the former is referred to as a *knee thoroughpin* and of the latter as a *tendinous windgall*.

Section IV: THE BLOOD-VASCULAR SYSTEM

The organs of circulation of the blood comprise the heart and blood-vessels.

The *heart* functions as a pump.

The *arteries* are thick-walled tubes which convey the blood from the heart to the tissues, and if cut a bright red blood escapes in a pulsating stream.

The *capillaries* are the microscopic end branches of the arteries which terminate in the tissues.

The *veins* are thin-walled tubes which convey the blood back to the heart, and if cut a dark red blood escapes in a steady flow. The walls of veins are much thinner than those of arteries and collapse when empty. In large veins valves are present which have thin free edges directed towards the heart thus ensuring the return flow of blood.

ARTERIES OF THE FRONT AND HIND LEG AND FOOT

The *large metacarpal artery* (common digital) conveys the blood to the leg and foot (*Fig. 28*). It descends down the metacarpus on the medial aspect of the digital flexor tendons and just above the fetlock divides to form the lateral and medial digital arteries.

The *digital arteries*, medial and lateral (*Fig. 29*), separate at an acute angle and pass down over the abaxial surface of the fetlock joint and descend along the edge of the digital flexor tendons to reach the inner aspect of the wing of the third phalanx where each divides into two terminal branches, the preplantar and plantar arteries.

The *preplantar artery* passes forward through the notch in the wing of the third phalanx, and along the preplantar groove on the laminal surface of the bone to supply the sensitive laminae.

The *plantar artery* passes along the plantar groove to enter the third phalanx through the plantar foramen and unites in the semilunar sinus with the corresponding artery of the opposite side to form the terminal arch. From this arch numerous branches pass throughout the bone and ramify in the corium of the wall and sole. The inferior arteries on each side anastomose to form the artery of the distal border of the third phalanx.

In addition to branches to joints, tendons and skin the digital arteries give off the artery of the first phalanx, of the digital cushion and the dorsal artery of the second phalanx.

In the hind leg the *large metatarsal artery* is a direct continuation of the anterior tibial artery. It descends in the groove, on the lateral aspect of the metatarsus, formed by the junction of the large and small metatarsal bone. A little above the button of the small metatarsal bone it passes to the posterior aspect of the metatarsus where it divides into the lateral and medial digital arteries which have the same arterial arrangement as in the front leg.

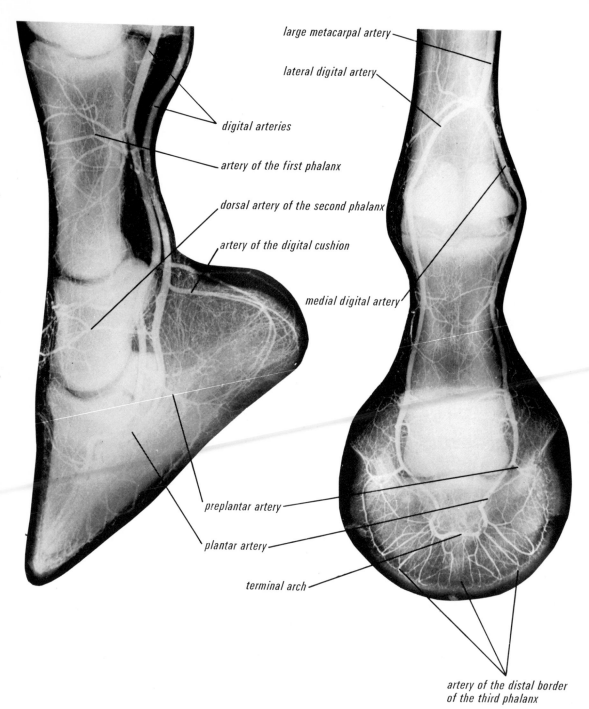

large metacarpal artery

lateral digital artery

digital arteries

artery of the first phalanx

dorsal artery of the second phalanx

artery of the digital cushion

medial digital artery

preplantar artery

plantar artery

terminal arch

artery of the distal border
of the third phalanx

Fig. 29. Arteriogram of the horse's foot.

VEINS OF THE FRONT AND HIND LEG AND FOOT

The veins of the foot comprise three distinct networks of vessels called the solar, laminal and coronary venous plexuses (*Fig. 30*). The veins of these plexuses communicate freely with one another and their branches converge to form the lateral and medial digital veins.

The *digital veins*, lateral and medial, ascend the limb in front of the corresponding digital arteries and unite just above the fetlock, between the deep digital flexor tendon and the suspensory ligament, to form a venous arch.

Three *metacarpal veins* arise from the venous arch. The *medial metacarpal vein* ascends the limb with the large metacarpal artery, the *lateral metacarpal vein* with the lateral plantar nerve, and the *deep metacarpal vein* between the suspensory ligament and medial small metacarpal bone.

The venous plexuses, venous arch and digital veins of the hind leg are arranged like those of the front leg.

It is interesting to note how the function of the foot assists in maintaining its venous circulation. When the foot takes weight it expands and in consequence the blood pressure in the veins is raised and they empty. When the foot is

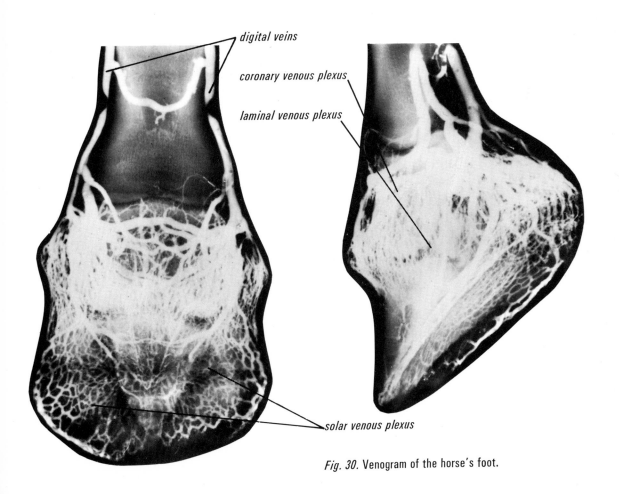

digital veins

coronary venous plexus

laminal venous plexus

solar venous plexus

Fig. 30. Venogram of the horse's foot.

raised the pressure is reduced and the veins fill. This action is so perfect that the digital veins and those of the foot are not provided with valves.

Section V: THE NERVOUS SYSTEM

The nervous system is a complex mechanism by which the various parts of the body are co-ordinated. It is divided into two parts. The central nervous system which comprises the brain and spinal cord and the peripheral nervous system.

Peripheral nerves are divided into two classes. *Afferent nerves* which conduct impulses from sense organs to the central nervous system, and *efferent nerves* which conduct impulses in the opposite direction.

NERVES OF THE FRONT AND HIND LEG
AND FOOT

The medial plantar nerve (*Fig. 28*), which is a continuation of the medial terminal branch of the median nerve, passes down the metacarpus on the medial aspect of the superficial digital flexor tendon, together with the large metacarpal artery. Towards the middle of the metacarpus it gives off a communicating branch which passes obliquely downwards over the flexor tendons to join the lateral nerve. At the fetlock joint the nerve divides into two digital branches.

(i) *The anterior digital branch* (*dorsal*) which passes forwards and divides into two to

ramify in the skin and corium of the hoof.

(ii) *The posterior digital branch* (*volar*) which descends along the border of the flexor tendons to supply the third phalanx, navicular bone, plantar cushion and corium of the sole.

The *lateral plantar nerve* is formed by the fusion of the terminal ulna nerve with one of the terminal branches of the median. It descends down the metacarpus along the lateral border of the deep digital flexor tendon behind the lateral metacarpal vein. About 1″ above the button of the lateral small metacarpal bone it is joined by the communicating branch from the medial plantar nerve. At the fetlock joint the nerve divides into two digital branches which ramify in an identical manner to the digital nerves on the medial aspect of the digit.

In the hind leg the *plantar nerves* result from the bifurcation of the tibial nerve. They descend in the metatarsal region, one on each side of the deep digital flexor tendon and accompanied by the metatarsal vein of that side. A little below the middle of the metatarsus the medial plantar detaches a small branch that winds obliquely downwards and laterally behind the superficial digital flexor tendon to join the lateral nerve just above the level of the button of the small metatarsal bone. At the fetlock both the medial and lateral nerves divide into two branches and have an identical distribution as like branches of the plantar nerves of the front leg.

CHAPTER THREE

The structure and
function of the
foot

THE *hoof* is the dense horny covering at the end of the digit and the term *foot* is used to describe the hoof and all the structures contained within it. The foot is a very specialised structure designed to resist wear, support weight and limit or prevent concussion.

The hoof is a continuation of the skin. The external foot or hoof which comprises the wall, sole, frog and periople is derived from the superficial layers of the skin or epidermis. The internal or sensitive foot which comprises the sensitive laminae, sensitive sole, sensitive frog and perioplic and coronary corium is derived from the deep layers of the skin or corium.

From this description of the formation of the hoof and sensitive foot it will be appreciated that the sensitive structures do not, as is sometimes stated, secrete the corresponding parts of the hoof.

Section I: THE EXTERNAL FOOT OR HOOF

The hoof which is non-vascular and insensitive is moulded over the sensitive structures and comprises the wall, sole and frog.

THE WALL

The wall is that part of the hoof which is seen when the foot is on the ground, and for description is divided into toe, quarters and heels (*Fig. 31*). The *toe* is the area in front, on either side of the midline, which passes into the *quarters* and which in turn pass into the *heels*.

The wall does not form a complete circle but is reflected inwards and forwards at an acute angle at the heels to form the bars (*Figs. 32 and 33*). The *bars* appear on the bearing surface of the foot as convergent ridges which are fused with the sole and united by the frog. By not completing the circle of the wall they allow for expansion of the foot and being part of the wall take weight and provide extra bearing surface and strength at the heels. They must be allowed to grow and develop normally. If they are cut away, as is sometimes practised, the foot is deprived of support at the heels and contraction results. The area of the sole between the wall and the bars is referred to as the "seat of corn".

The external surface is convex from side to side and slopes obliquely downwards. The slope is less at the quarters than at the toe, nearly upright at the heels and more marked on the medial than the lateral aspect of the foot (*Fig. 42*).

The surface is smooth and crossed by a number of waves or rings of horn (*Fig. 31*) which run parallel to the proximal border and indicate variations in the growth rate of the wall. The colour of the wall is governed by the colour of the skin at the coronet. If the skin is white it contains no pigment and in consequence the horn below it is white. White horn has the reputation of being brittle.

The periople (*Fig. 31*) is a thin layer of the epidermis which originates above the proximal border and develops as a rim of soft horn, light grey in colour, which bridges the junction between the epidermis and the wall. It is thickest proximally and gradually disintegrates as it grows down the wall; but at the heels it forms a wide cap to blend with the frog. When the hoof is dry the periople is not obvious, but when the

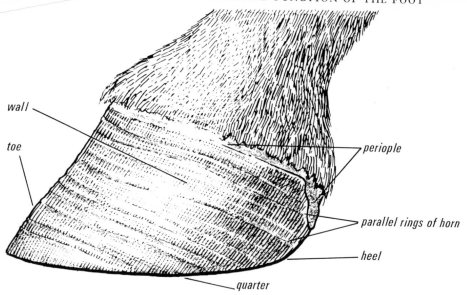

Fig. 31. The external foot or hoof – lateral aspect. Note the wavy growth of horn which appears as a number of rings parallel with the coronet and indicate alterations in the rate of growth.

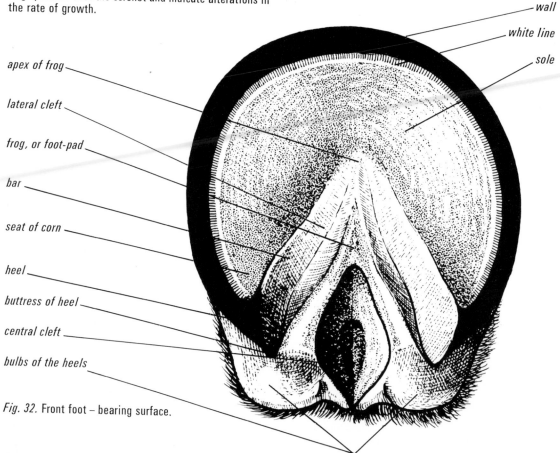

Fig. 32. Front foot – bearing surface.

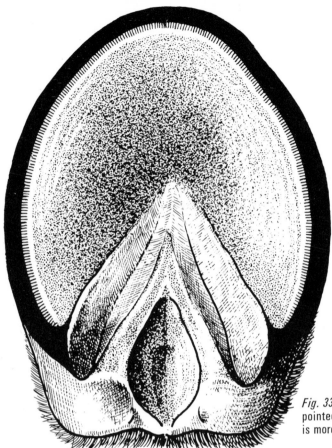

Fig. 33. Hind foot – bearing surface. A hind foot is more pointed at the toe, straighter at the quarters and the sole is more vaulted than in a front foot.

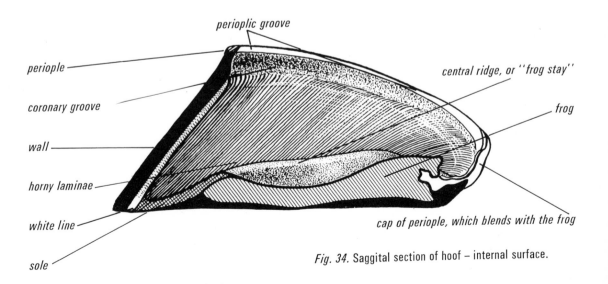

Fig. 34. Saggital section of hoof – internal surface.

feet have been exposed to moisture, a footbath for example, it is most conspicuous.

In addition to bridging the junction between dissimilar structures, the skin and wall and frog, the periople controls evaporation from the underlying horn. Therefore, it will be appreciated that care must be taken not to remove it by rasping because if this is persistently carried out it will result in excessive evaporation and brittle feet.

The internal surface (Fig. 34) is concave from side to side. It is traversed, in a vertical direction, by 500 to 600 horny laminae (leaves) which extend from the coronary groove to the bearing surface and on to the bars. Each horny lamina bears 100 to 200 secondary laminae. These insensitive laminae dovetail with the corresponding sensitive laminae of the foot to establish a very strong union.

It is interesting to note that as the horny laminae grow downwards there is a continual movement between them and the fixed sensitive laminae. Also, if a section of the wall is removed the exposed sensitive laminae are soon covered with a layer of horn. This observation was used to support the belief that the horny laminae are secreted by the sensitive laminae. This is not so; the layer of horn is the horny material that is secreted by the secondary sensitive laminae to establish contact with the secondary horny laminae.

The proximal or coronary border is thin and hollowed out to form the large coronary groove which lodges the coronary corium. Above the thin border is the perioplic groove which lodges the corium of the periople. These grooves merge at the heels.

The distal (bearing) border comes into contact with the ground and here its inner surface is united with the anterior border (periphery) of the sole (*Fig. 32*). This union is indicated on the bearing surface of the foot by a well defined white line.

The white line indicates the site of union between the insensitive laminae of the wall and the tubules of the sole. Between them is formed a soft plastic horn, yellowish in colour, which is presumably secreted by the corium of the sole. This soft horn, besides establishing a satisfactory union between wall and sole, permits the sole to yield slightly when weight is taken.

The white line is an important anatomical feature and a most helpful guide for the farrier. It indicates the thickness of the wall, the position of the sensitive structures, and these, considered with the slope of the wall, enable the farrier to assess the angle or pitch at which to drive the nails and secure a good hold without either pricking or causing pressure on the sensitive structures, a so-called "nail bind".

The wall is of equal thickness from the proximal to the distal border, but is thicker at the toe than at the heels (*Fig. 35*). The inner quarter is thinner than the outer except for the hind feet.

The rate at which the wall grows depends on a number of factors (*Fig. 36*). It grows evenly all round the proximal border at the rate of about $1''$ in 3 months. Therefore it takes, on average, from 9 to 12 months for the horn to grow from the proximal border to the toe, and to the heels about 6 months.

As the wall grows it undergoes compression and keratinisation and becomes hard and tough. Since the wall at the toe is longer and older than at the heels it is correspondingly harder. In the unshod foot the hard horn at the toe protects against friction and excessive wear, whereas the softer horn at the heels contributes to the expansion of the foot when it takes weight.

The rate at which the wall grows varies with individual horses. It grows more rapidly when a horse is at work than when it is confined to a stable. Also, the rate of growth appears to be influenced by weight bearing because, for example, when a portion of the wall is removed to relieve pressure from the shoe, that area of the wall will grow more rapidly than the rest which is in contact with the shoe.

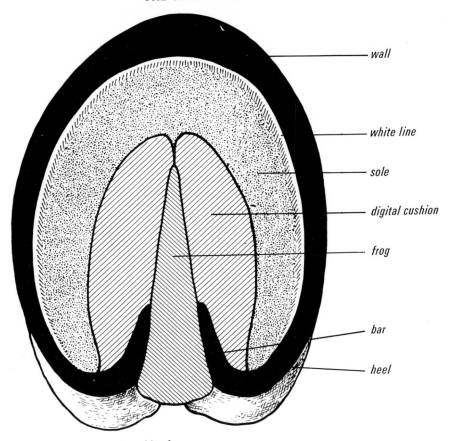

Fig. 35. Horizontal section of hoof.

Fig. 36. Rate of growth of the wall. The wall grows at the same rate around its proximal border A C. Therefore the horn along the line B D is the same age but obviously the horn at the toe E is older than the horn at the heels D.

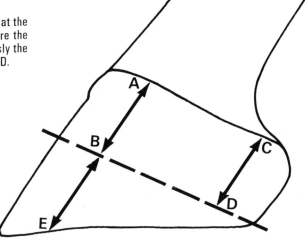

The rate of growth of the wall is not accelerated by any applications to its surface, but it can be stimulated by applying a blister to the coronet.

THE SOLE

The sole constitutes the greater part of the ground surface of the hoof and presents two surfaces and two borders (*Figs. 32 and 34*).

The external surface is arched or vaulted. This feature is more pronounced in the hind than in the front feet, but is subject to wide variation in different breeds.

The internal surface is convex and conforms to the concavity of the ventral surface of the third phalanx (*Fig. 37*). It is covered with numerous minute holes which lodge the papillae of the sensitive sole.

The anterior (convex) border is much thicker than the posterior border and its junction with the wall is indicated by the "white line".

The posterior (concave) border consists of two angular portions which lie between the wall and the bars and between them is a triangular space into which the frog fits.

The soles of heavy draught horses are generally flatter than those seen in riding horses and in ponies. The thickness of soles varies considerably; in some horses they are firm and rigid, whereas in others they are thin and yield to pressure. Growth of the sole differs from that of the wall as it exfoliates or flakes off when its fibres have attained sufficient length. This is a necessary feature of the sole if it is to maintain its natural vaulted configuration as it is not exposed to or worn away by friction.

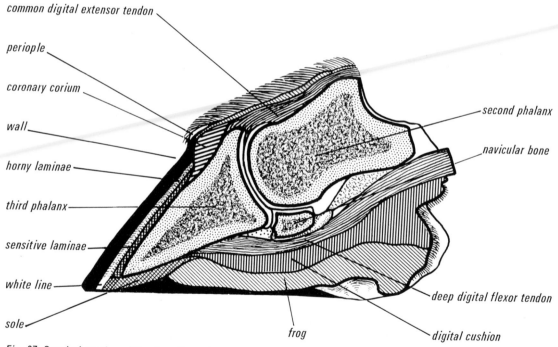

Fig. 37. Saggital section of the foot. Note that the third phalanx does not lie parallel with the bearing surface of the foot, but fits within the hoof, with its toe slightly lower than its angles.

The function of the sole is to protect the sensitive structures above it, to support weight and to bear weight around its anterior border. It will be noted that the sole is less dense and friction resistant than the wall and there are no sensitive structures directly above its anterior border. The vaulting of the sole is sufficient evidence to show that it is designed to support weight rather than bear weight, although that portion of the sole which is in contact with the wall is a weight bearing surface.

A normal healthy sole, because of its method of growth, is covered with flakes of horn. For the sake of appearance, some farriers pare down the sole until it looks neat and "eases under pressure" with the thumb. If the sole is to function effectively its protective thickness must be preserved, and to reduce it is a bad practice and to be deprecated.

THE FROG OR FOOT-PAD
The frog is a wedge-shaped mass of soft elastic horn having the character of india-rubber, which occupies the angle between the bars and the sole (*Figs. 32 and 33*). Its bearing surface should be in contact with the ground. It is described as having four surfaces, a base and an apex.

The bearing (external) surface has a shallow cleft posteriorly, termed the *central cleft*. This cleft is bounded by two ridges and between them and the bars lie deep depressions called the *lateral and median clefts*.

The internal surface has a central ridge or "frog stay" (*Fig. 34*). On each side of this ridge the surface is depressed and the whole surface is moulded on the digital (plantar) cushion, and covered with minute holes which lodge the papillae of the plantar cushion.

The base (posterior extremity) is depressed centrally with prominent eminences on either side, the *bulbs* of the heels.

The apex is a blunt point. It is wedged in the centre of the posterior border of the sole and lies a little in front of the middle of the bearing surface of the foot.

The lateral and medial surfaces are united with the sole and bars.

The frog contains more fluid than any other part of the hoof and this accounts for its soft pliable state. The apex which is much harder than the base acts as a sensory organ of touch by stimulating the nerve endings in the underlying digital cushion. Overgrowth of the frog is controlled by flakes of it separating when it attains a certain size and by being worn away by friction with the ground. The frog provides protection to the corono-pedal joint, and the aponeurosis of the tendon of the deep digital flexor, plays an important rôle in the anti-concussion mechanism of the foot, and its wedge shape contributes to providing a good foothold.

When the foot comes to the ground the frog takes the weight and is compressed. It is able to expand without being forced against the sole and bars because of the intervening space provided by the central and lateral clefts (*Fig. 32*). Also it is forced upwards and exerts pressure on the digital cushion. This in turn exerts pressure through the lateral cartilages on to the wall which expands (*Fig. 42*).

To function satisfactorily the frog must be normal in size and in a healthy state and to attain this it must be in contact with the ground. If it does not do so it soon atrophies, the heels converge and a contracted foot ensues. Atrophy of the frog can be remedied by pressure. However, it should be noted that the pressure exerted by fitting a bar-shoe is followed by little improvement. It is only when the intermittent pressure of natural weight bearing is established that the frog returns to its normal healthy state and contraction of the foot is halted.

THE STRUCTURE OF HORN
The horn of the hoof, which is almost completely keratinised, is composed of modified

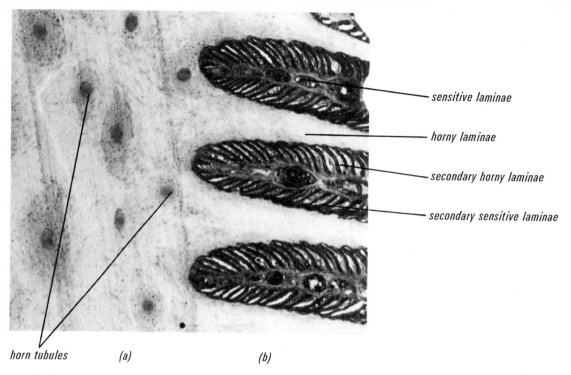

horn tubules   (a)   (b)

Fig. 38. Transverse section of the external and internal foot: *(a)* portion of the wall showing the horn tubules; *(b)* junction of the horny and sensitive laminae.

epithelial cells. The horn of the wall contains numerous tubules which are arranged in parallel and run from the proximal to the distal border (*Fig. 38*). The horn tubes of the sole have a similar disposition but those of the frog are slightly more tortuous. The horn of the frog is relatively soft, more elastic and not so keratinised as either the wall or the sole.

The water content of the hoof is an important factor which ranges from approximately 25% in the wall to 40% in the frog. The horn tubes contain fluid which is supplied from either the papillae of the corium or absorbed from the surface. Constant evaporation is taking place from the surface of the hoof and being replaced by these two processes. If evaporation is excessive then the hoof becomes brittle and cracks. On the other hand if evaporation is checked then excess fluid accumulates and the hoof becomes soft. For this reason, impervious oils and grease should not be applied to a normal healthy wall. It will be appreciated that the moisture content of the hoof is critical if it is not to become brittle and the elasticity of the foot is to be maintained.

Horn cells are dissolved by alkalies and therefore the harmful effects of ammonia present in decomposing urine and manure must not be overlooked in the management of horses' feet.

Horn is a bad conductor of heat and provides a very effective protection to the underlying structures against extremes of temperature. A normal hoof will withstand the effects of cold and the application of a red-hot shoe, provided it is held in contact for only a short time.

Section II: THE SENSITIVE OR INTERNAL FOOT

The corium or sensitive structures of the foot (*Figs. 39, 40 and 41*) are a modified part of the deeper layers of the skin which contain the blood vessels and nerves. They provide nutrition to the corresponding parts of the hoof.

The perioplic corium (perioplic ring) lies in the perioplic groove which is situated immediately above the proximal border of the coronary corium. It possesses fine papillae which supply nutrition to the periople.

The coronary corium (coronary body) is a thick, half-round structure situated above the sensitive laminae and lies in the coronary groove. Its surface is covered with long papillae which fit into openings of the coronary groove and supply nutrition to the wall.

The sensitive laminae (coronary laminae) which comprise both primary and secondary laminae are attached to the periostium of the laminal surface of the third phalanx and part of the lateral cartilages. They extend in a vertical direction from the coronary corium to the distal border of the bone and dovetail with the horny laminae of the wall to which they supply nutrition. The laminae at the toe are longer than those at the heels where they turn inwards to form the sensitive bars.

It is interesting to note that the weight of the horse is supported by the union of the horny and sensitive laminae. At stages of the gallop, for example, when the horse is supported by one leg only, its whole weight is taken by the dovetailing of these delicate structures. In relation to body size, the horse's foot is small, but due to the interleaving of 500 to 600 primary laminae and about 72,000 secondary laminae it encloses an area of approximately 8 square feet, thus keeping the functional surfaces of the internal foot within small proportions without affecting its strength.

The sensitive sole (corium of the sole) corresponds to the horny sole. It is firmly adherent to the periostium of the solar surface of the third phalanx and on its free surface has long papillae which penetrate the tubules of the sole to supply nutrition.

Fig. 39. The internal or sensitive foot – lateral aspect.

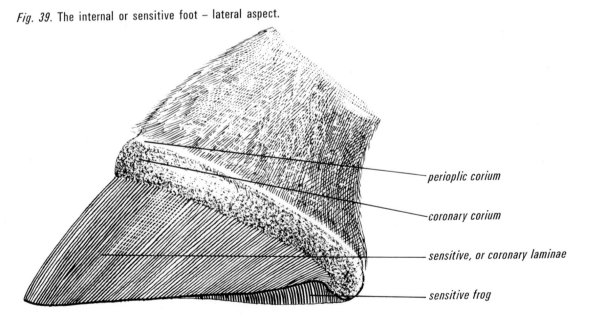

- perioplic corium

- coronary corium

- sensitive, or coronary laminae

- sensitive frog

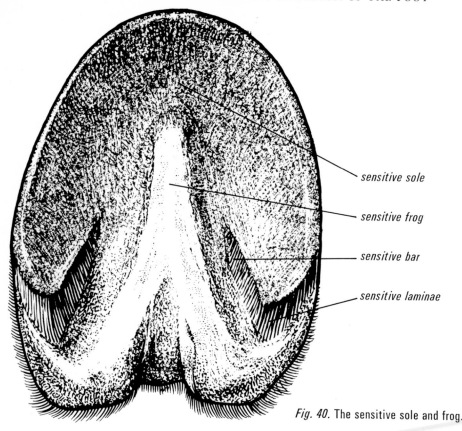

Fig. 40. The sensitive sole and frog.

The sensitive frog (corium of the frog) supplies nutrition to the digital cushion on which it is moulded and with which it blends.

The digital or plantar cushion is a wedge-shaped fibro-elastic pad occupying the posterior part of the foot and filling in the hollow of the heels (*Fig. 37*). It is firm yet yielding and possesses four surfaces, a base and an apex. The *superior surface* is applied to the tendon of the deep digital flexor, the *inferior surface* is moulded to the corium of the frog and the *lateral and medial* surfaces are related to the lateral cartilages. The *apex* lies anteriorly and is adherent to the tendon of the deep digital flexor at its insertion. The *base* is situated posteriorly, lies under the skin and is divided by a depression into two rounded masses called *bulbs of the heel.*

The digital cushion plays an important rôle in reducing concussion by expanding when the foot takes weight.

The sensitive structures of the foot, which receive their blood supply from the digital arteries, are very vascular and any wound results in profuse haemorrhage.

The nerve supply to the sensitive structures of the foot is from the terminal branches of the digital nerves.

Valuable as this nerve supply is in keeping the horse informed of the type of ground over which it is travelling, it is not essential to progression as all sensory nerves to the foot can be severed without seriously affecting the horse's locomotor efficiency or safety.

Section III: FUNCTIONS OF THE FOOT

The functions of the foot are two-fold. Firstly to reduce concussion and secondly to mitigate against slipping.

ANTI-CONCUSSION MECHANISM

The effects of concussion are minimised by the angular structure of the limbs and the movements of the foot when it comes to the ground and the weight of the horse passes over it. When examining the part played by the foot in reducing the concussion of weight-bearing, it must be considered as a whole because its various structures are interdependent. Since the posterior aspect of the bearing surface of the foot comes to the ground first, those structures which have the most important anti-concussion function are located posteriorly. The importance of the anti-concussion mechanism of the foot is readily appreciated when it is realised that a little more than one quarter of a horse's weight is supported by each front leg when it is standing, and at certain stages of the gallop the whole of its weight is supported by one foot.

The foot is protected from concussion by the yielding articulation of the corono-pedal joint, the slight descent of the third phalanx and the sole, the elasticity of the frog and digital cushion, the flexibility of the lateral cartilages and the expansion of the wall at the heels.

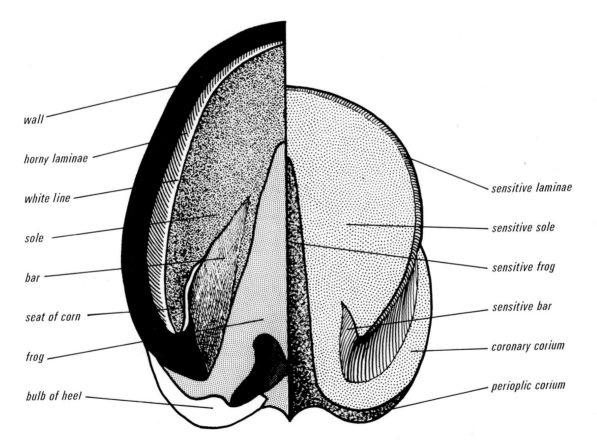

Fig. 41. Bearing surface of the foot. Half of the wall, sole and frog have been removed to illustrate their relationship to the sensitive foot.

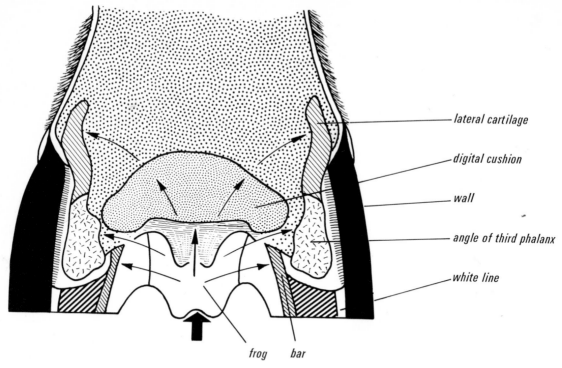

- lateral cartilage
- digital cushion
- wall
- angle of third phalanx
- white line

frog   bar

Fig. 42. Cross-section of the posterior aspect of the foot. When the foot takes weight the frog is compressed and expands. This results in pressure on the bars and digital cushion. These in turn press on the lateral cartilages which yield and is followed by expansion of the foot at the heels.

When the foot comes to the ground the weight is taken by the frog and posterior wall (*Fig. 42*). The frog is compressed and expands, more especially if it is well developed and the horse has low heels. This results in pressure on the digital cushion and the bars and these in turn press on the lateral cartilages which yield and force apart the thin wall at the heels. When weight is taken off the foot, the frog and digital cushion contract and the lateral cartilages and the wall return to their resting positions. The degree of expansion is slight and when measured in a front foot after lifting the opposite front foot the expansion will be in the order of $1/25''$. Naturally, when the horse is in motion the degree of expansion will be correspondingly increased. Horses with low heels and well developed frogs will register a greater degree of foot expansion than horses with high heels and poorly developed frogs. Indeed, if a frog is so small that it does not come into contact with the ground, then when weight is taken it is pressed downwards by the descent of the third phalanx. This results in the lateral cartilages being drawn inwards which, in turn, will contribute to the development of a contracted foot.

ANTI-SLIPPING MECHANISM

The bearing surface of the hoof is made up of the wall, sole and frog. The sole is concave or saucer shaped and like a saucer, due to its concavity and rim, it grips firmly when pressed into the ground. Indeed it can only be moved by a pull from above.

The frog, which is wedge shaped, with a groove running down its centre and one on either side, is the first part of the foot to come into contact with the ground. When a horse pulls up its feet are thrust forward and the frogs dig into the ground. The combination of a saucer shaped sole and wedge shaped frog assist a horse to maintain its balance and prevents slipping when it turns or pulls up sharply.

Section IV: PHYSIOLOGICAL SHOEING

The purpose of shoeing a horse is to protect its feet from excessive wear. If the anatomy and principles of the physiology of the foot are understood and applied when dressing a foot and when making and fitting a shoe, then normal function will be preserved and many of the harmful effects of shoeing overcome. To this end the following should be practised:

(i)   The wall should be reduced to the proportions that would result from the friction of normal wear of the unshod foot.

(ii) The outer edge of the shoe should conform with the outline of the wall.
      If the wall is rasped to make the foot fit the shoe the periople is destroyed, which makes the hoof brittle, bearing surface is lost, and less wall remains to secure the nails.

(iii) The sole should not be pared. It cannot be too thick to protect the internal foot.

(iv) Cutting out the bars or "opening up the heels" as this practice is commonly called, must not be practised. The bars are part of the wall and therefore their function is to take weight. Also, they play an important part in the anti-concussion mechanism of the foot.

(v)   The frog should not be trimmed. Unless it attains its normal size it does not come into contact with the ground, and unless it is compressed when weight is taken it cannot function properly.

(vi) The shoe must have a level foot surface and rest on the wall, bars and outer edge of the sole.

(vii) The shoe should be secured with as few nails as possible because they damage the horn. They should not be placed at the heels as this will limit normal expansion of the foot.

These, then, are the considerations which have to be taken into account to observe the rules of physiological shoeing. If these rules are not adhered to, the foot is unable to function normally and in time adverse changes will inevitably arise.

CHAPTER FOUR

Tools used by the farrier

THE tools employed by farriers are classified as "shoeing tools", which are used by the doorman to remove the shoe, prepare the foot and nail on the shoe, and "forge tools" which are used by the fireman at the fire and the anvil to make and fit the shoe.

Section I: SHOEING TOOLS

FARRIER'S SHOEING, DRIVING OR NAILING ON HAMMER (*Fig. 43*)

This hammer weighs 10 to 16 ozs. and is used for driving the nails, twisting off their points, forming the clenches and withdrawing nails. It has a large face and a short curved claw with the grip wide enough for withdrawing nails yet close enough for easily twisting off their points.

BUFFER OR CLENCH CUTTER (*Fig. 44*)

This tool is about 6″ long and made of steel. Many farriers make their own from an old rasp. The chisel-shaped end, which is about $1\frac{1}{2}$″ wide, is used with the shoeing hammer either to cut off or knock up the clenches before removing the shoe. Also, it is used for removing flakes of the horny sole and for raising the head of a badly driven nail sufficiently from the fuller for it to be gripped with the pincers and withdrawn.

The pointed end is used for punching out nails which have broken off and for cleaning out nail holes. The point should be shaped to conform with the shank of a horseshoe nail.

FARRIERS PINCERS (*Fig. 45*)

These pincers have handles 10″ to 12″ long and jaws 1″ to $1\frac{1}{4}$″ wide, which must be kept sharp. They are used for raising the branches of the shoe, levering off the shoe, withdrawing nails, cutting off any excess of a wrung-off nail, and to turn the clenches.

TOEING KNIFE (*Fig. 46*)

This knife is generally made by the farrier from an old rasp. It is about 10″ long with $2\frac{1}{2}$″ of one end ground sharp. This is used for lowering excessively overgrown feet by driving it through the wall with a mallet or the shoeing hammer. A useful tool, but skill and care are needed when using it because it can easily twist in the hand when struck and cut into the sensitive foot. This is particularly liable to happen when trimming the feet of young stock which are difficult to control and sensitive to the hammering.

HOOF CUTTER, HOOF TRIMMER OR PARER (*Fig. 47*)

This tool has handles 10″ to 12″ long with a pincer-like head having one jaw sharp and the other flat. It is safer to use than the toeing knife and in consequence some farriers use it exclusively for removing overgrown wall. When in use the flat jaw is placed on the outside of the wall with the sharp cutting jaw on the inside.

A hoof nipper which has both jaws sharp, is preferred by some farriers to the standard hoof cutter. Both tools are equally efficient and their choice is a matter of personal preference.

DRAWING KNIFE (*Fig. 48*)

This knife has a blade not more than $\frac{1}{2}$″ wide and is curved on flat. The point is bent over towards the inside of the curve for safety. The handle is made either of horn or wood and the butt has a V-shaped notch cut into it which in the case of wood has a metal inlay. Originally

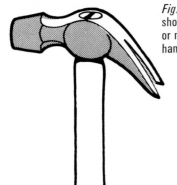

Fig. 43. Farrier's shoeing, driving or nailing-on hammer.

Fig. 44. Buffer or clench cutter.

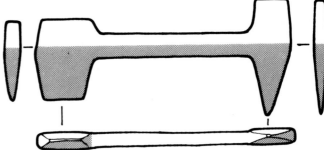

Fig. 45. Farriers pincers.

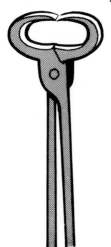

Fig. 46. Toeing knife.

Fig. 48. Drawing knife.

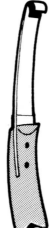

Fig. 47. Hoof cutter, hoof trimmer or parer.

the knife was designed for paring down the sole, a harmful practice which is now discarded.

It is used for lowering the wall, removing loose flakes of the sole and ragged pieces of the frog, and easing the sole in the angle between the wall and the bar. Also, it is used to remove a small piece of horn for the reception of a clip, a practice that is not to be recommended.

The posterior edge of the point is used for cleaning out the sole and clefts of the frog after removing a shoe and the butt of the handle is used to manipulate and press a hot shoe onto the foot when it is being fitted.

SEARCHER (*Fig. 49*)

This is a knife similar to the drawing knife but with a much thinner blade. As its name implies it is used for searching the foot, paring the horn around puncture wounds and cutting out corns.

Both the drawing knife and searcher are available in left and right-handed types.

FARRIERS RASP (*Fig. 50*)

This rasp must be long and wide to enable the farrier to obtain a level bearing surface. The standard farrier's rasp is 16″ long, half coarse and half file cut with serrated edges. The coarse cut surface is used for removing excessive wall, final levelling of the bearing surface and finishing off the clenches. The file cut surface is used for finishing off the shoe, hot rasping the heels and for shaping the clenches. The serrated edge is used for taking off the sharp outer edge of the wall, to prevent it splitting after the shoe has been nailed on.

Some farriers favour a tanged half-file rasp. These rasps have one surface coarse cut, the other file cut and are fitted with a wooden handle.

NAIL CLENCHER OR TONGS (*Fig. 51*)

This tool is specially designed for turning and bedding the clenches. It is particularly useful when working on young or sensitive horses which resent having their feet struck with the hammer.

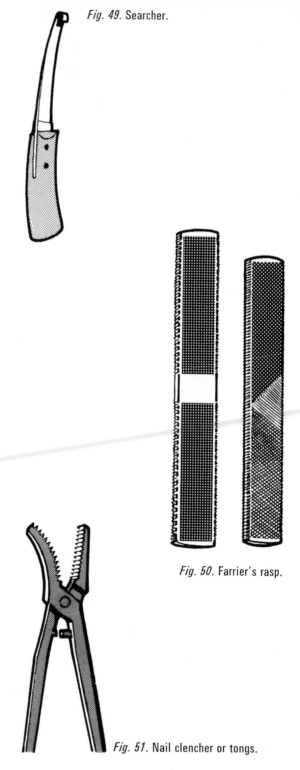

Fig. 49. Searcher.

Fig. 50. Farrier's rasp.

Fig. 51. Nail clencher or tongs.

In addition to all these tools a metal *ruler* is an essential for measuring the feet and the length of iron required to be cut off to make a shoe. Some farriers use a *divider* to measure the length of toe and a *hoof level* to check the angle of the wall, but most farriers consider that the preparation of the foot can be judged just as easily and accurately by eye.

Section II: FORGE TOOLS

ANVIL (*Fig. 52*)

The anvil used by farriers is designed to meet their special requirements. It is made of wrought iron, has a square body, a rounded "beak" and weighs from 2½ to 3 cwts.

The face or working surface which measures some 2' by 6" has a steel plate welded on to it and is used for "welding" and "drawing" iron. The beak is used for "turning" iron and shaping horseshoes.

At the base of the beak is a small square flat area, ½" below the face, termed the "table". It is softer than the face, having no steel plate welded on to it and is used when cutting iron with either the cold or the hot set to prevent their edges being blunted. The opposite end of the anvil is called the "heel" and is made thinner so that the farrier can work on a shoe with one branch under the face.

On the working surface, towards the heel of the anvil, are two holes which penetrate its entire thickness. One is a *square hole*, which is referred to as the *Hardie hole*. It takes the shank of bottom tools such as the hardie or the heel cutter and the farrier places the branch of the shoe over it when using the pritchel. The second is a *small round hole*, less than 1" in diameter, which is used to take the point of a punch or drift when making holes in the branch of a shoe for studs.

The farrier fixes his anvil with its face 27" to 30" from the floor and pitched slightly away from him so that scale and loose pieces of metal scatter with each hammer blow and fall on the floor. He places it in relation to the forge so that he can transfer hot iron from the fire to it with a lateral swing of his arm without having to move far and, thus, the iron does not have time to cool.

The anvil may be set in a cast-iron stand, but most farriers prefer to have them bolted to either a wooden bench or section of a tree trunk which is sunk some 2' in the ground. The springiness provided by the wood gives "lift" to the hammer after each blow which enables the farrier to strike more rapidly and with less effort.

An anvil is said to be set satisfactorily when a heavy blow on the beak does not move it and its quality is judged by its ring.

Fig. 52. Anvil.

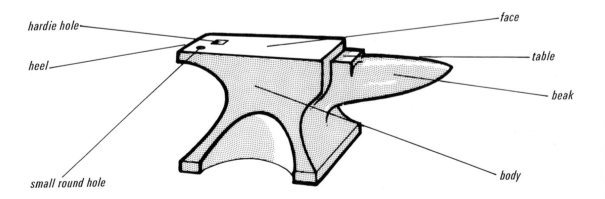

hardie hole

heel

small round hole

face

table

beak

body

TURNING HAMMER (*Fig. 53*)

This is the standard hammer used by the farrier at the anvil. It weighs $2\frac{1}{2}$ to 4 lbs, has one face flat and the other convex and is fitted with an ash or hickory shaft about 1′ in length. The flat face is used when working with tools and when the farrier is working with a striker he uses it to beat time on the anvil to indicate the force required from each blow. The convex face is used for forging and bending iron. On one side of the head is a ball or "lug" and on the other a "pein". These protuberances are used for starting and finishing off "drawing a clip".

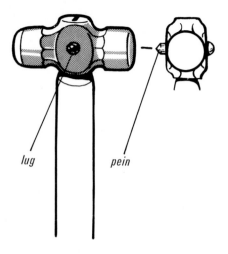

lug   pein

Fig. 53. Turning hammer.

Some farriers prefer to use an *engineer's riveting or ball pein hammer* (*Fig. 54*) for this work. The striking face of the hammer is flat and the other is a "riveting snub" which is commonly referred to as "bullnosed".

Fig. 54. Engineer's riveting hammer.

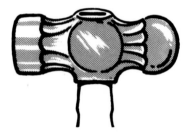

SLEDGE HAMMER (*Fig. 55*)

A sledge hammer weighs about 9 lbs, and has a 3′ shaft. The most common variety is the double-faced sledge, but straight pein and cross pein sledges are also used. The pein sledges have a flat striking face with the other wedge-shaped. If the angle of the wedge is sharp it is a "straight" pein and if rounded a "cross pein" sledge.

It is wielded by the striker under the direction of the farrier to weld hot metal and hammer it through a "tool" and for striking the stamp and fullering iron.

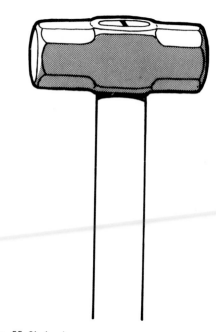

Fig. 55. Sledge hammer.

FIRE TONGS (*Fig. 56*)

These tongs are designed with 4″ jaws and 24″ to 30″ long handles, which enable the farrier to manipulate hot metal without having to be too close to the fire.

SHOE TONGS (*Fig. 57*)

These tongs are used by the farrier at the anvil for gripping and manipulating hot metal. They have shorter handles than fire tongs,

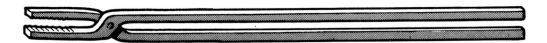

Fig. 56. Fire tongs.

ranging from 12″ to 18″ and with jaws from 1″
to 2″. This ratio of length of handle to jaw,
coupled with the handles being parallel when in
use, results in a most effective grip.

Fig. 57. Shoe tongs.

Two types are in use. Those with jaws which
shut close, called "inside shoe tongs" and are
used for grasping narrow bars and those with
open jaws called "outside shoe tongs" which are
used for handling thick moulds.

HOT SET (*Fig. 58*)

This is a chisel-shaped tool, about 4″ long
with a cutting edge $\frac{5}{8}$″ wide. It is used for cutting
heated iron bars and is set hammer fashion on a
handle.

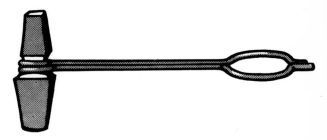

Fig. 58. Hot set.

COLD SET (*Fig. 59*)

This tool is similar in shape to the hot set but
is more massive and with a sharper edge. It is
used for cutting iron bars cold.

When using either a hot or cold set the work
is placed on the table of the anvil to preserve
the cutting edges.

Fig. 59. Cold set.

STAMP (*Fig. 60*)

This is a punch set hammer fashion on a
handle. It is used for making the nail holes and
therefore its point must be the same shape as the
head of the nail.

The stamp is held in position by the farrier
and either struck by the striker with a sledge
hammer or by the farrier himself using the flat
face of his turning hammer. It is struck at first
lightly and then more heavily until the point
almost penetrates the thickness of the shoe.

Fig. 60. Stamp.

FULLER OR FULLERING IRON (*Fig. 61*)

This is a blunt chisel set hammer fashion on a handle. It has one face flat and the other bevelled and is used to make a groove or crease around the edge of the ground surface of a shoe. When in use the bevelled face is directed outwards which enables the farrier to observe how fullering is progressing.

Fig. 61. Fuller or fullering iron.

The hot set, cold set, stamp and fuller are so-called "top tools" because they are laid on top of the work and then struck with the hammer. It was customary for these tools to be made with an oval hole through the centre to take a wooden handle, but the rigidity of this type of handle jars the holder considerably. This has been overcome by making the handle out of a thin metal rod which is bent around the waist of the tool.

HARDIE (*Fig. 62*)

This is a straight edged tool, weighing up to 2 lbs, shaped like a chisel and with a shank to fit the square hole on the face of the anvil. It is used to cut off lengths of iron bar which are placed over its edge and struck with the sledge hammer until they are cut through and broken off.

HEEL CUTTER OR HALF ROUND (*Fig. 63*)

This tool has a semi-circular cutting edge for cutting off and trimming the heels of a shoe and a shank to fit the square hole on the face of the anvil. Three or four sizes of heel cutter are required to meet the general range of shoes and when used the concave edge is directed away from the heel of the shoe (*Fig. 131*).

CONCAVE TOOL OR SWAGE (*Fig. 64*)

This tool is a mould through which a red hot bar of iron is slowly drawn by the farrier while at the same time it is struck with the sledge hammer to shape one side concave. It has a shank to fit the square hole in the face of the anvil.

The hardie, heel cutter and concave tool are so-called "bottom tools" because the work is placed on top of them and then struck with the hammer.

Fig. 63. Heel cutter or half round.

Fig. 62. Hardie.

Fig. 64. Concave tool or swage.

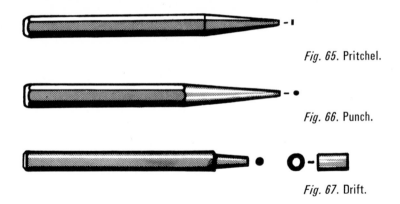

Fig. 65. Pritchel.

Fig. 66. Punch.

Fig. 67. Drift.

PRITCHEL (*Fig. 65*)

This is a long steel punch, with a point which is an accurate reproduction of the neck of the nail. It is used to finish off the nail holes commenced by the stamp and for carrying a hot shoe to the foot for fitting. When used for this purpose it is tapped into the nail hole of the outside toe.

The point of a pritchel soon becomes blunt and hence too large. When this occurs it is better to heat it and hammer it back into shape rather than grind a new point. Pritchels are made of tool steel which has a critical working heat. Therefore, the point should only be heated to a "red" heat before being hammered to shape, drawn out to a fine taper and finally shaped with a few "upsetting" blows on its point. If heated to a "white" heat the tip will break off when the pritchel is used and if worked to a "black" heat it will fracture. However, the life of the tip can be lengthened by hardening and tempering it rather than letting it cool in the air. If the tip is heated to "red" heat and then swirled around in oil or grease until it is cool it will have a silvery sheen, be very hard and shatter if struck. To temper the point, scrape off any burr, heat it in a low fire until it turns blue, then remove it and quench it in water.

PUNCH (*Fig. 66*)

The type used by farriers is round and is employed to make a hole through the heel of a shoe, before enlarging it with a drift to take a stud. It is used over the small round hole on the face of the anvil to avoid blunting the point and to prevent the branch of the shoe bending.

DRIFT (*Fig. 67*)

This tool resembles a punch. It is shaped to conform to the neck of a stud and is used to enlarge a hole already punched to take the stud. It is used over the round hole on the face of the anvil. The drift is first driven through the hole from the ground surface of the shoe and then from the foot surface. This results in a collar of metal forming around the hole on the ground surface which ensures a very tight fitting stud.

Section III: THE FORGE

Forges are of two types, static or portable. Basically both are the same in that air is blown through the hearth to create a concentrated fire capable of reaching welding heat.

The static forge has either a metal fire pan or a metal grate surrounded by firebricks and a cast iron back against which a sloping fire is built up some 10″ high and 18″ wide. Above the fire is the wide open base of the hood or cowl which tapers upwards into the chimney. At the other end of the forge is a cast-iron trough or "bosh" which is kept full of water and used for dowsing hot tools and quenching hot iron for tempering.

Good quality coal is the best fuel for the fire as it burns to coke which lasts well before becoming ash and produces little clinker. A good fire has a deep bed of coke maintained by the coal, which is heaped up around its edges, being gradually fed into the centre. The small concentrated fire of coke or "hot spot" of the hearth should be about 9″ deep and metal placed in it should lie about 6″ from the bottom so as not to be affected by the cold blast of air from the bellows or fan. If the fire becomes too intense the farrier regulates the heat by sprinkling it with cold water from the bosh. Scales of iron bind together with coke to form clinkers which give off no heat. Their formation is indicated by the fire tending to spread and when the fire is opened up they turn black and are easily recognised.

Air is blown through the fire by either bellows or a fan. Bellows are worked by hand and are double-acting, that is to say, with each upward and downward swing of the bellows arm a blast of air is produced which results in a continuous, not intermittent, draught of air through the fire.

Fig. 68. British "Alcosa" Heavy Pattern Circular Fan Forge. This is a popular type of hand forge for farriers. It has a fire pan 18″ in diameter and 6″ deep, is arranged for back blast and fitted with a hand geared fan having a 48.1 gearbox ratio.

Fans are driven by hand or an electric motor. The latter have an advantage because the draught of air can be regulated, set and maintained. To prevent the draught from disturbing the fire the farrier keeps this packed firm and packs coal around it to prevent it spreading.

The tools used to maintain the fire are the *stop poker* which is ½″ in diameter and is used to open up the fire and break up clinker; the *rake* which is designed for removing clinkers and keeping the fire together by raking the coal on to the fire at its edges, and the *fire shovel*, which has flat sides and is used for banking up the fire and tapping it down to keep it packed firm. All these tools have handles from 1½′ to 3′ in length.

When a farrier places a length of iron or the branch of a shoe in the fire it is referred to as "taking a heat" and it has to be heated to the correct temperature necessary for the work required to be done on it. The number of heats required to complete a specific job vary considerably and to a great extent are dependent on the technical skill and ability of the individual farrier.

Farriers do not measure the temperature of the heated iron in degrees centigrade or fahrenheit, but judge the temperature required, to perform specific tasks, by its colour. As is to be expected the term used to distinguish the various colours of heated iron varies in different parts of the country, but the following explanations will serve as a guide.

White or welding heat. The metal is white and gives off sparks. This heat is required for hammering iron into shape and for welding.

Bright red heat. The metal is just off white in colour. It is very pliable and easily worked. This heat is suitable for drawing clips, cutting off the heels and turning calkins.

Red or cherry red heat. The iron has a bright glow and the farrier uses this heat for most of his work. It is used for shaping and finishing off the shoe and for opening up the nail holes.

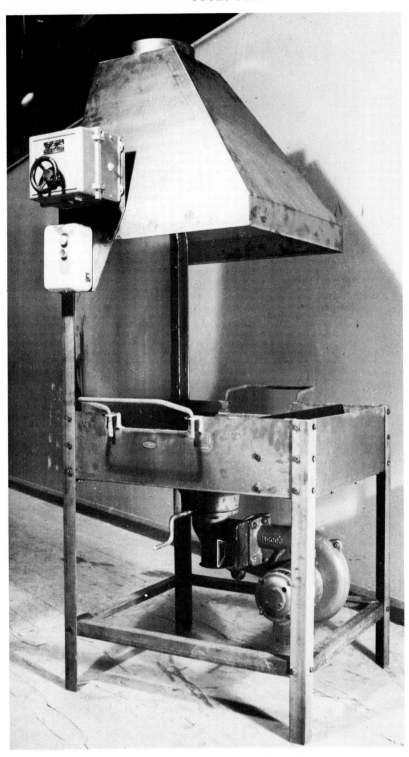

Fig. 69. British "Alcosa" Rectangular Motor Fan Forge. This is the type of forge commonly used at agricultural shows for farriery competitions. It is gas fired, has a fire pan $30\frac{1}{4}$" by $25\frac{3}{8}$" and 7" deep and gap sides which allows long bars to be heated. It is arranged for bottom blast which is provided by a universal ball bearing motor fan set fitted with a 1/6th h.p. motor wound for 220/240 volts.

Fig. 70. British "Alcosa" Farriers Portable Forge. The internal heating chamber is 9″ wide by 4″ high at the front, reducing to 1″ high at the rear and measures 12″ from front to back, and fired by either propane or calor gas. It is lined with a special quality refractory lining to provide a very intense heat from the fishtail burner, is encased in a heavy steel, weighs 50 lbs., is fitted with lifting lugs for ease of handling, and has a maximum heating up time of 8 mins.

Black or blue heat. The iron has a very faint glow. This heat is used for making minor changes in the shape of, and levelling the shoe.

It is common practice today for farriers to visit stables to shoe horses. This makes hot shoeing a problem because the farrier has to transport to the stables and set up a portable forge (*Figs. 68 and 69*) which is both inconvenient and time consuming. To a great extent these difficulties have been overcome by the introduction of the "Alcosa" furnace. Fired by either propane or calor gas it has been specially designed and developed for heating horseshoes, steel bars and small components (*Fig. 70*).

CHAPTER FIVE

The horseshoe and horseshoe nails

Section I: THE HORSESHOE

A HORSESHOE is described as having a *toe*, *quarters* and *heels*, and from toe to heel on each side is called a *branch* (*Fig. 71*). The *toe* is that portion between the first nail holes on each side, and that part of the branch between the last nail and the heel is called the *quarter*.

The whole substance of a shoe, that is the breadth and thickness of the metal, is referred to as the *web* and the width of the web as the cover. Therefore a shoe with a wide web is said to have "plenty of cover". A shoe has two surfaces, a *foot surface* which is in contact with the bearing surface of the hoof and a *ground* surface; and two *edges*, an inner and an outer.

Two front or two hind shoes comprise a *pair of horseshoes* and a pair of each is known as a *set*. The term *remove* is used to describe a partly worn shoe which has been taken off, cleaned up and put on again.

MATERIALS FOR MAKING HORSESHOES

Horseshoes have been made from a variety of materials which include rubber, vulcanite, plastic, brass and copper but wrought iron and mild steel are the most suitable. Wrought iron is almost pure iron containing not more than 2% of carbon with traces of phosphorus, sulphur and silicon. When heated it is easily worked and can be welded. Shoes made from old shoes of wrought iron are very hard-wearing. This increased hardness is due to the chemical changes which take place between the iron and the carbon in the fuel and not the hammering as is generally supposed.

When mild steel, which contains 1% to $1\frac{1}{2}\%$ of carbon, is heated it becomes ductile and malleable but if over-heated or rapidly cooled, it is rendered extra hard and brittle. Shoes made from mild steel are reputed to wear very smooth and to break easily. These disadvantages are not borne out in practice and today horseshoes made from mild steel are in general use.

Aluminium, which is a light metal and about one-third by weight of wrought iron, is used for racing plates.

Concave fullered steel and flat iron bar are the two materials in general use for making horseshoes.

CONCAVE FULLERED STEEL BAR

Width of Bar	THICKNESS OF BAR				
	$\times \frac{1}{4}''$	$\times \frac{5}{16}''$	$\times \frac{3}{8}''$	$\times \frac{7}{16}''$	$\times \frac{1}{2}''$
$\frac{1}{2}''$	★				
$\frac{5}{8}''$	★	★	★	★	
$\frac{3}{4}''$			★	★	★
$\frac{7}{8}''$					★

★ Indicates sizes available

Cross-section of bar :

FLAT IRON BAR

Width of Bar	THICKNESS OF BAR	
	$\times \frac{1}{2}''$	$\times \frac{7}{16}''$
$\frac{7}{8}''$	★	
$1''$	★	★

★ Indicates sizes available

Cross-section of bar :

THE DESIGN OF HORSESHOES

The type of shoe fitted varies according to the horse and the work it is expected to perform, but a number of basic design features are common to all shoes.

The width of the shoe is related to the natural bearing surface of the foot and should cover the wall, white line and outer border of the sole. The average width of a shoe is about twice the thickness of the wall but it should be a little wider at the toe where wear is greatest and a little narrower at the heels so as not to impinge on the frog. A shoe which is too wide predisposes to grit and stones lodging under it and when worn is conducive to slipping.

The thickness of the shoe is related to its size. If it is too thick it raises the foot excessively from the ground which reduces normal frog pressure; in addition, excessively large nails are required to fit the deep nail holes. To preserve the balance of the foot the shoe must be of uniform thickness. If the toe is excessively thick, it puts strain on the flexor tendons and is conducive to stumbling. On the other hand, if

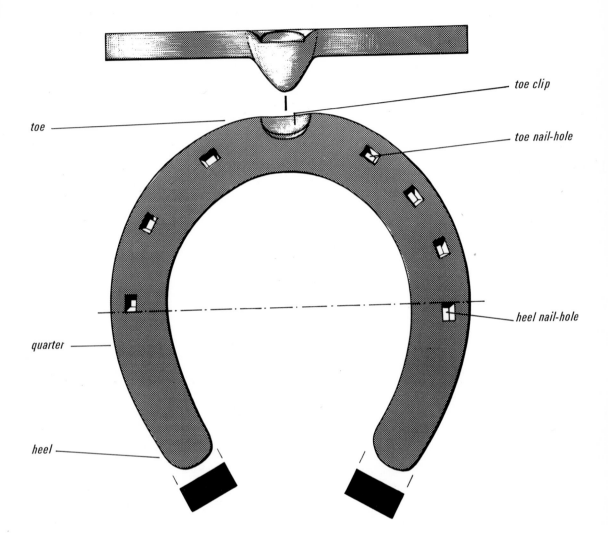

Fig. 71. Standard horseshoe with a plain foot and ground surface and correctly placed nail-holes. In each branch three nail-holes are stamped anterior to an imaginary line which divides the shoe into two equal parts, with the heel nail-hole in the outer branch placed just posterior to this line.

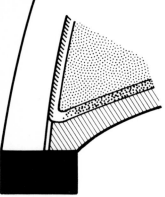

Fig. 72. Section of a shoe with a plain flat foot surface.

Fig. 73. Section of a shoe with foot surface sloped outwards.

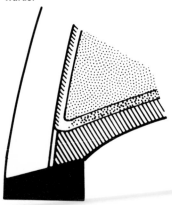

Fig. 74. Section of a seated-out shoe.

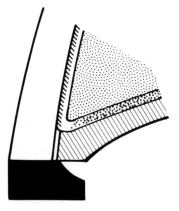

the heels are excessively thick they tend to straighten the pastern, raise the frog off the ground and in time can lead to an overshot joint.

The foot surface of the shoe is that which supports the hoof. There are a number of varieties, each with its special features.

A plain flat surface (*Fig. 72*) which covers the wall, white line and border of the sole, provides a firm basis for the foot to rest on and is suitable for all normal front and hind feet.

A surface sloped outwards (*Fig. 73*) was introduced to prevent contraction of the foot by contributing to expansion. In practice this is not attained and lameness results.

A seated-out surface (*Fig. 74*) has the inner edge sloped to relieve pressure on the border of the sole. Seated-out shoes have the disadvantage that grit and stones accumulate under them and in heavy going they are liable to be sucked off.

A shoe which is so extensively seated-out that only a narrow rim of the foot surface remains is called a *saucer shoe* (*Fig. 75*). Saucer shoes were designed for the treatment of severe cases of dropped sole but today are of little more than historical interest. The narrow foot surface makes it difficult to fit and nail them on. All too soon the wall either overlaps the edge of the shoe and splits, or comes to rest within the edge of the shoe and is compressed with resulting lameness.

The ground surface of the shoe has to be considered in relation to the foothold it provides, its wearing properties and its support for the nails.

A plain stamped shoe (*Fig. 72*) has a flat level ground surface which wears well and is only broken by the nail-holes.

A concave shoe (*Fig. 76*) has the inner edge of the ground surface sloped. This makes it lighter than a plain stamped shoe with the same

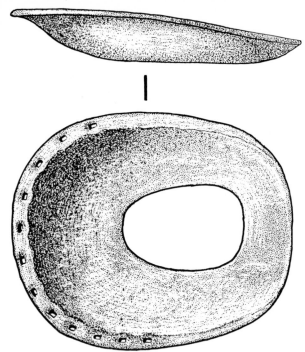

Fig. 75. A saucer shoe.

width of foot surface, gives a better foothold and reduces suction in heavy going.

A convex shoe (*Fig. 77*) has the inner edge of the ground surface thicker than the outer edge by as much as $\frac{1}{4}''$. This shoe is used for horses which wear out their shoes quickly. The inner edge is worn first and saves the outer edge and nail heads for later wear.

Fig. 76. Section of a concave shoe.

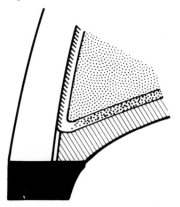

A fullered shoe (*Fig. 78*) has a groove or crease round the ground surface which creates two ridges. This improves the foothold and prevents slipping, but does not wear as well as a plain flat surface. As the nail-holes are stamped in the groove the nail heads are supported only on two sides, but this has the advantage that the exactness of their fit can be seen and the removal of single nails facilitated.

It is not customary for shoes made from plain bar iron to have the fullering extended around the toe and on to the heels as this deprives the shoe of wear where it is most required. When machine-made fullered shoes are altered the groove is liable to be closed and, unless it is

Fig. 77. Section of a convex shoe.

Fig. 78. Section of a fullered shoe.

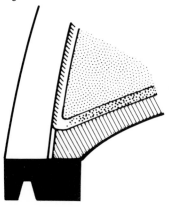

opened up, the heads of the nails cannot be driven home and after a little wear they become loose.

A fullered shoe is often said to be lighter than a plain shoe but this is a fallacy when the shoe is made from plain iron bar as no metal is removed in its making.

A concave fullered shoe (*Fig. 79*) combines the advantages of concaving and fullering and is the most popular general purpose shoe for hunters, hacks and ponies.

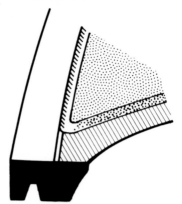

Fig. 79. Section of a concave-fullered shoe.

The Rodway shoe (*Fig. 80*) has two parallel grooves around the ground surface which create three ridges. The nail-holes are stamped in the outer groove. This shoe was introduced with the idea that three ridges would improve the foothold, but in practice it is not an improvement on the fullered shoe with one groove and two ridges and wears no better.

The weight of the shoe is important and, generally speaking, the lighter the shoe the better but obviously it must be related to wear.

The extent to which heavy shoes tire a horse is all too frequently overlooked. The shoe for a heavy draught horse weighs about 5 lbs., and, therefore, if the horse takes 30 strides per minute it has to make the necessary effort to raise 150 lbs., for each leg, a total of 600 lbs., for all four legs. At the end of an average day's work of 4 hours at the walk, this comes to over 60 tons. When it is realised that this extra weight of the shoes is at the end of a long arm level, it is easy to appreciate the expenditure of effort necessary for a horse to perform a day's work and the contribution made by heavy shoes to the stresses on the limbs and the horse's fatigue.

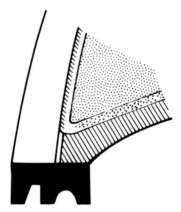

Fig. 80. Section of a Rodway shoe.

The wear of the shoe depends on numerous factors; the material from which the shoe is made, the surface of the ground and roads travelled over, the work performed and the conformation and action of the individual horse.

A set of shoes on average should last 4 to 5 weeks or a distance of between 100 and 350

miles. Horses wear out their shoes more quickly when working on macadamised and concrete roads which provide a poor foothold and especially when they are wet. The pace at which a horse works and the type of vehicle it draws also has a marked effect on the length of wear of its shoes. The shoes of heavy draught horses working at a slow pace ($2\frac{1}{2}$ mph) have a longer life, both in respect of time and distance, than horses working at a trot (6 mph) because of the friction created by slipping and pulling up more sharply. In addition, the type of vehicle plays its part. A vehicle with free moving shafts gives a horse more freedom when placing its feet, thereby reducing slipping, than a vehicle with rigid shafts.

A horse with a normal action will wear its shoes evenly with the exception of the outside of the toe which always is more worn. Hind shoes wear out more rapidly than front shoes and some horses will wear out their shoes twice as fast as others.

Horses which wear out their shoes faster than average should not be fitted with a heavier shoe but shod with either a wide web shoe or a convex shoe. However, uneven wear of a shoe is a different problem and correction should be made by altering the form and distribution of the iron by turning up the worn part, for example the toe.

FULLERING

Fullering is the term used to describe making a groove, crease or furrow round the ground surface of the shoe in which the nail-holes are stamped. The groove is made with a fullering iron and is either complete when it extends round the shoe from heel to heel, or incomplete when it is confined to the region of the nail-holes leaving the toe and heel plain.

The fullering iron is held with its bevelled face towards and about $\frac{1}{8}''$ from the outer edge of the shoe. This enables the farrier to see and regulate the depth and angle of the groove. As he draws the fullering iron along with a slight rocking movement, from the heel to the toe of each branch, it is struck either by the farrier himself using the turning hammer or by his assistant wielding a sledge hammer and driven into the shoe. A groove made close to the outer edge of the shoe is referred to as "fine fullering" and when distant, "coarse fullering".

The fullering iron is positioned slightly further from the outer edge of the shoe at the toe than at the heels and is held at an angle corresponding with the slope of the wall. Thus, a groove is made which conforms in position and angle to the thickness and slope of the wall which greatly assists in the correct stamping of the nail-holes.

The groove should be uniform in width and between a half and two-thirds the thickness of the shoe in depth (*Fig. 81*). A groove can be too

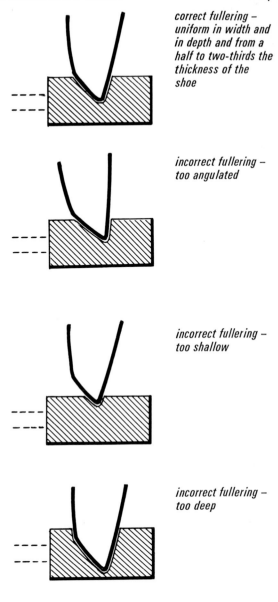

correct fullering – uniform in width and in depth and from a half to two-thirds the thickness of the shoe

incorrect fullering – too angulated

incorrect fullering – too shallow

incorrect fullering – too deep

incorrect fullering – too narrow and too deep

Fig. 81. Fullering.

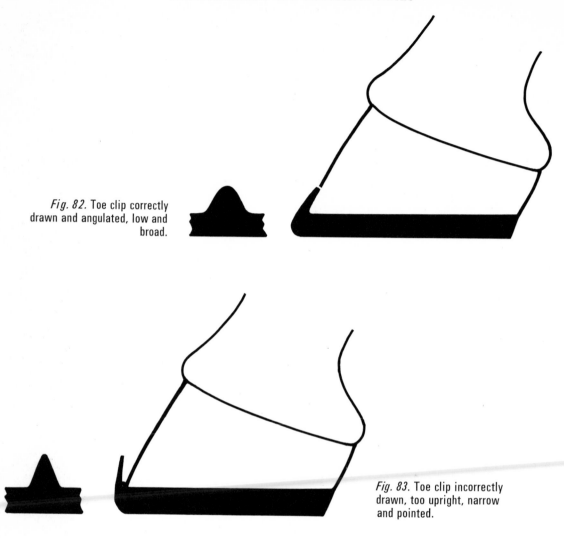

Fig. 82. Toe clip correctly drawn and angulated, low and broad.

Fig. 83. Toe clip incorrectly drawn, too upright, narrow and pointed.

angulated, too wide or too shallow when it fails to support the nail-heads. If it is too deep and narrow it is easily closed during alterations to the shoe.

CLIPS

A clip is a thin triangular projection drawn from the outer edge of a shoe at the toe, quarter or heel.

A correctly drawn and angulated clip should be low and broad, rest accurately against the wall and not exceed in height double the thickness of the shoe (*Fig. 82*). A narrow pointed clip does not give adequate support and should the shoe become loose it is all too easily trodden on and may puncture the foot. Care must be taken when drawing a clip that a ridge is not left on the foot surface to cause pressure and result in lameness (*Fig. 83*).

The surface of a clip is flat and, therefore, for a toe clip to be accurately fitted it may be necessary to reduce the curvature of the wall slightly with a few strokes of the rasp. The removal of a piece of the wall for the reception of a clip (*Fig. 84*), or drawing a clip vertical and hammering it into position after the shoe has been nailed on (*Fig. 85*), are undesirable practices which can injure the foot.

If a single toe clip is drawn it is placed at the centre of the toe, but when two are drawn they are placed one on either side of the toe between the first and second nail holes. Toe clips assist in obtaining an exact fit and steadying the shoe when the nails are driven; quarter clips prevent the shoe being displaced sideways and heel clips are used sometimes on surgical shoes.

CALKINS

A calkin is formed either by turning down or welding a piece of steel to the heel of a shoe. Calkins provide a good foothold on soft ground and country roads and assist draught horses to back and hold back loads, but are of little advantage on modern roads.

Calkins, by raising the heels, reduce frog pressure and unbalance the foot. The higher and more anteriorly the calkins are placed the more

Fig. 84. The removal of a piece of the wall for the reception of the toe clip is an undesirable practice.

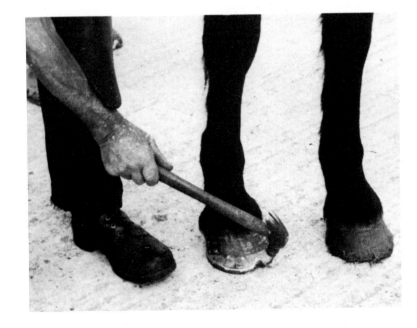

Fig. 85. A correctly drawn clip does not require to be hammered into position.

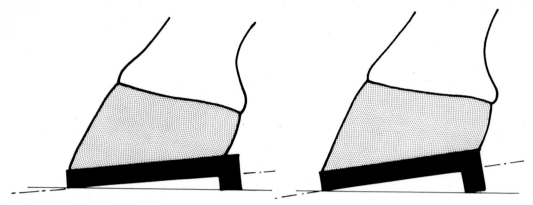

Fig. 86. Calkins unbalance the foot and reduce the frog pressure. The higher the calkins and the more anteriorly they are placed the more serious the effects.

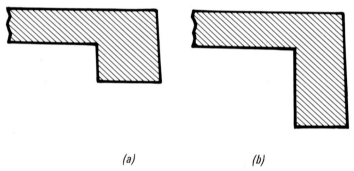

(a)   (b)

Fig. 87. (a) A good calkin – low, broad and square, set at right angles and not more than twice the thickness of the shoe; *(b)* a poor calkin – too high and too narrow.

Fig. 88. Calkins result in excessive wear at the toe. The dotted line illustrates that a lot of iron is wasted because the toe is worn through before the shoe is worn out.

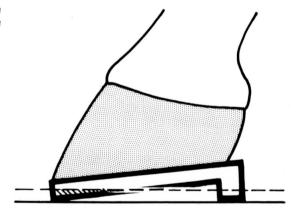

serious the effects (*Fig. 86*). Calkins should be low, broad and square, set at right angles, not more than twice the thickness of the shoe and both of the same height (*Fig. 87*).

Inevitably, calkins result in excessive wear at the toe which is worn through before the shoe is worn thin, thus wasting a lot of iron (*Fig. 88*). To counter this the toe can be made thicker, but unless the branches are made correspondingly thinner it only increases the weight of the shoe. The maximum wear of a shoe with calkins is obtained by turning up the toe, thus bringing into wear a larger proportion of the branches, but it makes the preparation of the foot and fitting the shoe more difficult.

It is not customary to fit calkins on front shoes, but when they are used, on draught horses for example, it is in conjunction with a toe-piece to preserve the balance of the foot. Riding horses shod behind with calkins should have the inside calkin replaced by a wedge heel to prevent brushing.

Care must be taken to ensure that the calkin and wedge heel are equal in height and that the calkin is not too high, as it tends to catch and twist the foot.

TOE-PIECES

A toe-piece is a rod of iron or mild steel welded across the toe of a shoe (*Fig. 89*). To make a toe-piece a rod of iron is selected and from one end the length of iron required is cut half through but not detached. Next, the toe-piece to be and the toe of the shoe are brought to a white heat.

Finally, the toe-piece is placed in position across and a little behind the toe, welded with a few light blows and broken off.

In some areas it is customary for draught horses to be shod with a toe-piece and calkins. The toe-piece not only provides a firm foothold to start loads, but also restores the unnatural position of the foot caused by the calkins. In addition, as the wear of the branches between the toe and the heels is reduced a lighter shoe can be fitted.

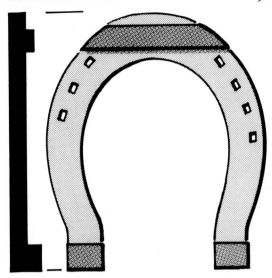

Fig. 89. Draught horseshoe with toe-piece and calkins.

Section II: NAIL-HOLES

The correct stamping of nail-holes is a most important operation because their size and shape determine the fit of the nail head and their position and angulation the direction taken by the nail as it passes through the wall (*Fig. 90*).

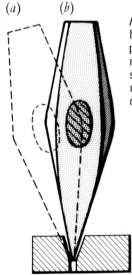

(*a*)   (*b*)

Fig. 90. Stamping the nail-holes. *(a)* stamp angulated – position used for stamping nail-holes at the toe; *(b)* stamp held upright – position used for nail-holes at the quarters and heel.

Nail-holes are made with a stamp from the ground surface of the shoe and finished off with a pritchel. Because the point of the stamp is the same shape as the nail-head, and the point of the pritchel an accurate reproduction of the neck of the nail, the nail-hole is an exact counterpart of the head and neck of the nail.

The stamp is struck, at first lightly and then more heavily, until its point almost penetrates the shoe. The holes at the toe are angulated slightly to conform with the slope of the wall (*Fig. 91* [*a*]), whereas those at the heels and quarters are more upright (*Fig. 91* [*b*]). A very upright inside heel may require the heel nail-hole to be directed slightly outwards. Nail-holes pitched excessively outwards are unsatisfactory as the nail obtains very little hold (*Fig. 91* [*c*]).

The stamped nail-holes are completed by being punched out with the pritchel, over the square hole on the face of the anvil. The shoe is then turned over and the holes "back pritchel-led" to remove any rough edges or "burr". A perfect countersink is thus completed, into which the head and neck of the nail will fit exactly and with the opening on the foot surface directly over the white line.

A nail-hole stamped in a fullered shoe only supports the nail-head on two sides, but in a plain stamped shoe it is supported on all four sides and provided the fit is exact the nail is immovable. Nail-holes should be stamped a little smaller than the nail-head to allow for the nail-head to be left projecting about $\frac{1}{8}''$ when the nail is driven hard home.

Sometimes, when back-pritchelling, the neck of the nail-hole is made a little larger than that of the nail. This enables the pitch of the nail to be varied when driven. Seemingly this is an advantage, but as the neck of the nail-hole is too large, nail slack occurs below the countersink which results in the shoe becoming loose before it has worn thin (*Fig. 92* [*a*]). On the other hand, if the neck of the nail-hole is on the small side, it is assumed that a really secure fit will be obtained when the nail is driven home. This is not the case because the ridge produced by the back-pritchelling either strips or pinches the

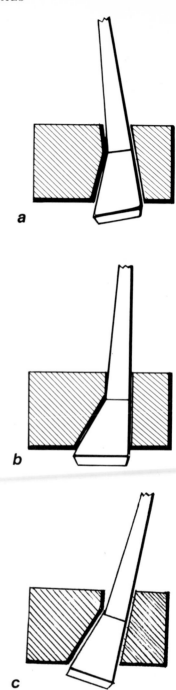

Fig. 91. Nail-holes. *(a)* slightly angulated or pitched nail-hole suitable for the toe; *(b)* upright nail-hole suitable for quarters and heels; *(c)* excessively pitched nail-hole, unsatisfactory, provides little hold.

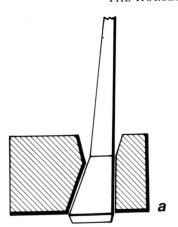

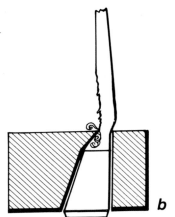

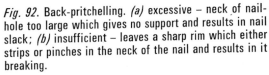

Fig. 92. Back-pritchelling. *(a)* excessive – neck of nail-hole too large which gives no support and results in nail slack; *(b)* insufficient – leaves a sharp rim which either strips or pinches in the neck of the nail and results in it breaking.

neck of the nail which soon breaks and is followed by a loose shoe (*Fig. 92* [*b*]). In addition, if the nail-hole is too small or the nail-head too large and projects excessively it quickly wears away, leaving too little head to carry the shoe (*Fig. 93* [*a*]) and if the nail-hole is too large or the nail-head too small, then nail slack occurs and results in a loose shoe (*Fig. 93* [*b*]).

Nail-holes should be evenly spaced $\frac{3}{4}''$ to $1\frac{1}{4}''$ apart and distributed in the anterior half of front shoes and the anterior two-thirds of hind shoes. A front shoe with 7 nail-holes has 3 stamped in the inner and 4 in the outer branch. In each branch 3 holes are stamped anterior to an imaginary transverse line dividing the shoe into two equal parts. The heel nail-hole in the outer branch is placed just posterior to this line and, in consequence, the 4 nail-holes in the outer branch are spaced closer together than the 3 in the inner branch (*Fig. 71*). Too many nail-holes placed too close together weaken a shoe.

Fig. 93. (a) Nail-hole too small. The nail-head projects excessively and quickly wears away, leaving too little head to carry the nail; *(b)* nail-hole too large. Nail-head has no hold which results in slack and a loose shoe.

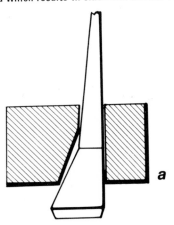

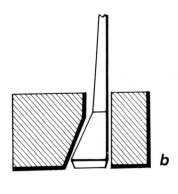

In addition to their spacing, nail-holes are related to the outer edge of the shoe. Nail-holes placed near the outer edge are described as "fine" and those near the inner edge as "coarse" (*Fig. 94*). A nail driven through a "fine" nail-hole may split the horn and has to be driven excessively high to obtain a good hold, whereas one through a "coarse" nail-hole passes close to the sensitive foot and may lead to a nail-bind. Nail-holes require to be fine when the shoe is fitted close and coarse when it is fitted full.

It is common practice to stamp 5 nail-holes in small shoes, 5 to 7 in medium sized shoes and 7 to 8 in heavy draught shoes and racing plates. It is not necessary to increase the number of nail-holes in direct relation to the size of the shoe because the nails used are proportioned to the size and weight of the shoes.

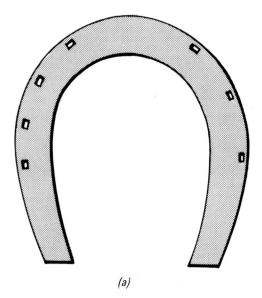

(a)

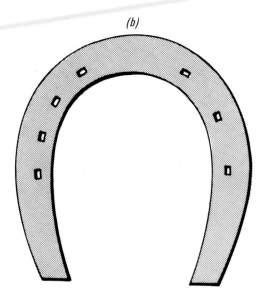

(b)

Fig. 94. Placing of nail-holes. *(a)* near the outer edge are described as "fine" and *(b)* near the inner edge as "coarse".

Section III: HORSESHOE NAILS

Handmade horseshoe nails are a relic of the past except for the occasional frost-nail. Today, machine made nails are in general use and are more perfect in all respects than the best hand made nails (*Fig. 95*).

Machine made nails are smooth and polished and made from the best mild steel. They can be driven through the hoof without breaking, buckling or splitting, but yet are sufficiently ductile not to snap when the point is turned over or wrung off. The shank of a nail should be sufficiently ductile to withstand being bent 4 or 5 times through 90° without breaking.

The head, neck, shank and point of a horseshoe nail are all designed to meet its special requirements.

The head is wedge shaped, with the outer surface flat and the inner sloped to the neck. This surface may be roughened or checkered for ease of identification. Nail-heads of this shape fitting accurately into the countersunk nail-holes will secure the shoe firmly until they have worn away. Nails with flat heads can only secure a shoe by their shanks and, in consequence, as soon as the heads have worn away the shoe becomes loose.

The neck is the junction between the head and the shank.

The shank extends from the neck to the point, has two surfaces and is twice as wide as it is

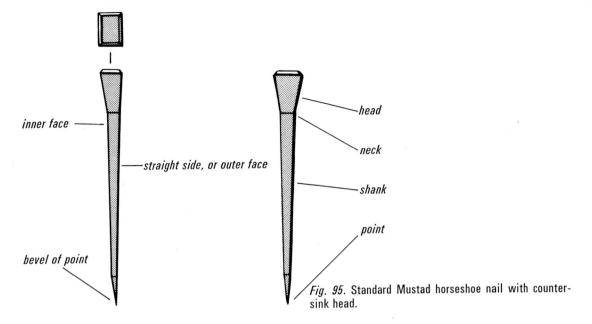

inner face

straight side, or outer face

bevel of point

head

neck

shank

point

Fig. 95. Standard Mustad horseshoe nail with counter-sink head.

thick. It is slightly curved in length to ensure that the nail will take a straight and not a curved course through the horn.

The point is bevelled on the inner face. A nail with a short bevel emerges low down on the wall, whereas one with a long bevel can be driven much higher. This is to no advantage, as such a point easily bends or turns and when wrung off sufficient may not remain to form a clench.

Basic to the design of a horseshoe nail is its slightly curved shank and bevelled point. When the nail is driven the bevel forces the point towards the straight side or outer face of the shank. Therefore the nail must always be driven with its straight side or outer face towards the outer edge of the shoe which makes

certain that the point will turn away from the sensitive foot and emerge on the outside of the wall (*Fig. 96*).

The size of horseshoe nails is denoted by numbers ranging from 2 to 12. The numbers correspond to the weight in lbs., of 1000 nails. For example, 1000 nails of size 6 weigh 6 lbs. Therefore, the higher the number the larger the nail. The difference in length between each size is approximately $\frac{1}{8}''$.

The Mustad horseshoe nail is the only variety remaining in general use. Sizes 3, 4 and 5 are suitable for most ponies, sizes 5 to 8 for hacks and hunters and sizes 8 to 10 for draught horses. Size 3 can be used for racing plates but three sizes of special nails are available and designated 2P, 3P and $3\frac{1}{2}$P. They are respectively $1\frac{3}{8}''$, $1\frac{9}{16}''$ and $1\frac{3}{4}''$ long.

MUSTAD HORSESHOE NAILS

Size	2	3	4	5	6	7	8	9	10	11	12
Length	$1\frac{5}{8}''$	$1\frac{3}{4}''$	$1\frac{7}{8}''$	$2''$	$2\frac{1}{8}''$	$2\frac{1}{4}''$	$2\frac{3}{8}''$	$2\frac{1}{2}''$	$2\frac{5}{8}''$	$2\frac{3}{4}''$	$2\frac{7}{8}''$

Fig. 96. A horseshoe nail must always be driven with its straight side, or outer face, towards the outer edge of the shoe. This ensures that the point will turn away from the inner face of the shank and the sensitive foot. *(a)* correctly pitched nail emerges about a third of the way up the wall and gives a secure hold; *(b)* nail pitched excessively inwards resulting in a "pricked" foot; *(c)* nail pitched excessively outwards obtains little hold.

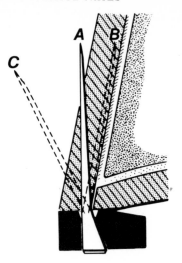

The smaller the nail the better provided its holding ability is consistent with, and in relation to, the size and weight of the shoe. It is bad practice to drive small nails excessively high to obtain a good hold or to use excessively large nails which tend to split and weaken the horn.

The number of nails used to secure a shoe should be the minimum necessary, but since nails of the right size and correctly placed cause little damage to the horn it is better to have one nail too many rather than one too few and risk loosing a shoe.

To secure a shoe with nails can be considered an undesirable practice and in consequence alternative methods have been investigated. Numerous ideas have been tried ranging from special toe and quarter clips to metal bands. Without exception all these methods have failed to prevent the loss of shoes and the metal bands wear groves in the hoof. No nail-less shoe has been invented which can be attached so securely to the foot either by mechanical means or by adhesives to make it a practical proposition. Invariably, they cause more serious injuries to the foot than those resulting from the loss of a shoe.

For all practical purposes properly driven nails cause no harm to the foot and obtain a more than adequate hold to secure the shoe. Caulton Reeks (1906) records three cases of avulsion of the entire hoof. The horses were engaged in shunting and the heel of a shoe was either caught between two converging rails or trapped by a waggon wheel. The horse sensing its foot trapped made a violent effort to release it and pulled it out from the imprisoned hoof. The effectiveness of correctly driven nails to secure a shoe requires no further support.

CHAPTER SIX

Types of horseshoes

WHEN a farrier selects a shoe he has to take account of the class of horse, its size, weight and the work it performs. Any modifications to the shoe that may be necessary for an individual horse can be ascertained by observing its action, its conformation, the shape of its feet and examining the wear of its shoes.

Section I: MACHINE MADE HORSESHOES

Machine made horseshoes are no better or more durable than the best hand made shoes but have the advantage that a good model can be repeated. They have regularity of form, a true foot surface and save the farrier valuable time by reducing manual labour. They are manufactured either by bending a length of iron bar or mild steel around a block or are drop stamped by a heavy hammer in a die. As a rule, front shoes are better shaped than hind shoes which tend to have the toes and quarters too rounded.

The chief disadvantage of machine made shoes relates to the nail-holes. All the nail-holes are stamped upright in exactly the same position in every shoe of the same pattern and size. Upright nail-holes give the farrier little freedom in pitching the nails and to overcome this defect he back pritchels the holes with all the inherent disadvantages this entails. In addition, all the nail-holes are stamped at the same distance from the edge of the shoe which means that the use of "fine" and "coarse" stamped nail-holes cannot be taken advantage of to meet the needs of individual horses.

Machine made shoes, with the exception of racing and training plates, are of three basic types. The plain stamped shoe, the three-quartered fullered shoe and the concave fullered shoe. These shoes are made in a whole range of styles, weights and sizes and can be supplied with heels cut and rounded, clips drawn, double calkins, double wedges, wedge heel and calkin; hind shoes have the nail-holes more widely spaced to facilitate drawing double toe and quarter clips. This range of shoes enables a suitable set to be selected for the majority of horses and fitted cold.

PLAIN STAMPED SHOE
(Fig. 97 [a] and [b])

Shoe Code No.	Shoe Width	SIZE OF BARS FROM WHICH SHOE IS MADE								
		$\frac{3}{4}'' \times \frac{7}{16}''$	$\frac{3}{4}'' \times \frac{1}{2}''$	$\frac{7}{8}'' \times \frac{7}{16}''$	$\frac{7}{8}'' \times \frac{1}{2}''$	$1'' \times \frac{7}{16}''$	$1'' \times \frac{1}{2}''$	$1'' \times \frac{5}{8}''$	$1\frac{1}{8}'' \times \frac{7}{16}''$	$1\frac{1}{8}'' \times \frac{1}{2}''$
1	$4''$	★	★							
3	$4\frac{1}{2}''$	★	★	★	★					
5	$5''$	★	★	★	★	★	★	★		
7	$5\frac{1}{2}''$	★	★	★	★	★	★	★		
9	$6''$			★	★	★	★	★	★	★
11	$6\frac{1}{2}''$			★		★	★	★	★	★
13	$7''$					★	★		★	★
15	$7\frac{1}{2}''$					★			★	★

★ Indicates sizes obtainable

Fig. 97 (a). Plain stamped shoe, machine made. Front
shoe with toe clip and heels tapped to take studs.

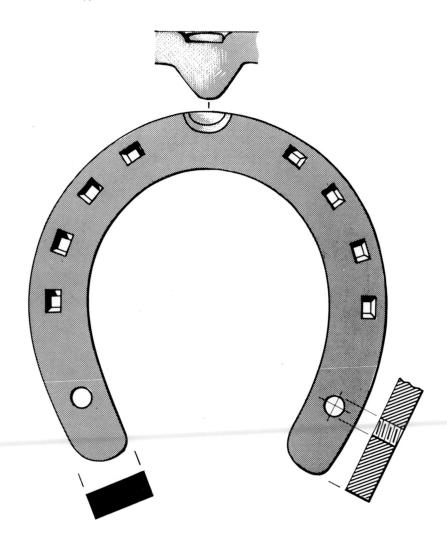

Cross-section of shoe:

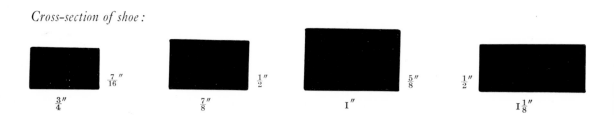

$\frac{3}{4}''$ $\frac{7}{16}''$ $\frac{7}{8}''$ $\frac{1}{2}''$ $1''$ $\frac{5}{8}''$ $\frac{1}{2}''$ $1\frac{1}{8}''$

Fig. 97 (b). Hind shoe with clips drawn and heels tapped
to take studs.

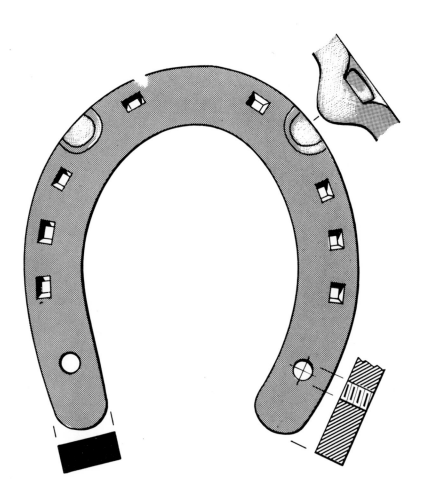

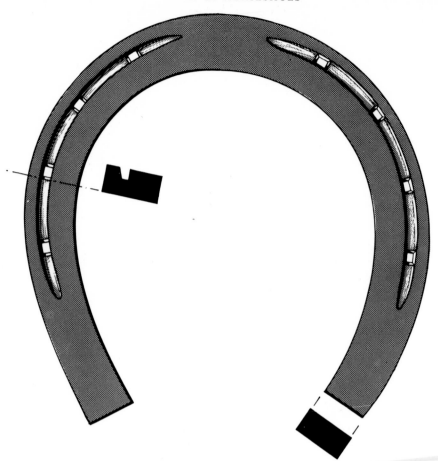

Fig. 98 (a). Three-quarter fullered shoe, machine made.
Front shoe.

THREE-QUARTER FULLERED SHOES
(*Fig. 98 [a] and [b]*)

Shoe Code No.	Shoe Width	SIZE OF BARS FROM WHICH SHOE IS MADE						
		$\frac{5}{8}'' \times \frac{5}{16}''$	$\frac{5}{8}'' \times \frac{3}{8}''$	$\frac{3}{4}'' \times \frac{3}{8}''$	$\frac{3}{4}'' \times \frac{7}{16}''$	$\frac{3}{4}'' \times \frac{1}{2}''$	$\frac{7}{8}'' \times \frac{7}{16}''$	$\frac{7}{8}'' \times \frac{1}{2}''$
I	$4''$	★	★	★	★	★		
3	$4\frac{1}{2}''$	★	★	★	★	★		
5	$5''$	★	★	★	★	★	★	★
7	$5\frac{1}{2}''$			★	★	★	★	★
9	$6''$				★		★	★
11	$6\frac{1}{2}''$				★		★	★
13	$7''$						★	★

★ Indicates sizes obtainable

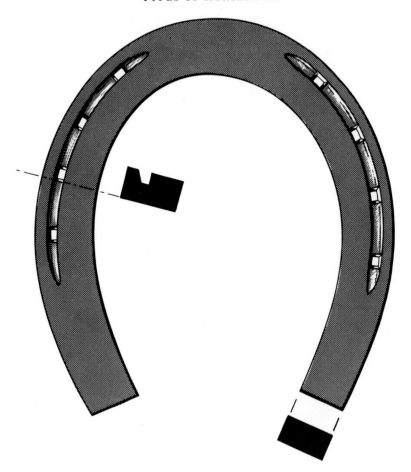

Fig. 98 (b). Hind shoe. The heels have been left long so that they can be trimmed to length or turned to form calkins.

Cross-section of shoe :

$\frac{3}{8}''$

$\frac{5}{8}''$

$\frac{7}{16}''$

$\frac{3}{4}''$

$\frac{1}{2}''$

$\frac{7}{8}''$

Fig. 99 (a). Concave fullered shoe, machine made. Front shoe.

CONCAVE FULLERED SHOES
(*Fig. 99 [a] and [b]*)

Shoe Code No.	Shoe Width	SIZE OF BARS FROM WHICH SHOE IS MADE								
		$\frac{1}{2}'' \times \frac{1}{4}''$	$\frac{5}{8}'' \times \frac{1}{4}''$	$\frac{5}{8}'' \times \frac{5}{16}''$	$\frac{5}{8}'' \times \frac{3}{8}''$	$\frac{5}{8}'' \times \frac{7}{16}''$	$\frac{3}{4}'' \times \frac{3}{8}''$	$\frac{3}{4}'' \times \frac{7}{16}''$	$\frac{3}{4}'' \times \frac{1}{2}''$	$\frac{7}{8}'' \times \frac{1}{2}''$
0	$3\frac{1}{2}''$	★	★	★	★					
1	$4''$	★	★	★	★	★	★	★	★	
2	$4\frac{1}{4}''$	★	★	★	★	★				
3	$4\frac{1}{2}''$	★	★	★	★	★	★	★	★	
4	$4\frac{3}{4}''$	★	★	★	★	★	★	★	★	
5	$5''$	★	★	★	★	★	★	★	★	★
6	$5\frac{1}{4}''$	★	★	★	★	★	★	★	★	★
7	$5\frac{1}{2}''$	★	★	★	★	★	★	★	★	★
9	$6''$						★	★	★	★

★ Indicates sizes obtainable

Fig. 99 (b). Hind shoe. The heels have been left long so that they can be trimmed to length or turned to form calkins.

Cross-section of shoe:

Section II: RACING PLATES

Racehorses require the lightest shoe possible to protect the foot and provide a good foothold, but it must be strong enough not to twist, bend or break. There are two common varieties of racing plates and both are made of aluminium: the standard racing plate with a single groove and the so-called "double grip" which has two grooves and is reputed to give a better foothold.

Racing plates have bevelled or "pencilled off" heels. Front shoes are fitted close and short to prevent brushing and the shoe being wrenched off.

Hind shoes are set well back to prevent over-reaches, and whether the heels are plain, with a calkin on the outside heel and a plain inside heel or a calkin on each heel, is decided by the going and the horse's action.

Front and hind shoes are secured with 6 or 7 nails, with the heel nails placed well back to prevent the shoe from spreading or bending. A set of plates weighs from 6 to 8 ozs.

For training, slightly heavier concave fullered shoes, made of mild steel, are fitted.

The size of calkin permitted is governed by the Jockey Club rule No. 149 which relates to shoeing for racing, and states:

> "No horse shall enter the parade ring or run in shoes which have protrusions on the ground surface other than calkins on the hind, limited to $\frac{1}{4}''$ in height. The use of American type toe-grab plates or with a sharp flange is forbidden whether or not modified in any way".

It should be noted that the term "protrusion" includes nail-heads which should be long enough only to hold the shoe or plate and, therefore, prohibits the use of oversize nails to provide extra grip or take the place of a calkin.

ALUMINIUM RACING PLATES
(Fig. 100 [a] and [b])

Shoe Code No.	Shoe Width	SIZE OF BAR FROM WHICH SHOE IS MADE		
		$\frac{7}{16}'' \times \frac{1}{4}''$	$\frac{1}{2}'' \times \frac{9}{32}''$	$\frac{1}{2}'' \times \frac{5}{16}''$
1	$4''$	★	★	
2	$4\frac{1}{4}''$	★	★	
3	$4\frac{1}{2}''$		★	★
4	$4\frac{3}{4}''$		★	★
5	$5''$		★	★
6	$5\frac{1}{4}''$		★	★
7	$5\frac{1}{2}''$		★	★
8	$5\frac{3}{4}''$		★	★

★ Indicates sizes obtainable

Cross-section of shoe:

 $\frac{1}{4}''$ $\frac{7}{16}''$

 $\frac{9}{32}''$ $\frac{1}{2}''$

 $\frac{5}{16}''$ $\frac{1}{2}''$

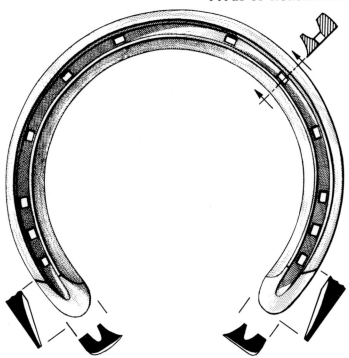

Fig. 100 (a). Racing plates, aluminium, machine made. Front shoe with bevelled or ''pencilled'' heels.

Fig. 100 (b). Hind shoe with a plain inside heel and a calkin on the outside heel.

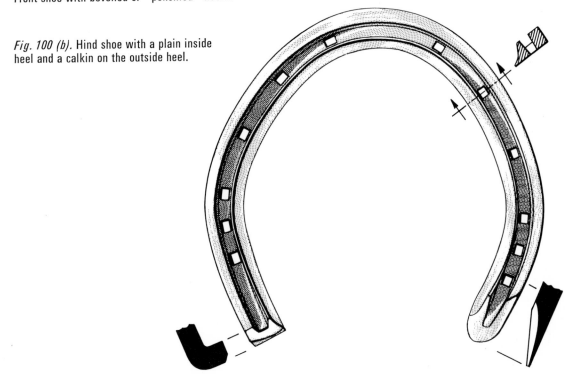

STEEL CONCAVE TRAINING AND RACING PLATES

Shoe Code No.	Shoe Width	SIZE OF BARS FROM WHICH SHOE IS MADE			
		$\frac{1}{2}'' \times \frac{1}{4}''$	$\frac{5}{8}'' \times \frac{1}{4}''$	$\frac{5}{8}'' \times \frac{5}{16}''$	$\frac{5}{8}'' \times \frac{3}{8}''$
0	$3\frac{1}{2}''$	★		★	★
1	$4''$	★	★	★	★
2	$4\frac{1}{4}''$	★	★	★	★
3	$4\frac{1}{2}''$	★	★	★	★
4	$4\frac{3}{4}''$	★	★	★	★
5	$5''$	★	★	★	★
6	$5\frac{1}{4}''$	★	★	★	★
7	$5\frac{1}{2}''$	★	★	★	★

★ Indicates sizes obtainable

Cross-section of shoe :

Steeplechasers require a shoe as light as possible but sufficiently strong to withstand hitting obstacles without twisting or bending. These requirements are met by a mild steel shoe, the same pattern as a single groove racing plate and weighing 12 to 16 ozs. per set.

Front shoes may have a toe clip and bevelled heels which are fitted close and short. Hind shoes are set well back, may have double toe-clips and have either two small calkins or a wedge heel and calkin. As for racing plates, each shoe is secured with 6 or 7 nails but the heel nails are not placed quite so far back.

Section III: HUNTER, POLO AND HACK SHOES
(*Fig. 101 [a] and [b]*)

A hunter has to jump, gallop and turn at speed. To meet these demands a shoe is required which provides a good foothold and remains secure on heavy going. To this end a concave fullered shoe with a plain flat foot surface is the most satisfactory.

Front shoes have a toe-clip and the inner branch is fitted close to prevent brushing. The heels should be a little shorter than the bearing surface, about $\frac{1}{8}''$ and bevelled at the same angle as the heels of the foot to reduce the chance of being struck and wrenched off.

Hind shoes have the toe slightly squared or rounded on both edges and double toe-clips. These features allow the shoe to be set back to prevent over-reaches and the flexor tendons of the front limb being struck. It is customary for the shoe to have a wedge heel and calkin or two calkins in which case the inner calkin is fitted close and sloped slightly downwards and inwards.

A set of shoes weighs from $3\frac{1}{2}$ to 4 lbs.

Show jumpers have to be able to twist and turn at speed and to pull up sharply. Competitions are held both out-of-doors and in indoor arenas and horses have to meet the challenge of changes in the siting of obstacles and great variations of pace. These problems are met by shoeing show jumpers with the concave fullered hunter shoe but with the heels tapped to take studs. The position of the studs and the types used is

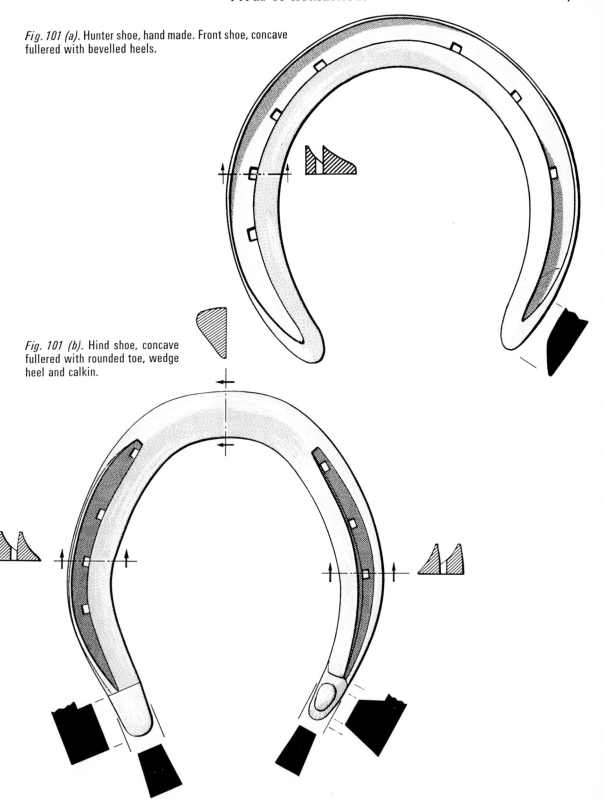

Fig. 101 (a). Hunter shoe, hand made. Front shoe, concave fullered with bevelled heels.

Fig. 101 (b). Hind shoe, concave fullered with rounded toe, wedge heel and calkin.

very much a matter of personal preference, the going and the performance required of a horse in a particular competition or jump off.

Front shoes have heels bevelled at the same angle as the heels of the foot and are fitted as for hunting shoes. If one stud is fitted it is placed in the outer branch either between the two heel nails or at the heel, and when two studs are fitted, one is placed at each heel.

Hind shoes have the heels cut off at an obtuse angle and fitted as for hunter shoes. When two studs are fitted one is placed in each heel and when only one then it is placed in the outside heel.

POLO SHOES

A polo pony requires a shoe which provides a good foothold for pulling up and turning sharply at the gallop, when it brings its weight back onto its hocks and uses its hind legs as a pivot.

The shoe fitted has to comply with the Hurlingham Polo Club rules as laid down under the section Equipment for Ponies and which states:

(i) "Rimmed shoes are allowed, but the rim may only be on the inside of the shoe.

(ii) Frost nails and screws are not allowed, but a calkin, fixed or movable, is permissable provided this is placed only at the heels of the hind shoes. The fixed or movable calkin shall be limited in size to a $\frac{1}{2}''$ cube."

Note: The movable calkin is allowed so that when it becomes worn it can be replaced by a fresh one without re-shoeing. The essence of this permission is that the movable calkin should resemble, as far as possible, the recognised form of fixed calkin, and does not permit the fixing of any fancy shaped spike, nor the placing of the calkin anywhere except at the heels of the hind shoes.

The polo or rimmed shoe (*Fig. 102*) is made from concave mild steel bar and fashioned in a

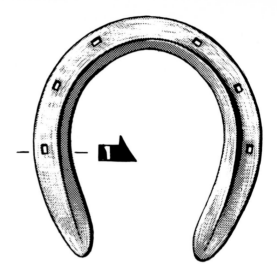

Fig. 102. Polo shoe, front, hand made.

special tool. The foot surface is flat but the ground surface has a sharp rim round the inside edge which gives an excellent grip on turf.

Front shoes have bevelled heels and the inside branch is fitted close. Hind shoes have rounded solid toes and are set back. The outer heel has a small square calkin and the inner heel has either a narrow calkin or is left plain.

The polo shoe is rarely used today. Its place has been taken by the concave fullered hunting shoe with the heels of the hind shoes tapped to take studs.

HACK SHOES

Hacks are rarely used for more than a few hours each day and do a lot of road work. For this reason they require heavier shoes than hunters.

Front shoes are concave fullered, similar in shape and fitted as for a hunter shoe except that the heels project about a $\frac{1}{4}''$ beyond the bearing surface and are cut off at a more obtuse angle.

Hind shoes are either plain or concave fullered. The toe is square or rounded and the shoe is set back a little to prevent over-reaches.

A low calkin or square stud is placed at each heel to secure a good foothold. Sometimes it is suggested that these modifications are not necessary because hacks by and large are worked at a more leisurely pace than hunters and calkins do little to secure a firm foothold on modern roads. This may well be true of calkins but cannot be said of the modern stud with its hard tungsten carbide core which gives a good foothold on any type of road.

A single toe clip in front and either a single or double toe clips behind are optional. A set of shoes weighs from 4 to 4½ lbs.

Riding ponies are shod all round with concave fullered shoes. Front shoes have the heels cut off level with the bearing and at the same slope as the heels of the foot. The inner branch is fitted close.

Fig. 103. Rodway double fullered shoe, hand made. Front shoe, *(a)* the ground surface has two parallel grooves and three ridges, and the nail-holes are stamped in the outer groove; *(b)* the foot surface is seated but this is not usual.

Hind shoes are set back a little with the heels cut off square. They are either left plain, fitted with low square studs or tapped to take studs to meet the requirements of various activities.

Toe clips in front and behind are optional. A set of shoes weighs from 2 to 2½ lbs.

Section IV: CARRIAGE AND DRAUGHT HORSE SHOES

Carriage horses tend to wear their shoes harder than saddle horses and especially the toes of the hind shoes. At one time the double fullered Rodway shoe was popular but it did not live up to its expectations of providing a better foothold and increased wear (*Fig. 103*). Carriage horses are shod traditionally with plain fullered shoes in front and plain stamped shoes behind

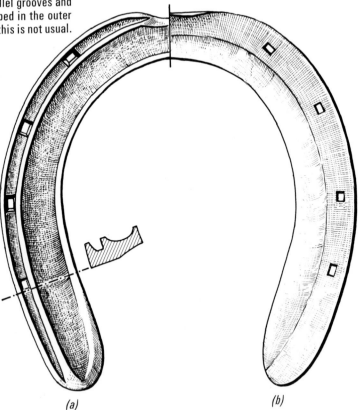

(a)   (b)

with calkins; but today they are often shod with concave fullered all round. Front shoes have the heels left long, but should not extend more than a $\frac{1}{4}''$ beyond the bearing surface and are cut off at an obtuse angle. Hind shoes require plenty of cover at the toe to combat wear and either have a calkin at each heel or a square stud.

Trap ponies are shod with the same pattern shoes as those for carriage horses. For driving competitions the heels of the hind shoes should be tapped to take the studs of choice to suit the particular terrain.

DRAUGHT HORSE SHOES
(Fig. 104)

Draught horses have to haul, start and back loads. The type of shoe fitted varies with the district and the road surface.

For all general purposes a plain stamped shoe

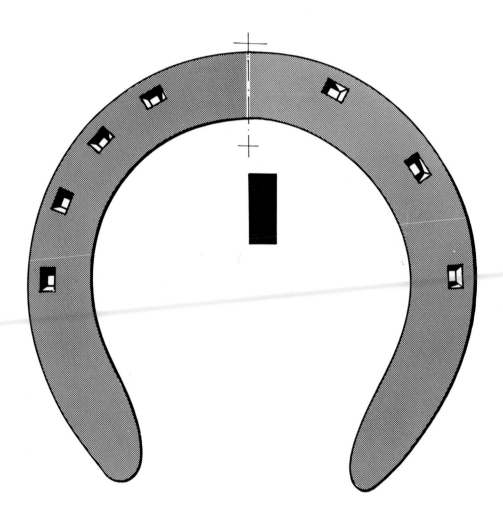

Fig. 104 (a). Draught horseshoe, hand made. Front shoe, plain stamped.

in front and a plain stamped shoe behind with a thickened toe and calkins is satisfactory. As draught horses work at a slow pace brushing is not a problem and, in consequence, the heels of both front and hind shoes can be left long and fitted wide to provide a firm base on which the foot can rest.

In some towns it is the practice to shoe heavy draught horses, both in front and behind, with a toe-piece and calkins (*Fig. 89*). This method of shoeing provides a good foothold, especially on paved streets and maintains a normal balance of the foot but deprives the frog of normal weight bearing.

On the smooth surfaces of modern roads toe-pieces and calkins provide no extra grip or foothold and once a horse has become accustomed to this type of shoe it takes some time to adapt to a flat shoe. A set of shoes weighs from 16 to 20 lbs.

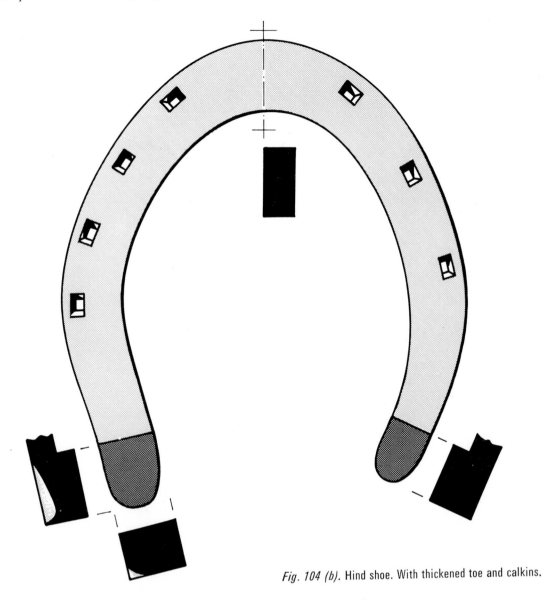

Fig. 104 (b). Hind shoe. With thickened toe and calkins.

Bevelled shoes are fitted when heavy draught horses are competing at shows and in the sale-ring. Bevelling is a modification of the outer edge of the shoe which is shaped to be continuous with, and at the same slope as, the wall (*Fig. 105*). Therefore the ground surface of the shoe is much wider than the foot surface and may extend as much as $\frac{3}{4}''$ beyond the circumference of the wall.

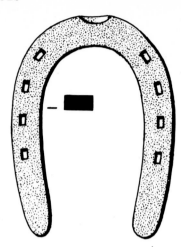

Fig. 106. Mule shoe. Front shoe, plain stamped and narrow with long heels.

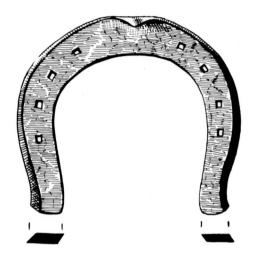

Fig. 105. Bevelled front shoe, hand made.

Bevelled shoes certainly enhance the appearance of the horse's feet by making them appear larger but are unsuitable for normal work.

Section V: MULE OR DONKEY SHOES (*Fig. 106*)

The anatomy and physiology of the mule or donkey's foot is the same as for the horse. In comparison with the horse the mule's foot is long and narrow, the donkey's even more so. It is more rounded at the toe, the sole is more vaulted and the heels are very upright and high. The wall is thicker and the horn more dense.

Mules and donkeys are frequently worked both under load and in draught without shoes. Then, the only attention their feet require is for the edge of the hoof to be kept rounded off with a rasp to prevent it splitting, and for the toe to be kept short and the heels lowered.

In wet weather and when working on modern roads shoeing is necessary. A mule or donkey shoe is a plain stamped shoe which is narrower and lighter than the pattern used for horses. As a rule the heels of both front and hind shoes are left plain, although on occasions the heels of hind shoes are turned down to form calkins. Each shoe is secured with 5 or 6 nails which have to be short with a strong shank as the standard horseshoe nail is invariably buckled by the hard horn of the mule or donkey's hoof.

CHAPTER SEVEN

Making a horseshoe

To make a front shoe and a hind shoe with a wedge heel and calkin from concave fullered iron bar, a farrier has to employ all the techniques, with the exception of fullering, which are basic to his craft for bending, turning and shaping metal.

Farriers in the practice of their craft, as is only to be expected, acquire and develop their own individual and preferred techniques. The methods to be described will serve as a practical guide, which obviously can be modified by individuals in the light of experience to meet their own acquired skills of handling and manipulating metals.

To describe making a shoe, concave fullered iron bar is chosen because today it is used for practically all shoes with the exception of those for heavy draught horses. No guidance will be given regarding the heat at which the metal is worked or the number of heats required to complete a specific task because this is dependent, in no small measure, on each farrier's method of working coupled with his speed and efficiency.

Section I: CUTTING OFF THE CORRECT LENGTH OF IRON BAR
(*Figs. 107 to 112*)

The length of iron bar required to make a shoe is estimated as follows:

Measure the width of the foot and the distance from the toe to the heel along the line of the frog, in inches.

Whichever is the greater, multiply the figure by 2 and add $1\frac{1}{2}''$ for concave fullered and $1''$ for plain iron bar.

Fig. 107. Measuring and marking off a length of concave fullered iron bar with rule and chalk.

Fig. 108 (above). Cutting off the length of iron bar required with a cold set.

Fig. 109 (above right). Locating and marking the centre of the cut off length of iron bar using a length of an old three-sided file.

Fig. 110 (right). Taking the first heat. Shoes are generally made in pairs.

Fig. 111 (below right). The white hot length of iron bar is cleaned with a wire brush to remove the scale. This improves the finished shoe and prevents sparks flying off when the metal is worked which can burn the farrier's hands or face.

Fig. 112. Length of iron bar cleaned and ready for making into a shoe.

Section II: MAKING A FRONT SHOE
(*Figs. 113 to 145*)

FIRST STAGE (TURNING THE TOE)

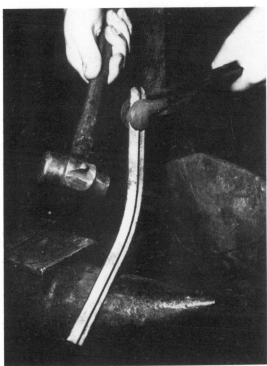

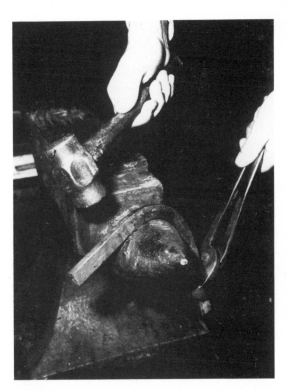

Fig. 113. The length of iron bar is held over the beak of the anvil and struck with the turning hammer, alternately on each side of the centre of the concave surface, until bent to an angle of 90°.

Fig. 114. The toe of the shoe is turned and finished off over the beak of the anvil.

Fig. 115. Completed first stage. The toe is at an angle of 90°.

SECOND STAGE (FORMING THE HEEL AND TURNING THE OUTSIDE BRANCH) *Fig. 116.* The end of the outside branch is closed on edge to form the outside heel.

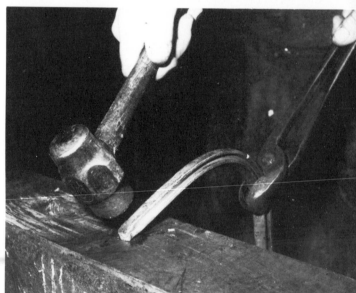

Fig. 117. The outside heel is tapered to an angle of 45°.

Fig. 118 (above). The outside branch is turned to shape over the beak of the anvil.

Fig. 119 (above right). Completed second stage. Outside branch turned and heel formed.

THIRD STAGE (STAMPING THE NAIL-HOLES)

The stamp is struck lightly at first and then more heavily until its point almost penetrates the thickness of the web. It is held so that the angle of each nail-hole corresponds with the slope of the wall and the point will emerge on the foot surface to correspond with the outer edge of the white line.

Fig. 120 (right). The stamp is held upright at the heel so as to produce a "fine" hole on the foot surface.

Fig. 121 (below right). The stamp is held at an angle at the toe so as to produce a "coarse" hole on the foot surface.

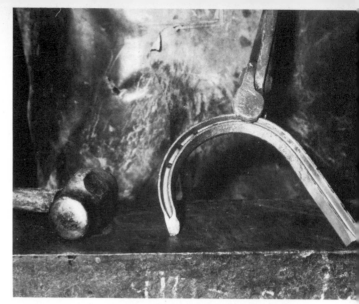

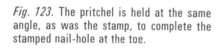

Fig. 122. The pritchel is held upright, as was the stamp, to complete the stamped nail-hole at the heel.

Fig. 123. The pritchel is held at the same angle, as was the stamp, to complete the stamped nail-hole at the toe.

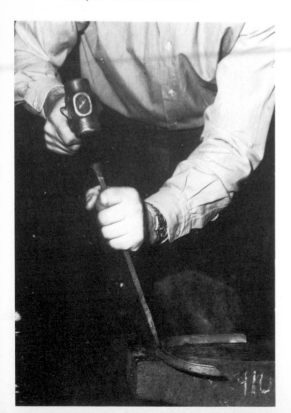

Fig. 124 (opposite page, top). Completed third stage. Note the position of the heel nail-hole just posterior to the toe-half of the shoe.

FOURTH STAGE (FORMING THE HEEL AND TURNING THE INSIDE BRANCH)

Fig. 125 (opposite page, centre. The inside heel is tapered to an angle of 45° and closed on edge.

Fig. 126 (opposite page, bottom right). The outside edge of the branch is knocked over to prevent brushing.

Fig. 127. The inside branch is turned to shape over the beak of the anvil.

Fig. 128. The heel nail-hole is stamped upright as for the outside branch.

Fig. 129. The toe nail-hole is stamped at an angle as for the outside branch.

The nail-holes are completed with the pritchel in exactly the same manner as described for the outside branch.

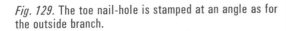

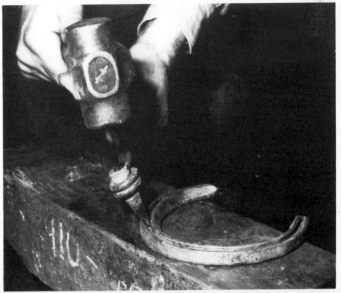

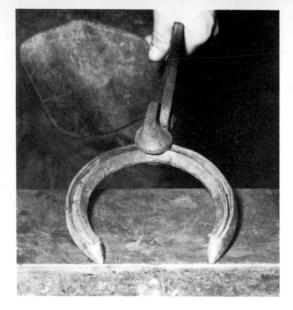

Fig. 130. Completed fourth stage. Both branches turned, heels formed, outside edge of inner branch knocked over and closed and nail-holes stamped and pritchelled.

TRIMMING THE HEELS

If the heels of a shoe are too long they are cut off to length either using a heel cutter or a special tool.

Fig. 131. The heel of the shoe is heated to a red heat and cut off with the heel cutter. The ground surface of the heel is placed on the heel cutter and directed away from the concave cutting edge.

Fig. 132. Alternatively the heel of the shoe is heated to a red heat, placed on the face of the anvil with the ground surface uppermost and then trimmed to length using a special tool which is made from an old rasp by curving it on length and sharpening the end.

FIFTH STAGE (DRAWING THE TOE CLIP)
(i) *Standard method*

Fig. 133. The centre of the toe is marked, held over the heel of the anvil and the clip commenced by striking the mark with the "lug" on the turning hammer.

Fig. 134. Taking down the metal.

Fig. 135. Levelling the foot surface at the back of the clip.

Fig. 136. Commencing to draw the clip.

Fig. 137. Drawing the clip being completed.

(ii) *Using a punch*

Fig. 138. The centre of the toe is marked and a "bubble" is drawn with a punch.

Fig. 139. The "bubble" is placed over the small round hole on the body of the anvil and extended.

Fig. 140. Drawing the clip is completed over the heel of the anvil.

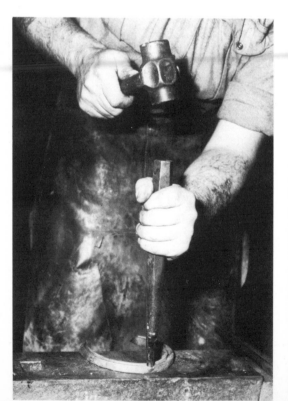

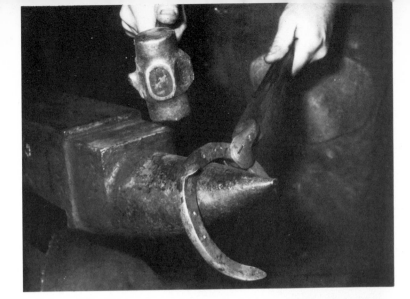

Fig. 141. The toe clip is set and finished off.

SIXTH STAGE (FINISHING OFF THE SHOE)

Making the shoe is now complete, but the best hammer work can be improved by a few judicious strokes of the rasp around the clips and heels, over the surfaces and along the edges.

Fig. 142. Rasping the heels.

Fig. 143. Removing the "rag" from the foot surface at the heels.

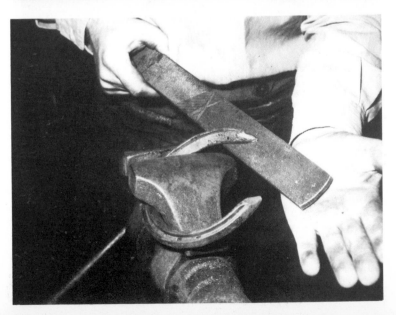

Fig. 144. Completed shoe, foot surface. The foot surface is level, note especially at the back of the toe clip, and the "cover" is not reduced at the heels.

Fig. 145. Completed shoe, ground surface. Well balanced shoe. The toe clip is centred, nail holes correctly placed and spaced and the inside edge is knocked over and closed to prevent brushing.

**Section III:
MAKING A HIND
SHOE**
(*Figs. 146 to 150*)

Fig. 146. The length of iron bar is turned to shape. The toe is formed at a more acute angle than for a front shoe and then it is "knocked over".

Fig. 147. Outer branch completed. The heel is square with the inside edge chamfered so that the width of the foot surface is retained without the heel impinging on the frog.

Fig. 148. Inner branch completed. The heel is shaped as for a front shoe and with the brushing edge knocked over and closed.

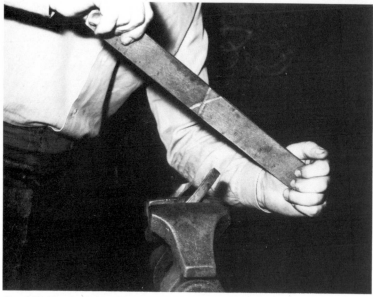

Fig. 149. Finally the heels are dressed and finished off with a few strokes of a rasp.

Fig. 150. Completed shoe, ground surface. Shoe well balanced. Toe knocked over, outer heel square with inside edge chamfered, inside heel tapered to an angle of 45° and the brushing edge knocked over.

Section IV: MAKING A HIND SHOE WITH A WEDGE HEEL AND CALKIN
(Figs. 151 to 163)

FIRST STAGE (MAKING THE WEDGE HEEL ON THE INSIDE BRANCH)

Fig. 151 (below). About an inch of one end of the length of iron bar is heated, held vertical on the face of the anvil and struck to "upset" it.

Fig. 152 (right). The amount of "upsetting" required to make a wedge heel.

Fig. 153 (below right). Commencing to draw the wedge heel.

Fig. 154. The wedge heel is set with a half-round concave tool.

Fig. 155. Rasping and finishing off the wedge heel.

Fig. 156. The completed wedge heel.

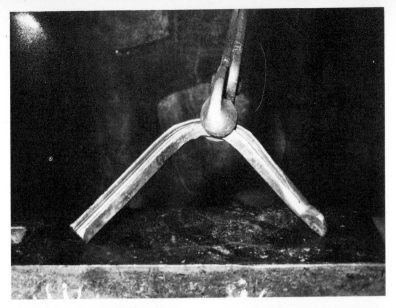

SECOND STAGE
(TURNING THE TOE)
Fig. 157. The toe is turned and knocked over in exactly the same manner as described for making a standard hind shoe.

THIRD STAGE
(MAKING THE CALKIN AT THE OUTSIDE HEEL)
Fig. 158. The foot surface is creased over the edge of the anvil.

Fig. 159. The shoe is reversed and the heel turned up, at almost a right angle, to form the calkin.

Fig. 160. The turned up heel is knocked back to shape.

Fig. 161 (a), (b) and (c). The various positions in which the shoe is held while striking the heel to shape the calkin.

Fig. 161 (b).

to move its legs in alignment with its body. The toe is pointed forward and the foot set down flat (*Fig. 183* [*a*]).

Defects of limb conformation and of the pastern foot axis alter the flight of the foot and result in the following abnormalities of gait.

Paddling (*Fig. 184* [*a*]). The foot moves forwards, outwards and then inwards in a circular movement. This results in the foot landing and breaking over on the outside toe which results in excessive wear of the outside quarter. This action is seen in horses with a toe-in conformation (*Fig. 183* [*b*]).

Winging (*Fig. 184* [*b*]). The foot moves forwards, inwards and then outwards in a circular movement. This results in the foot landing and breaking over on the inside toe which results in excessive wear of the inside quarter. This action is common to horses with a toe-out conformation (*Fig. 183* [*c*]) and is a cause of brushing.

Plaiting (*Fig. 184* [*c*]). This term is used to describe the action when a horse moves its foot across and inwards to land more or less in front of the opposite foot. It is seen in horses with a narrow base toe-out conformation and is conducive to stumbling.

To assess a horse's length of stride, the flexion of its joints and its co-ordination in raising a front foot to clear the approaching hind foot, it has to be examined passing the observer.

A normal action is characterised by the foot breaking over at the toe with the flight of the foot following a smooth arc which reaches its peak as it passes the opposite leg (*Fig. 185* [*a*]).

If the horse has a sloping pastern foot axis the break over of the foot is delayed and, in consequence, reaches the peak of its arc of flight before it passes the opposite leg (*Fig. 185* [*b*]). Horses with this conformation have a slightly increased stride, keep their feet close to the ground and are comfortable to ride.

On the other hand, if the horse has an upright pastern foot axis, the foot breaks over quickly and reaches the peak of its arc of flight after it has passed the opposite leg (*Fig. 185* [*c*]). Horses with this conformation have a slightly reduced stride and bring their feet to the ground at a sharp angle. This increases concussion which is conducive to joint problems and makes the horse an uncomfortable ride.

Section IV: WEAR OF THE SHOE

Defects of conformation and abnormalities of feet always affect work and performance. The most important defects are those of the pastern foot axis, toe-in and toe-out, which result in abnormal wear of the shoe.

Therefore, before fitting a new set of shoes the wear of the old shoes must be studied. Wear provides valuable information regarding any defects of conformation or abnormalities of gait and any faults in the previous preparation of the foot or in the making of the shoe. It is upon the state of wear of a shoe that much information is

Fig. 184. Abnormalities of gait:

(a) Paddling;
(b) winging;
(c) plaiting.

(a)   (b)   (c)

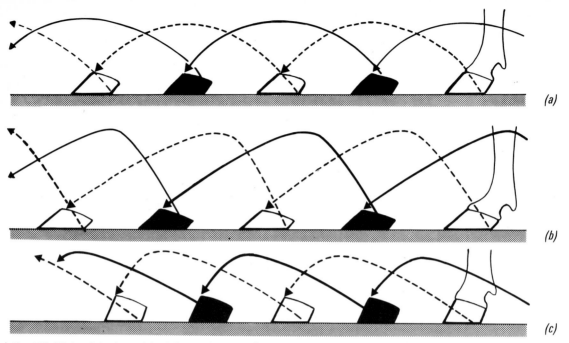

Fig. 185. Flight of the foot with: *(a)* normal pastern foot axis; *(b)* sloping pastern foot axis; *(c)* upright pastern foot axis.

gleaned towards the preparation of the foot and the selection of the correct shoe.

When a shoe has worn evenly it indicates that the foot has been reduced to its correct proportions and the type of shoe is suitable. Some horses, with a normal action, wear out their shoes more quickly than average and in these cases a wider or a convex shoe rather than a thicker shoe should be fitted.

Unevenness of wear results from a variety of causes. It may be due to faulty preparation of the foot, fitting the wrong type of shoe, abnormal conformation of limb or pastern foot axis, or the horse's gait, whereby it goes on its toe or heels.

If the toe of the shoe is excessively worn it may be due to a number of causes. The toe of the foot is too long, the shoe has excessively high calkins, or the horse goes on its toe to alleviate pain, as is seen in cases of navicular and bone spavin disease. Correction is by turning up the toe of the shoe, out of the line of wear, to re-

semble the worn surface of the old shoe. Excessive wear should never be compensated for by increasing the thickness of a shoe.

Excessive wear of a shoe at the quarters is due either to an uneven bearing surface or an abnormal pastern foot axis with a toe-in or toe-out conformation. If the wear is due to the former then all that is required is to lower the foot on the appropriate side to normal proportions. When the wear is due to a toe-in conformation it can be rectified by the margin of the wall at the inside toe, back almost to the quarter, being reduced and rounded off and the shoe fitted close to the inside toe and quarter; but on the outside from the quarter to the heel, it should be fitted a little wider than normal. The toe clip should be drawn towards the outside rather than the centre of the toe. For a toe-out conformation the reverse procedure should be adopted.

When the heels of a shoe are excessively worn it is generally due either to chronic laminitis or low ringbone disease. Increasing wear in these cases should be attempted not by increasing the thickness of the heels of the shoe but rather by lowering the heels of the foot, as much as safety will allow, and fitting a shoe a little long at the heels. If these simple measures do not suffice, consideration will have to be given to fitting a surgical shoe.

Section V: REMOVING A SHOE
(*Figs. 186 to 199*)

To remove a shoe, the clenches are first cut off with a buffer and then, using the pincers, the shoe is eased at the heels and along each branch until it is loose, when it is grasped at the toe and pulled backwards across the foot and off.

Care must be taken to ensure that the clenches are cut off cleanly, as a rough clench pulled through the wall causes unnecessary damage. Any nail stubs embedded in the wall must be removed by punching them out either with the point of a buffer or with a new nail which has had its point cut off. A nail striking a stub may buckle and penetrate the sensitive foot, or force the stub against the sensitive foot causing pressure, pain and lameness.

FRONT FOOT

Method of picking up a left front foot and positioning it.

Fig. 186. Stand close to the horse's shoulder, face to the rear, run the left hand firmly but unhurriedly down the posterior aspect of the limb.

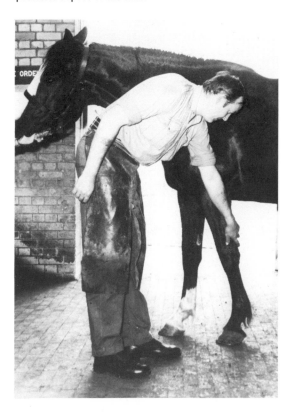

Fig. 187. Raise the foot by grasping the leg around the pastern.

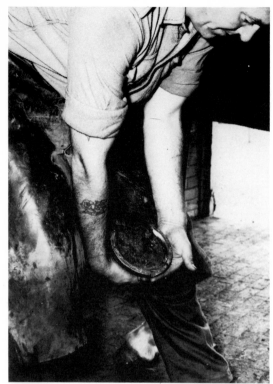

Fig. 188 (left). Take a step forward with the left leg, and at the same time bring the horse's foot under the knee and hold it in both hands.

Fig. 189 (below left). Left front foot correctly positioned. Note the position adopted by the farrier to secure the foot. Knees slightly bent and brought together with the toes turned in.

Method of removing a front shoe.
Fig. 190. The clenches are cut off with a buffer. The blade is held close against the wall to prevent cutting into it.

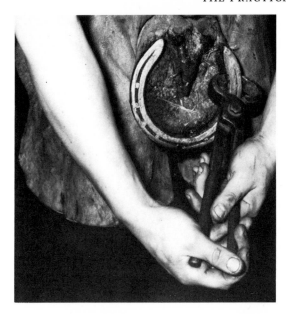

Fig. 192. The toe of the shoe is grasped with the pincers and removed by pulling it upwards, backwards and off across the foot.

Fig. 191 (left). The inside heel of the shoe is raised by closing the jaws of the pincers under it and prising downwards towards the toe. The outside heel is next eased in like manner.

This manoeuvre is continued alternately, along each branch, until all the nails are partly withdrawn and the shoe is loose.

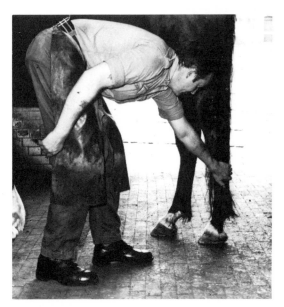

HIND FOOT
Method of picking up a left hind foot and positioning it.

Fig. 193. Stand close in to the horse's side, facing to the rear, and run the left hand firmly but unhurriedly across the quarters and down the posterior aspect of the limb to just above the fetlock joint.

Fig. 194 (above). Raise the leg by pulling it forwards and, immediately the foot is off the ground, take a step forward and support it in the right hand.

Fig. 195 (above right). Left hind foot correctly positioned. The farrier has taken a step forward with his left foot and placed the leg across his left thigh with the foot resting against his right knee.

Fig. 196 (below right). Cutting off the clenches on the outside of the left hind foot. Note the position of the hand holding the buffer and the method of using the wrist to support the foot.

The hind shoe is then removed using exactly the same method as described for a front shoe.

METHOD OF WITHDRAWING THE NAILS
INDIVIDUALLY

When it is necessary to remove each nail individually, the clenches are cut off and the heels raised as described for removing a front or hind shoe. Then the raised heel is given a sharp knock with the closed jaws of the pincers to extrude the head of the nail from the countersink. It can then be grasped with the pincers and withdrawn. The nails are dealt with in this manner on each side alternately, until all have been withdrawn and the shoe removed.

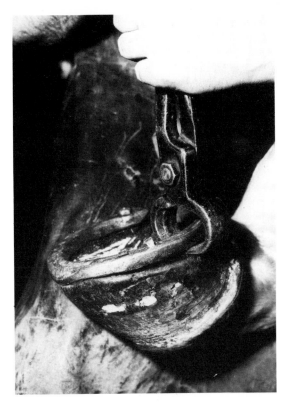 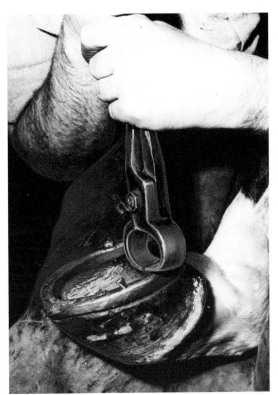

Fig. 197 (above). The jaws of the pincers are closed under the heel of the shoe which is raised by pushing the handles downwards and towards the toe.

Fig. 198 (above right). The raised heel of the shoe is knocked back into position by striking it with the closed jaws of the pincers which results in the head of the nail being extruded.

Fig. 199. The extruded head of the nail is grasped with the pincers and withdrawn.

Section VI: DRESSING THE FOOT
(*Figs. 200 to 219*)

The normal proportions of the unshod foot are maintained by wear. But once a shoe is fitted the foot is protected from friction and continues to grow except for slight wear at the heels. This is due to the friction between the heels and the shoe as a result of the normal expansion of the foot and can result in the heels being lowered by as much as 1/6″ in a month. It is this lowering of heels, coupled with overgrowth of the wall at the toe, which gradually alters the pastern foot axis and the normal balance of the shod foot.

After removing the shoes and before proceeding to prepare the foot, its shape and proportions must be studied and any defects noted that will have to be taken into account when dressing the foot.

First, with the horse standing on a level surface, the balance of the foot in relation to the length of toe and height of heel is examined. Then, with the foot raised, (*Fig. 200*) the bearing surface is examined for irregularities of outline and unevenness.

The old adage that: "The shoe should be made to fit the foot and not the foot the shoe" is only a half-truth. They are complementary, as the foot and shoe have to be fitted to each other. Indeed, to fit a shoe to a foot which has not been correctly prepared may be more injurious to the horse than fitting the foot to the shoe.

STAGE I. ATTENTION TO THE FROG AND SOLE

For the frog to play its important rôle in the anti-concussion mechanism of the foot it must be large, firm and prominent, but not project beyond the bearing surface at the heels by more than the thickness of the shoe.

The frog should be pared only to remove any ragged or loose tags, (*Fig. 201*) or in the treat-

Fig. 200.

Fig. 201.

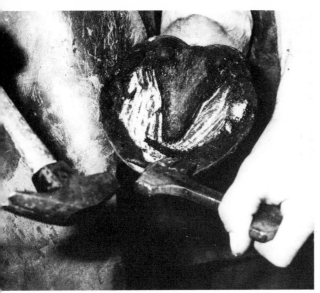

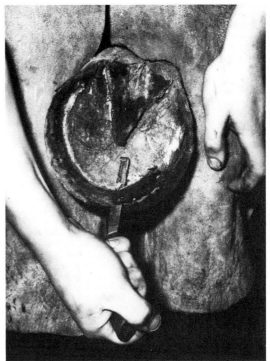

Fig. 202 (above).

Fig. 203 (right).

Fig. 204 (below right).

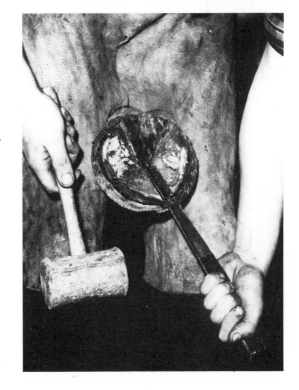

ment of thrush. But it may be trimmed lightly to allow free use of the hoof pick in the clefts.

The sole protects the foot against injury and excessive paring is a bad and unnecessary practice. Only flakes of the sole that have failed to shed should be removed (*Fig. 202*).

STAGE II. LOWERING OVERGROWN FEET

It is not always easy to decide how much of an overgrown foot requires to be taken down when levelling the bearing surface. This can be resolved by cutting away a thin strip of dead horn from the inner edge of the wall and exposing the white line (*Fig. 203*).

A slight overgrowth of horn is easily reduced with a drawing knife, but if it is excessive then either a toeing knife or hoof cutter is required. Using a toeing knife requires care and practice, (*Fig. 204*) because it easily twists in the hand and can cut through the wall and sole into the sensitive foot. On the other hand hoof cutters are easy to use, are safe in unskilled hands and leave a more level surface.

 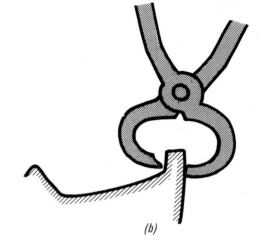

(a)   (b)

Fig. 205. Hoof cutters: *(a)* correctly held. The handles are perpendicular and with the cutting edge on the inside to control the depth of the cut; *(b)* incorrectly held. The depth of the cut is not controlled and an uneven surface results.

Hoof cutters are used with the handles held perpendicular to the bearing surface and with the cutting edge on the inside so as to control the depth of cut (*Fig. 205*). The excess horn is removed by commencing at one heel, with half a cut at a time to leave a smooth surface, and taking increasingly deeper cuts, working towards the toe (*Fig. 206*). Then, with gradually decreasing cuts, working around to the other heel.

STAGE III. THE PREPARATION OF A LEVEL BEARING SURFACE

The final preparation of the foot for the shoe comprises reducing it to its normal proportions and rasping a level bearing surface.

Rasping. Rasping is carried out in a continuous circular movement. A right-handed person holds the handle of the rasp in his right hand and places his left hand, palm down, over the other end which acts as a guide. To dress a near fore or near hind foot, commence at the outside heel and quarter and for the off fore and off hind at the inside heel and quarter. Then gradually work round to the opposite quarter and note that as the toe is passed it becomes necessary to change the position of the hands. A left-handed person reverses the method.

The preparation of a level bearing surface using a rasp is conveniently described in four steps.

Fig. 206. Hoof cutters being used to lower the wall. Always start at one heel and work towards the toe.

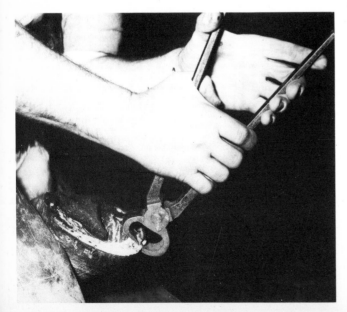

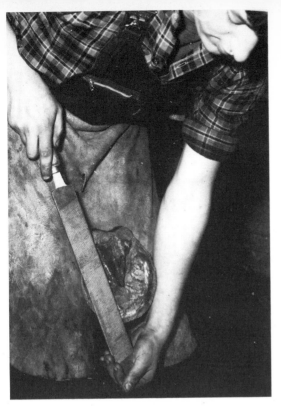

Fig. 207. *First step.* The outer aspect of the bearing surface is rasped along the line from heel to toe.

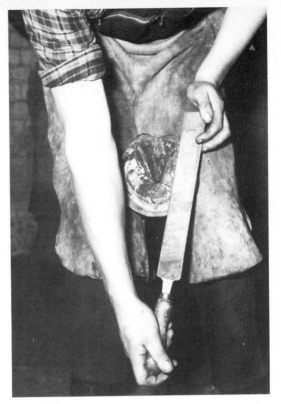

Fig. 209. *Third step.* The inner aspect of the bearing surface is rasped along the line from toe to heel. Note that the farrier has changed the position of his hands.

Fig. 208. *Second step.* The bearing surface is rasped across the quarters and toe.

Fig. 210. *Fourth step.* The edge of the wall is lightly rasped round, using the file surface of the rasp, to remove its sharp edge which prevents the hoof from breaking or splitting.

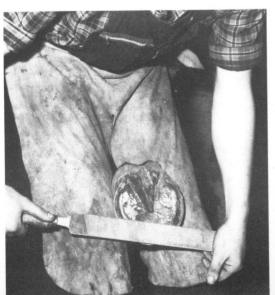

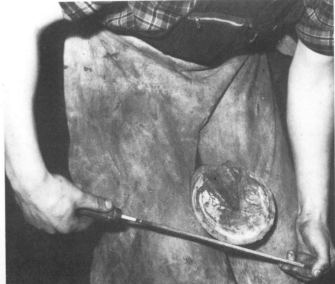

Fig. 211. Method of positioning a hind foot to rasp the bearing surface.

Fig. 212. Overlowering the inner quarter by raising the handle of the rasp.

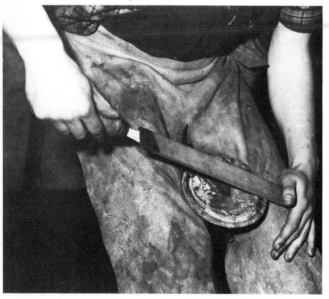

Faults in using a rasp. At all times the rasp must be held level and used with full strokes. If not, more horn will be removed from some areas than others and result in an uneven bearing surface (*Figs. 212 to 214*).

To prepare a level bearing surface, in the majority of cases, it is only necessary to remove as much horn as has grown since the last time the horse was shod. But before commencing this task it is essential to check the balance of the foot in relation to the pastern foot axis and decide where and how much horn will require to be removed in relation to the following conditions:

(i)   *Toe too long.* If this is due to excess horn at the toe the pastern foot axis is not straight but broken back at the coronet (*Fig. 180 [a]*). This defect puts excessive strain on the flexor tendons and predisposes to stumbling.

    In these cases the foot axis is corrected by shortening the toe as much as common sense dictates and nature permits.

(ii) *Heels too high.* This results in an upright or stumpy foot and if it is due to excess horn at the heels then the pastern foot axis is not straight but is broken forward at the coronet (*Fig. 180 [b]*). This defect throws the knee forward, straightens the pastern, puts extra weight on the front of the foot, shortens the bearing surface and reduces frog pressure. In these cases the foot axis is corrected by lowering the heels.

(iii) *Heels too low.* In these cases the bearing surface is increased and the excessive slope of the foot puts extra weight on the back of the foot. To correct the foot axis the quarters are lowered slightly, the toe a little more and the heels not touched at all. In severe cases it may be advisable to fit a shoe with thickened heels.

(iv) *Broken-in and broken-out (Figs. 215 [a] and [b])* are terms used to describe an excessive growth or overlowering of one side compared with the other. These cases are corrected by lowering the wall on the appropriate side.

When correcting these defects to obtain a normal pastern foot axis and level bearing surface it is important to lower the excess of horn first. If, for example, there is an excess of horn at the toe and the heels are lowered first, it may be impossible to remove a corresponding amount from the toe to balance the foot; to correct the mistake a shoe with thickened heels or even calkins may have to be fitted.

It is not possible to lay down hard and fast rules for balancing the feet. The best guide is to work towards obtaining a normal pastern foot axis, but it must not be overlooked that there are marked variations in the shape and form of normal feet. Some horses normally have high heels, others are long at the toe, but in these cases the pastern foot axis is a straight line and to attempt to reduce such feet to an ideal standard shape only causes untold harm. In addition to correcting the pastern foot axis it must not be overlooked that maintaining a level bearing surface is of equal importance.

A badly dressed foot is not only altered in shape but also in position, relative to the leg, which in turn influences the action of the limb. Some farriers check their work by measuring the distance from the coronet to the bearing surface with a ruler, the width of the foot with dividers and the angle at the toe with a hoof gauge, but the majority of craftsmen depend on their eyes, experience and expertise when preparing a foot for a shoe.

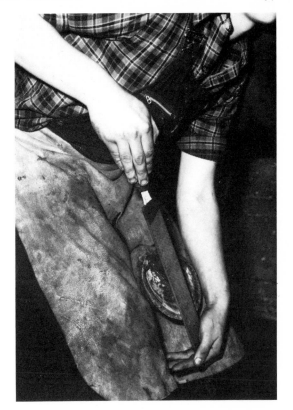

Fig. 213 (above right). Overlowering the wall at the toe by raising the handle of the rasp.

Fig. 214 (right). Overlowering the outer quarter by dropping the handle of the rasp.

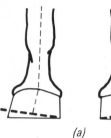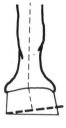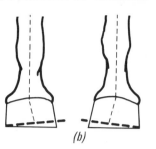

(a)

Fig. 215. (a) Broken-in foot, excessive growth of the outside of the hoof; *(b)* broken-out foot, excessive growth of the inside of the hoof.

(b)

FEATURES OF A CORRECTLY DRESSED FOOT

(i)   The weight is evenly distributed over the foot. When viewed from the front (*Fig. 178* [*a*]), the transverse plane at the coronet is parallel with the lower border. Both sides of the wall are of equal height and the plantar surface is at right angles to the foot axis.

(ii) When viewed from behind (*Fig. 178* [*a*]), both heels are the same height and the base of the frog just touches the ground.

(iii) When viewed from the side the toe, quarters and heel are proportionate and the pastern foot axis is in a straight line (*Fig. 180* [*c*]).

Fig. 216. A correctly dressed foot – bearing surface is level, frog and sole lightly trimmed, bars preserved and seat of corn lightly pared to prevent pressure from the shoe.

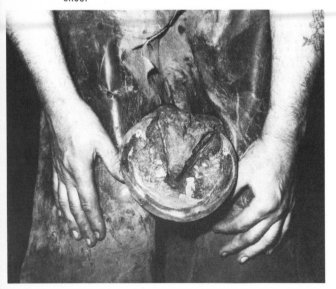

(iv) The length of the toe and the heels is preserved to produce a proportionate foot with a level bearing surface (*Fig. 216*). The bars are preserved and the sole at the seat of corn is lightly pared to prevent pressure.

FAULTS IN DRESSING THE FOOT

Paring the frog. On no account should the frog be pared for neatness or in the mistaken idea that it is injured by contact with the ground. If it is pared down to such an extent that it does not make contact with the ground it cannot function normally, soon atrophies and leads to a contracted foot.

Paring the sole. The sole must not be pared except to remove undesquamated flakes of horn. The mistaken idea that descent of the sole was fundamental to expansion of the foot led to the practice of paring out the sole until it eased or yielded under thumb pressure. This not only deprives the foot of its normal protection but also reduces the bearing surface provided by the margin of the sole.

Over-lowering the toe. This decreases the slope of the foot, raises the heels and reduces the bearing surface. The foot axis is broken forward which throws the knee forward, straightens the pastern and puts extra weight on the front of the foot, while the high heels prevent normal frog pressure.

Over-lowering the heels. This is a common fault as it is easier to rasp the heels than the toe. It increases the slope of the foot, the length of the toe (which can be a cause of stumbling) and the bearing surface. The foot axis is broken back which puts extra weight on the back of the foot and increases the strain on the flexor tendons. On no account should the heels be over lowered to obtain frog pressure as this unbalances the foot and the adverse effects outweigh any benefits that might accrue.

Over-lowering the bearing surface. This is particularly liable to happen when flat and spreading feet are dressed and is followed by the horse being foot-sore for a few days.

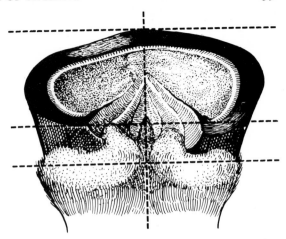

Fig. 218. Uneven bearing surface. The toe and opposite heel have been overdressed.

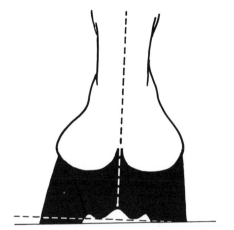

Fig. 217. One side of the foot has been over-dressed.

Uneven bearing surface. This occurs when one side (*Fig. 217*) is over-dressed. This results in an excessive amount of weight being taken on the higher side and, if not corrected, in course of time the foot will become twisted.

Also, it is not uncommon for one side of the toe and the opposite heel to be over-dressed (*Fig. 218*) which leads to uneven pressure distribution. A badly dressed foot is due either to inexperience or careless use of the rasp.

Opening-up the heels. This is the term used to describe cutting away the bars to make the foot appear wider. By breaking the continuity of the bearing surface, the wall turns inwards at the heels which deprives the foot of an important part of its anti-concussion mechanisms and leads to contraction.

Rasping the wall. This is often done with the best of intentions to remove any roughness or ridges and to give the foot a neat smooth finish. But it should be kept to a minimum and not carried out above the clenches as it removes the periople which increases evaporation and renders the horn hard and brittle. Rasping below the clenches reduces the bearing surface and the nail holding capacity of the wall.

The term "dumping" or "stumping-up" the toe is used when an excessive amount of the wall at the toe is rasped away. This is a bad practice as it reduces the bearing surface and exposes the underlying soft horn which becomes brittle.

Fig. 219. Dumping. The shoe is set back and the protruding wall at the toe is rasped away to make the foot fit the shoe, and give it a neat appearance.

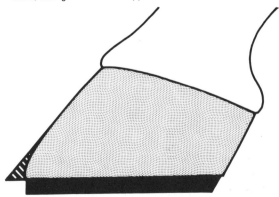

Dumping is basically a fault in dressing the foot and fitting the shoe. The shoe is made smaller in circumference than the wall, which is rasped away to make the foot fit the shoe and, hence, it looks small and neat (*Fig. 219*). Dumping can be justified to a limited extent when a shoe has to be set back, and also on flat and sloping feet so that the nails can be pitched higher to secure a better hold.

Section VII: FITTING THE SHOE
(*Figs. 220 to 237*)

When a shoe is fitted its foot surface has to be adapted to the bearing surface of the hoof (surface fitting) and its outer edge has to correspond to the circumference of the wall (outline fitting).

An exact fit between shoe and foot ensures that the pressure of weight bearing is equally distributed over the whole of the bearing surface. Thus the shoe can be said to resemble very closely a continuation of the wall, an ideal arrangement to prevent wear and, at the same time, any interference with normal function.

SURFACE FITTING

Surface fitting comprises adapting exactly the foot surface of the shoe to the bearing surface of the foot.

A horse with normal feet and action wears the toes of its shoes excessively and, therefore, it is basically correct to fit shoes which conform in shape to the worn shoes. This requires fitting a shoe with a rolled toe and altering the bearing surface accordingly. Such shoes are economical regarding wear and in reducing concussion, but are difficult to make and fit. Therefore, for all practical purposes, an exact and satisfactory fit is obtained by simply fitting two level surfaces together.

Injuries caused by uneven pressure are most likely to occur at the toe and the heels. Pressure at the toe is due either to the bearing surface of the wall being reduced to below the level of the sole, or to the foot surface of the shoe being raised on its inner edge. Horses with flat feet tend to have a prominent sole, especially at the

toe, which can be relieved of excessive pressure either by prudent paring down or by fitting a seated-out shoe.

OUTLINE FITTING

Outline fitting is the adaption of the shoe to the length and breadth of the hoof, with the outer border of the shoe corresponding to the outline of the bearing surface.

Close fitting. The edge of the shoe is brought within the circumference of the wall and the projecting horn is rasped away until the wall is flush with the shoe. This gives the appearance of neatness but it is a bad practice because valuable bearing surface is lost, less wall remains to secure the nails and it contributes to brittleness and cracks.

Fig. 220. Shoe left on too long. The heels of the shoe have moved forward off the wall and bars, and come to rest on the seat of corn, causing pressure and bruising.

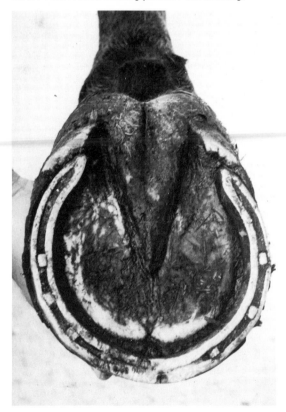

However, it is proper to fit the inside heel close on horses used for fast work, to prevent brushing and speedy cutting.

Wide fitting. The shoe is fitted wide or full to the hoof so that the edge of the shoe projects beyond the circumference of the wall. This gives added protection, but the advantage is slight and is outweighed by brushing and tread injuries.

It is customary for heavy horses to be fitted with shoes wide at the heels, to provide a firm base for support. In this case the upper edge is rounded off or "boxed-up". In addition, for show purposes, heavy draught horses are often fitted with bevelled shoes (*Fig. 105*) to make their feet appear larger.

Length of shoe. It is important that the heels of the shoe extend back to the end of the horn to cover the wall and the bars. During growth of the wall, the heels of the shoe gradually move forward and come to rest on the seat of corn to cause pressure and bruising (*Fig. 220*).

It is common practice to fit front shoes with the heels extending slightly beyond the extremity of the horn and to bevel them off to conform with the angle of the heels (*Fig. 221*). For horses which work at fast paces it is customary to fit shoes with heels which extend to just within the termination of the horn and to cut them off at a

more acute angle. This is referred to as "pencilled heels" (*Fig. 222*).

Heels too long. Shoes with heels too long are liable to be trodden on by a hind foot and be pulled off, or may result in a fall. Also, long heels can injure the point of the elbow when the horse is lying down.

Heels too short. If the heels are too short some bearing surface is lost and, as the foot grows, they will, all too soon, come to rest on the seat of corn.

HOT SHOEING

Horn is a poor conductor of heat and therefore a hot shoe can be applied to the horse's hoof without causing pain or injuring the underlying sensitive foot. Obviously a hot shoe should not be held in contact with the foot any longer than is absolutely necessary to decide on any alterations to the shoe or bearing surface to ensure a correct fit. If the method is abused by applying the shoe too hot or holding it in contact until it beds itself into the horn, then a burnt sole will result, especially if the horn is thin.

When a shoe is fitted hot, it is applied at a dull red heat to the bearing surface. The horn is charred in relation to the areas of contact thus revealing any irregularities between the two surfaces. If the bearing surface is uneven the

Fig. 221. The heels of a front shoe should extend slightly behind the bearing surface and be bevelled off at the same angle as the heels.

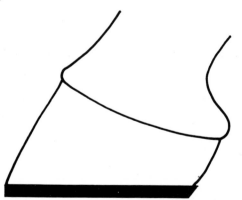

Fig. 222. The heels of a front shoe for horses used for galloping should end just within the bearing surface and be bevelled off obliquely.

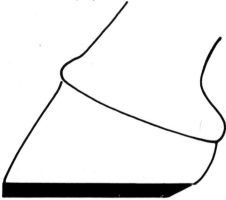

charred areas are taken down with either a drawing knife or a rasp and if the shoe does not fit exactly it is taken back to the anvil and altered.

This procedure is followed until a perfect surface and outline fit is obtained.

In addition, the charring of the horn fibres reduces the absorption of moisture and softens and expands the horn which makes driving the nails easier and secures them more firmly when the horn contracts.

The advantage of hot shoeing over cold shoeing can be summed up by stating that it enables the shoe to be fitted more accurately and retained more securely.

FITTING A SHOE HOT

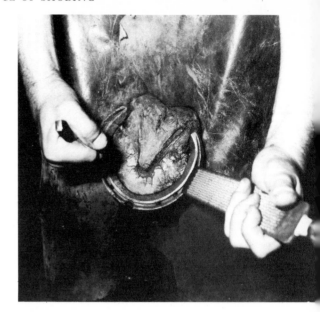

Fig. 224. The end of a rasp or handle of a drawing knife is used to position the hot shoe.

Fig. 225. The horn is unevenly charred. This indicates that either the bearing surface of the foot or the foot surface of the shoe, or both, are not level. If it is the shoe that is not level then the whole of one side and the opposite heel is charred.

Fig. 223. The shoe at a dull red heat, is carried on a pritchel to the foot and tried on.

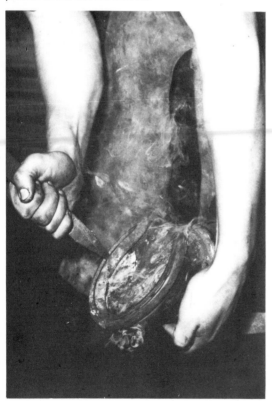

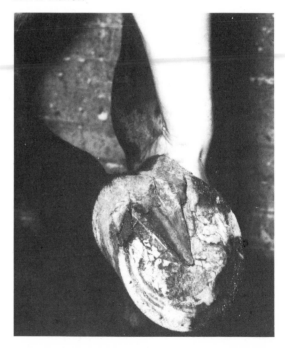

Fig. 226. The bearing surface of the foot is evenly charred to a dark-honey colour. This indicates even contact between the foot and shoe provided the foot surface of the shoe is true. A rim of charred horn is removed with a drawing knife to relieve pressure on the sole.

Fig. 227. The seat of corn is eased to the depth of about 1/10th of an inch below the level of the wall and the bar, to prevent any pressure from the heel of the shoe.

COLD SHOEING

Machine made shoes are regular in form, have a level foot surface and are generally fitted cold. All shoes have to be altered to obtain a perfect fit and when fitting a cold shoe it is possible only to alter its outline slightly and its foot surface not at all.

In the majority of cases a suitable machine made shoe can be selected from the wide range available and with the limited alterations possible a satisfactory fit can be obtained.

Cold fitted shoes are more liable to become loose than are those fitted hot because an exact fit between the foot and shoe surfaces cannot be obtained. Unless an exact fit is obtained the uneven pressure results in a slight rocking of the shoe which gradually raises the clenches and the shoe becomes loose.

Methods of altering the shape of a cold shoe. Farriers develop their own individual methods and techniques for altering the shape of ready-made cold shoes. The following methods illustrate the basic principles of altering the outline of a cold shoe using the face and beak of an anvil.

Fig. 229. Opening a heel over the beak of an anvil.

Fig. 228. Opening the toe over the beak of an anvil.

Fig. 230. Closing the toe over the beak of an anvil.

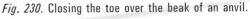

Fig. 231. Closing a heel over the beak of an anvil.

Fig. 233. The shoe being levelled on the face of an anvil

Fig. 232. Closing a shoe using the face of an anvil. This method is incorrect because it does not shape the shoe.

Fig. 234. Method of holding and positioning a shoe to check whether its surfaces are level.

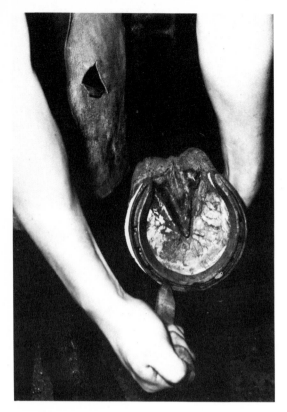

Fig. 235.

Fig. 236.

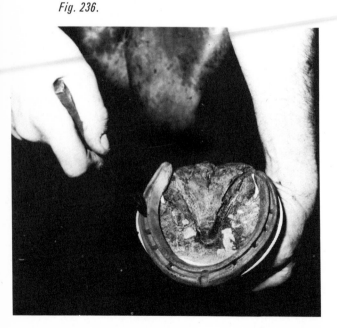

FAULTS IN OUTLINE FITTING

The outer branch of the shoe is fitted too close and the inner heel is too wide (*Fig. 235*).

Toe clip not centred. Both branches fitted too close. Outer heel is too long and the inner heel is too short (*Fig. 236*).

FAULTS IN SURFACE FITTING

Easing the heels. This term is used to describe the practice of lowering the foot surface of the heels of a shoe (*Fig. 237*). This practice arose from the erroneous idea that by lowering the

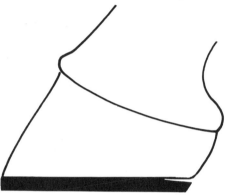

Fig. 237.

heels of the shoe, the heels of the foot would be relieved of weight bearing which would allow expansion. This is a bad practice because bearing surface is lost and abnormal pressure is concentrated at a point where the foot and shoe should be in level contact.

Excessive burning of the horn. This is sometimes done with the idea of obtaining a solid bed for the shoe. It is a mistake because the excessively charred horn crumbles away and the shoe becomes loose.

Section VIII: NAILING ON A SHOE AND FINISHING OFF
(*Figs. 238 to 235*)

A number of important points have to be

taken into account when nailing on a shoe and unless due attention is paid to them, a well made shoe, accurately fitted to a correctly prepared foot, will soon become loose.

The nails selected must be proportionate to the size of the shoe and the foot. If too large they will split the horn and if too small the shoe will not be secured. Nails should be driven parallel to the horn fibres and no nail should be driven to enter or cross a crack. If the feet are broken the nail-holes should be stamped so that the nails can be driven through sound horn. Only the minimum number of nails necessary to secure the shoe should be used. Most shoes can be secured with seven nails, four in the outside and three in the inside branches.

Opinions differ as to whether the first nail to be driven should be at the toe or the heel. If a toe nail is driven first, it is argued that this permits the shoe to be swung and the heels accurately positioned. Those who drive a heel nail first argue that if the first nail is driven at the toe it tends to move the shoe backwards. The nail should enter the wall at the white line and be pitched to emerge about one third of the way up the wall to obtain a secure hold. If the point of the nail emerges too high up the wall, "coarse nailing", it can prick or press on the sensitive foot and cause lameness. If it emerges too low, "fine nailing", a secure hold is not obtained. As the wall at the toe is about twice as thick as at the heels the nails at the toe can be driven correspondingly higher.

The farrier judges the direction the nail is taking by the sound, resistance encountered and the feel transmitted by the hammer. As the nail passes outwards from the soft horn at the white line to the hard horn so the sound changes. A soft sound indicates that the nail is running in an old nail hole or crack or is entering the soft horn of the wall and proceeding towards the sensitive foot. As soon as the farrier is sure the nail is on its proper course, and when he has driven it about two-thirds of its way, he puts his finger on the spot where he expects the point to emerge and strikes some sharp blows. This turns the point of the nail away from its bevel to

emerge on the outside of the wall.

Generally speaking, a short and thick hold of the wall by a nail is better than driving it shallow and high. Ideally no more of the wall should be included within the grasp of the nail than is likely to be removed at the next shoeing, thus maintaining a constantly sound wall. The height that a nail can be driven depends on the condition of the wall, the number and position of the old nail-holes and the size and shape of the foot.

Immediately each nail has been hammered home the protruding point is either twisted off, using the claw of the shoeing hammer, or cut off about $\frac{1}{8}''$ from the wall with clench cutters.

When all the nails have been driven they are "drawn-up". The closed jaws of the pincers are placed under the edge of each stub of the cut off nail and at the same time the nail head is given a few sharp blows with the shoeing hammer.

This draws the shank of the nail well up into the wall and at the same time turns the stub over to form a clench.

NAILING ON THE SHOE

Fig. 238. The shoe is held in the fitted position and the first nail, the inside heel nail, is driven.

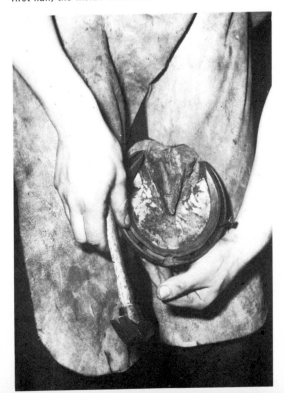

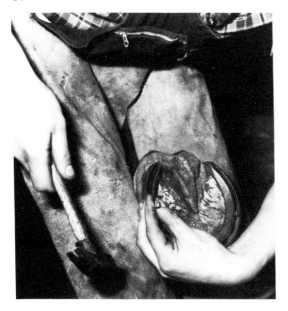

Fig. 239 (above). The second nail, the outside heel nail, is driven. It is important to make any adjustments to the outline fitting before driving this nail which fixes the shoe in its permanent position. The remaining nails are then driven on each side alternately.

Fig. 240 (above right). Immediately each nail is hammered home the protruding point is twisted off using the claw of the hammer. Care must be taken to leave enough of the shank to form the clench.

Fig. 241 (right). When all the nails have been driven and the points wrung off, the closed jaws of the pincers are pressed firmly upwards against the stubs and the heads driven home by repeated blows of the hammer. This draws up the nail to tighten the shoe on the foot and at the same time turns over the protruding stub to form a clench.

METHODS OF HOLDING THE FOOT
FOR CLENCHING UP

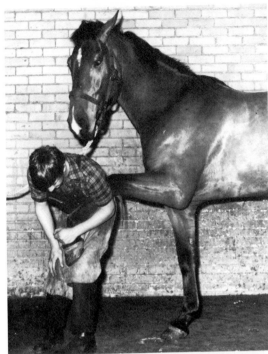

Fig. 242. To work on the outside of a left front foot, the farrier draws the leg forward and rests it on his left knee.

When working on the inside of the foot, the farrier faces in the opposite direction and rests the foot on his right knee.

Fig. 243. An alternative method of positioning a front foot for clenching up is to draw it forward and rest it on a tripod.

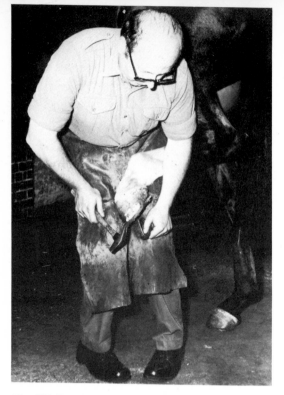

Fig. 244. To work on the outside of a left hind foot, the farrier draws the leg forward, and with his back to the horse rests its foot on his left thigh.

Fig. 245. To work on the inside of a left hind foot, the farrier draws the leg forward, and facing forwards rests its foot on his right thigh with his right arm over the leg to hold the foot in position.

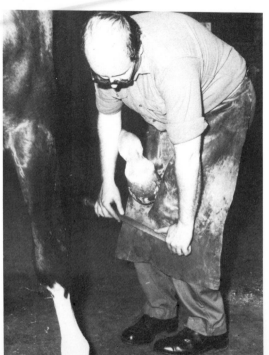

Fig. 246. The split horn underlying the clench is smoothed off with the file edge of the rasp, care being taken not to cut a notch.

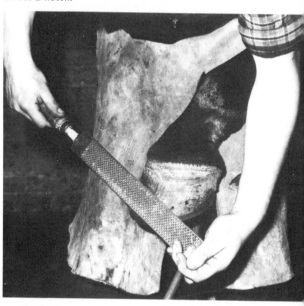

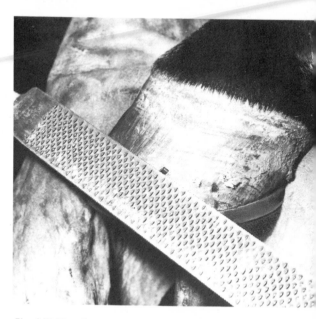

Fig. 247. The clench is shaped with the file edge of the rasp. It should be slightly bevelled and equal in length to the width of the shank. It is designed to hold the shank securely and not for stapling the shoe to the hoof.

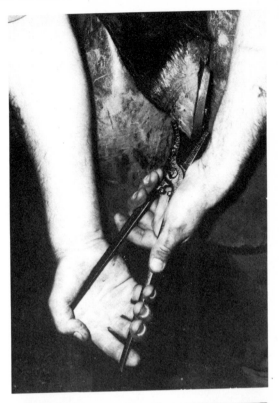

Fig. 248 (above). The clench is turned and bedded by tapping it with the hammer until it lies flat against the wall. At the same time the closed jaws of the pincers are pressed firmly upwards against the head of each nail in turn to prevent it being driven back.

Fig. 249 (above right). An alternative method of turning the clenches is to use clenching tongs. Note the position of the farrier's hands. The left hand holds the clenching tongs firmly against the wall whilst with his right hand he closes the handles. Clenching tongs are particularly useful for young and nervous horses, and for horses with sensitive feet which they resent being hammered.

Fig. 250 (right). The clenches are smoothed off with the file side of the rasp, care being taken not to weaken them by excessive rasping, and the edge of the wall is under-rasped to give it a final finish.

ACCIDENTS WHEN NAILING ON A SHOE

Pricks occur when the nail is mis-directed and penetrates the sensitive foot. This causes pain and the horse snatches its foot away. When the nail is withdrawn a little blood may escape from the nail-hole and the nail be discoloured.

Pricks are most liable to occur if the horse is restive and particularly if coupled with an excessively rasped wall, shoe fitted close, coarse nail-holes or the nail driven with the straight side to the inside (*Fig. 251*).

Treatment consists of pouring some tincture of iodine into the hole and administrating a prophylactic dose of tetanus antitoxin unless the horse is protected against tetanus. If the lameness has not completely disappeared within two or three days then the nail-hole must be opened up to provide drainage and combined with hot foot baths and antibiotic therapy.

Nail bind is the term used when a nail has been driven sufficiently close to the sensitive foot to cause pressure, pain and lameness. The effects are not always immediate and may be delayed for 1 to 3 days. The condition is diagnosed by tapping the horn over the line of each nail until pain is evinced which indicates the offending nail. In the majority of cases the condition is evident within 12 to 24 hours and all that is required is to withdraw the nail and rest the horse for a couple of days. In long standing cases the withdrawal of the nail may be accompanied by a discharge. In these cases the holes must be immediately opened up to provide drainage, combined with hot foot baths, and antibiotic therapy and a prophylactic dose of tetanus antitoxin.

POINTS TO BE OBSERVED WHEN EXAMINING A NEWLY-SHOD HORSE

Foot on the ground (Fig. 252).

(i) Clenches are even, flat and broad. Nails not driven into old nail holes or cracks and pitched higher at the toe than at the heels.

(ii) Both front and hind feet should be pairs, be the same size and shape and with the same pastern foot axis.

(iii) No rasping of the wall. A little always occurs below the clenches when they are rasped off smooth.

(iv) No dumping of the wall. Especially at the toe of front feet to conceal a badly fitted shoe.

(v) Clips low and broad and the toe clip centred.

(vi) Shoe fits the outline of the foot. Heels of correct length.

Fig. 251. A very carelessly driven nail which caused a nail bind. Not only was it driven with its straight side to the inside but also its point did not emerge to be twisted off and a clench formed.

Fig. 252.

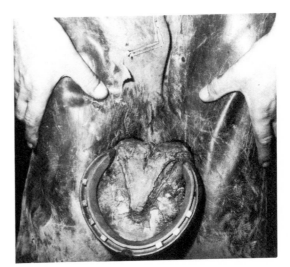

Fig. 253.

Foot lifted off the ground (Fig. 253).

(i) Nails driven home and the heads fit the countersinks.

(ii) No unnecessary paring of the frog and sole.

(iii) Heels not opened up.

(iv) Toe clip centred and in line with the point of the frog.

(v) The sole has been eased at the seat of corn.

(vi) No daylight between the foot and the shoe which indicates an unevenness of either the bearing surface of the foot or the foot surface of the shoe.

(vii) Shoe fits the foot and the heels do not interfere with the function of the frog.

(viii) The shoe is properly finished off.

Finally the horse is trotted up for signs of lameness.

CHAPTER NINE

Care of the feet

Section I: THE SHOD HORSE

SHOES prevent the hoof from being worn away by friction but interfere with the normal expansion and contraction of the foot. For feet to be kept in a healthy state they require to be picked out at least twice daily, morning and evening, and on each occasion the horse returns from work. In addition, the shoes have to be removed every 4 to 6 weeks to balance the foot and maintain a normal pastern foot axis.

In the care of horses' feet a number of general factors have to be taken into account, such as whether the horse is stabled in a loose box or stall, the type of bedding and the amount and type of exercise. Stable hygiene is most important and care must be taken that horses in stalls do not stand with their hind feet in dung and urine which softens the horn and predisposes to thrush. When feet are picked out extra care must be taken to keep the space between the shoe and the sole, especially if the shoe is seated-out, and the clefts of the frog free of all grit and dirt. If the frog is overgrown some judicious trimming is permissible to expose the clefts and facilitate picking out.

It is not always appreciated that for feet to function normally the moisture content of the hoof must be maintained. When horses are stabled for long periods and during dry weather the hoof is unable to make good the moisture lost by evaporation, and in consequence it becomes dry and hard, loses its elasticity and easily cracks. If the feet are washed daily sufficient moisture will be absorbed to make good this loss. A hard brush should not be used for this purpose as it will remove the periople. A considerable amount of moisture is absorbed by the sole and the frog and a convenient method of replacing it, when circumstances permit, is to pack the feet with wet clay.

The importance, necessity and advantages of applying impervious materials, such as ointments and oily dressings, to stimulate growth and keep the feet healthy, merits careful consideration. There is no evidence to show that they stimulate growth. Their action is related directly to controlling the delicately balanced evaporation and absorption of moisture by the hoof. Under ordinary conditions the continuous application of an impervious material to the hoof prevents evaporation and in consequence the horn becomes soft and crumbly. In wet conditions it has the opposite effect and by controlling the excessive absorption of moisture it prevents the horn becoming too soft. On the other hand in dry conditions it can be used to prevent or delay the loss of moisture and if dry and brittle hooves are soaked in water to replenish their moisture content, this can be followed by an application to help retain it. These objects can best be attained by applying a thin film of vaseline or lanoline to the wall, sole and frog.

The hoofs of shod horses can be kept healthy and their normal elasticity maintained by picking out their feet regularly, providing dry standings and beddings, washing as necessary and the judicious application of vaseline or lanoline to maintain the moisture content of the horn within its normal limits.

THRUSH

This is a disease of the frog which is characterised by a foetid discharge from the central and sometimes the collateral clefts, associated with disintegration of the horn. It is more common in hind than in front feet and in horses with poorly developed and atrophied frogs. It does not cause lameness, except in neglected cases when the underlying sensitive foot becomes exposed.

The cause of thrush is not known, but it is invariably associated with poor stable management, stalls and loose boxes not regularly mucked out, and wet standings. Failure to pick out the feet favour its development.

It is a preventable disease and in the first instance attention must be directed to improving stable management and general hygiene. Clean, dry loose boxes and standings, regular use of the hoof pick and attention to shoeing to ensure frog pressure are all called for.

Local treatment comprises paring away all diseased and loose horn, keeping the clefts of the frog clean and dry and either instilling an astringent powder, such as a mixture of 1 part of powdered copper sulphate to 2 parts of boric powder each morning and evening, or packing the clefts with tow and Stockholm tar every 2 to 3 days.

Section II: THE UNSHOD HORSE

It is customary to turn out all types of working horses for a few months during the summer. This not only gives them a rest and improves their general condition, but allows their shoes to be removed which gives the hooves a chance to grow without being damaged by nails.

Without the protection of a shoe the hoof is worn away by friction and the rate of wear depends on the quality of the horn and the state of the ground. Whether the horse is out at grass or confined to a yard, its feet require attention every 4 to 6 weeks. Normal growth is not always controlled by friction, and in many cases the toe requires to be shortened and the heels lowered to maintain a normal pastern foot axis and the edge of the wall rounded off with a rasp to prevent it from splitting or pieces breaking away. To prevent excessive wear and the horse becoming foot-sore a little more of the wall should be left than is customary when dressing a foot to fit a shoe. During the dry season in hot countries, horses are worked on unmetalled roads without hind shoes and mules are not shod. In these conditions it is most important to carry out routine inspections. The edges of the walls must be kept rounded off to prevent them from splitting, the feet kept balanced and the animals examined at the trot to make sure they are not becoming foot-sore. If there is a spell of wet weather or the animals have to be worked on metalled roads, the hooves are rapidly worn down and shoeing becomes necessary.

TIPS (*Fig. 254*)

These are short or half shoes which protect the anterior half of the foot. They prevent the wall at the toe from wear whilst permitting the posterior half of the foot and the frog to bear

Fig. 254. A standard tip.

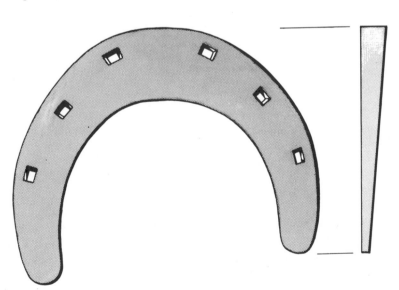

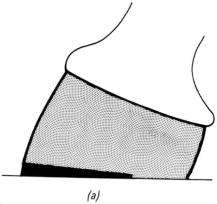 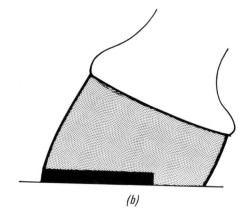

(a)   (b)

Fig. 255. (a) The standard tip is fitted by lowering the front half of the foot so that when the tip is fitted the ground surface of the tip and the unprotected posterior half of the foot are level; *(b)* The Charlier tip. A strip of the lower border of the wall is removed and the tip embedded in it.

normal weight. For these reasons they are sometimes fitted to front feet when horses are turned out to grass, but they have their disadvantages. They are not easy to fit, frequently become loose and have to be removed at regular intervals so that the overgrowth of wall at the toe can be reduced and the normal pastern foot axis restored.

There are two types of tip. The standard tip (*Fig. 255* [*a*]) which is gradually thinned off towards its heels and the modified or Charlier tip (*Fig. 255* [*b*]) which is let into the wall. The Charlier tip has no advantages over the standard type, requires considerable skill to fit and is little more than a relic of the past.

All tips are retained with 4 or 5 nails and require to be fitted full to prevent the growth of wall from spreading over them and splitting.

Section III: YOUNG STOCK

When foals are given free exercise ordinary wear keeps their feet within normal proportions; but if they do not get sufficient exercise or are confined to small paddocks their feet soon become overgrown. If the toes are too long a sloping fetlock develops which upsets the balance of the foot and predisposes to stumbling.

But more frequent, and more important, is the development of high heels. This results in loss of frog pressure, contracted and weak heels which curl inwards, followed by a twisted or deformed foot.

Defects of conformation are all too frequent and it is essential they are recognised and dealt with as soon as possible. Congenital defects of the pastern foot axis cannot be cured, but by intelligent use of the rasp the defect can be controlled and prevented from getting worse. It is most important that any corrections carried out are done gradually so that the leg can adjust to the abnormal strains and stresses imposed on it. The most common defects requiring early and regular attention are:

(i) *Straight in front.* In these cases the heels are slightly raised and in consequence are not worn down and continue to grow. This is followed by the fetlock becoming gradually straighter, contraction of the flexor tendons, and unless the heels are lowered the condition can progress to knuckling of the fetlock joint.

(ii) *Toe turned-in.* When the foal advances its foot it swings it outwards and lands on the outside edge of the wall causing excessive wear (*Fig. 183* [*b*]). This results in overgrowth of the inside wall and heel which, unless kept rasped down to maintain a level bearing surface, leads to an exacerbation of the defect.

(iii) *Toe turned-out.* In these cases the exact opposite to a turned-in toe (*Fig. 183* [*c*]) pertains and is dealt with in like manner but by keeping the outside wall and heel rasped down to maintain a level bearing surface.

Attempts are frequently made to correct limb defects by altering the bearing surface of the foot.

In this connection it must be pointed out that the leg and the foot act one upon the other and in a young growing animal its bones are moulded in relation to the pressures placed on them. Therefore, if attempting to correct a congenital limb defect by altering the alignment of the limb, it is preferable to alter the limb axis with a shoe rather than mutilate the bearing surface, which should be kept level at all times.

CHAPTER TEN

Prevention of slipping, and winter shoeing

Section I: METHODS TO PREVENT SLIPPING

THE methods employed to give horses a secure foothold include special shoes, calkins, wedge heels, toe-pieces, studs and a variety of pads.

Special shoes with various notches, projections or transverse ridges on the ground surface (*Fig. 256*) and shoes grooved to take a length of rope or a cord of rubber have been tried (*Fig. 257*). These shoes diminish slipping to some degree but their disadvantages outweigh any hoped for advantages. The sharp ridges soon wear smooth, the grooved shoes are difficult to make and nail on and the groove does not retain the rope or rubber securely which quickly wears out.

In practice not one of these shoes provides a better grip than the standard concave fullered shoe and really they are only of historical interest.

Shoes with a toe-piece and calkins for draught horses, and with a wedge heel and calkin for riding horses have stood the test of time as the most satisfactory methods of providing a secure foothold. But these shoes take skill and time to forge and, therefore, more simple, less time consuming and more economical methods are required. These requirements have been met, in no small measure, by the introduction of a range of horseshoe studs. These studs have been designed to meet the requirements of all types of horses and conditions of work and in addition to providing a good grip they reduce the wear of the shoes.

HORSESHOE STUDS

Studs are available in a whole range of sizes to suit ponies, hacks and harness horses and of different shapes to meet the special requirements of various sports such as show jumping and other events.

The standard studs for routine non-slip purposes are low and broad, which allow the frog to function normally and are tapered so that once fitted they remain permanently in the shoe (*Fig. 258*). It is common practice to insert one stud in each heel (*Fig. 259*).

The durability of these studs greatly increases the life of the shoe and, under normal conditions, they can be expected to last for a minimum of 350 miles for hacking and hunting, and 250 miles for light draught work. As these studs wear down they continue to retain their non-slip properties because of a centre core of tungsten carbide, a very hard metal, which wears down much more slowly than the surrounding metal and persists as a projection (*Fig. 260*).

In some cases, if it is considered that the standard stud raises the heels of the shoe excessively, then the *plug type stud* is used (*Fig. 261*). These studs are countersunk into the shoe, until level with the ground surface. As the surrounding metal and the heel of the shoe wear down the hard tungsten core remains to provide a good grip and prevent slipping (*Fig. 262*).

For sporting activities such as show jumping and horse trials in particular, which require studs to be exchanged quickly to meet the changes of pace and ground conditions, the screw-in type stud is used (*Fig. 263*).

Fig. 256. An anti-slipping shoe. This shoe has transverse ridges on its ground surface.

Fig. 257. A rope shoe. This shoe has a groove on the ground surface into which a tarred rope is inserted.

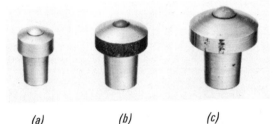

(a)   (b)   (c)

Fig. 258. Standard tapered studs. Type (a) for small ponies and light-weight hunters; type (b) for hacks, hunters and light harness horses; type (c) for heavy draught horses.

Fig. 259. A concave fullered hunter shoe with a standard type stud fitted in each heel.

Fig. 260. A well worn shoe fitted with standard type studs. As the studs wear down the tungsten carbide core persists as a projection and prevents slipping.

Fig. 261. Standard plug type studs which are countersunk into the shoe level with the ground surface. They combine the advantage of flat shoeing and prevent slipping.

Fig. 262. A well worn shoe fitted with plug type studs. As the heel of the shoe wears down the tungsten carbide core persists to provide a good grip and to prevent slipping.

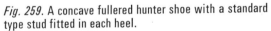

Fig. 263. Standard screw-in type studs. *(Above left)* type suitable for hacks and hunters; *(above right)* for jumping and eventing.

Fig. 264. The Mordax horseshoe nail *(right).*

Fig. 265. A hole is punched from the foot surface of the shoe.

Fig. 266. The hole is completed by reverse punching from the ground surface of the shoe. This produces a complete collar of support around the hole.

Another non-slip device is the "Mordax" horseshoe nail. This nail is identical in shape to the standard horseshoe nail but has been developed on the same principle as a stud. It has a core or pin of tungsten carbide which projects just above the surface of its head (*Fig. 264*). When used, the nail must be driven until it is flush with the ground surface of the shoe, otherwise when the soft metal of the nail head wears away the tungsten carbide pin may be lost. These nails are available in sizes 6, 7 and 8 and one nail inserted at each heel is generally sufficient.

Method of punching a hole to take a standard type stud.

This is conveniently described in five steps.

Fig. 267. The hole is enlarged to size with a drift, the same shape and size as the shank of the stud.

Fig. 269. The stud inserted, and driven home in the outside heel of a hind shoe.

Method of making and tapping a hole to take a screw-in type stud.

Fig. 268. The stud is inserted and driven in with a special tool, made to fit its shape.

Fig. 270. A hole is either drilled or punched from the ground surface of the shoe.

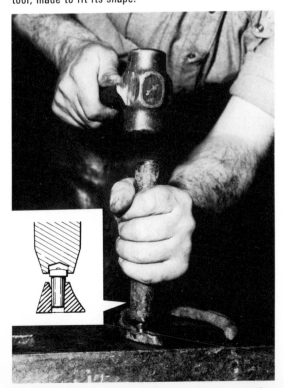

Fig. 271. The hole previously made is tapped to cut the threads.

Fig. 272. Hole tapped and screw-in stud being inserted.

Fig. 273. An outside heel stud inserted and tightened with a spanner until the sharp edge lies at right angles to the heel of the shoe.

HORSESHOE BORIUM

This is the trade name for tungsten carbide crystals packed into a tube of mild steel. The metal tube acts as a bond which enables the tungsten carbide crystals to be deposited on a shoe by welding. This produces a rough surface which prevents slipping and at the same time reduces the wear of the shoe.

As the soft bonding metal wears away the particles of tungsten carbide left exposed must be large enough to remain prominent and provide a good grip. To meet this requirement a screen size of 8 to 10 is required. If smaller particles, sizes 10 to 30 are used, their hardness satisfactorily reduces the wear of the shoe but the surface rapidly becomes smooth and its non-slip properties are lost.

Applying horseshoe borium. Rods of horseshoe borium are supplied in 14″ lengths and $\frac{1}{8}$″, $\frac{3}{16}$″ and $\frac{1}{4}$″ in diameter. The latter are the most suitable for treating horseshoes. Shoes must be fitted and cleaned before the borium is applied.

(i) The area of the shoe to which borium is to be applied is heated, either with an oxy-acetylene torch (*Fig. 274*) or in the forge fire, until it is at white heat and the surface begins to melt (*Fig. 275*).

(ii) The end of the borium rod is preheated, applied to the molten metal of the shoe and the tungsten carbide crystals puddled over the surface of the shoe until the desired area is covered (*Fig. 276*).

(iii) Finally, the treated area is heated with the flame to melt and flatten the bonding metal and leave the crystals exposed (*Fig. 277*).

(iv) The treated shoe is left to cool slowly. If it is quenched and cooled quickly it becomes very brittle and easily chips and flakes if altered cold.

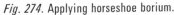

Fig. 274. Applying horseshoe borium.

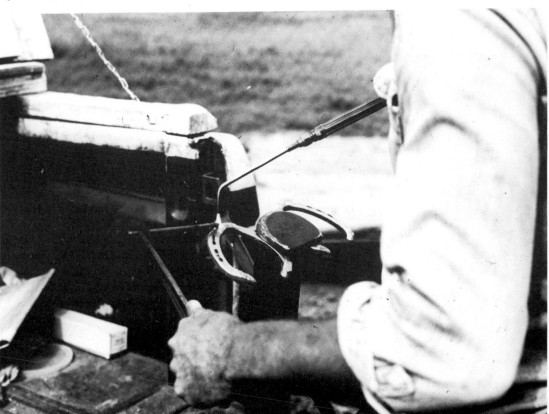

Fig. 275. Branch of shoe heated in the forge fire to a white heat and held on the face of the anvil, for applying the horseshoe borium.

Fig. 276. The end of the borium rod is preheated, applied to the molten metal of the shoe and the tungsten carbide crystals are puddled over the surface.

Fig. 277 (above). The treated area is finally heated with the oxy-acetylene torch to melt and flatten the bonding metal, and to leave the crystals of tungsten carbide exposed.

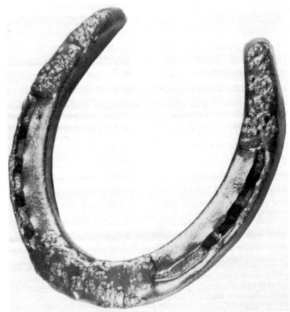

Fig. 278 (right). Shoe treated with horseshoe borium at the toe, between the first two nail-holes, and at the heels, from the heel nail-holes to the end of the branch.

The amount of horseshoe borium required to treat a shoe depends on the purpose for which the horse is required. Horses used across country, for example, will only require a spot on each heel to prevent slipping. Whereas horses which do a lot of road work will require a liberal covering of the toe and heels (*Fig. 278*) not only to provide a good foothold but also to prevent wear. In these cases the outer edge of the shoe at the toe, between the first two nail holes and from the heel nail holes to the end of the shoe are treated to a height of about a $\frac{1}{4}''$. It is important that all deposits of horseshoe borium are of equal thickness so as to preserve the balance of the shoe.

Shoes treated with horseshoe borium provide a better grip and last 4 or 5 times as long as a standard plain shoe (*Fig. 279*), but this advantage leads, all too often, to shoes being left on far too long. The increased life of the shoe results in a gradual increase in the size of the nail holes which necessitates using increasingly larger nails each time the horse is shod. This can lead to split hooves and loose shoes. In time the normal movements of the heels wear a groove which produces an uneven foot surface that is difficult to correct. Also, horseshoe borium is expensive and shoes once treated are difficult to shape and level.

In spite of these disadvantages horseshoe borium has an important part to play in the management of horses by providing a secure foothold, preventing wear and prolonging the life of the shoe.

Horses with a normal action invariably wear the toe of their shoes excessively. This can become a real problem when horses are doing a lot of road work because this excessive local wear necessitates the shoes being replaced before they are worn out. Various methods are

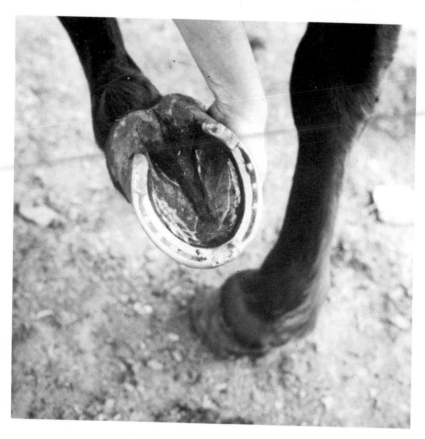

Fig. 279. The horse has been shod with the shoe illustrated for five months. Wear has been minimal and sufficient horseshoe borium remains to provide a good grip.

used to combat this problem. A rod of stainless steel or tungsten carbide welded into the toe is very effective, but an application of horseshoe borium or a plug type stud inserted on either side of the toe is equally effective and has the added advantage of improving the foothold.

Section II: WINTER SHOEING

During most winters, spells of cold weather can be expected when the roads are covered with snow or ice. Fortunately these conditions rarely persist for more than a few days at a time and, therefore, only temporary measures have to be taken to prevent horses from slipping and to keep them at work.

The methods employed comprise modifications to the shoes, the use of frost nails and the fitting of studs. Each method has its advantages and disadvantages in relation to the conditions

ing and leads to unnecessary damage to the hoof.

FROST NAILS

The use of frost nails is a cheap and quick method of preventing horses from slipping and they can be inserted without any special tools or the services of a farrier.

Frost nails are of two basic types. Both types have a large head which is either pointed or wedge shaped. One type has a flat under surface of its head (*Fig. 281* [*a*]) and therefore is only retained by its shank, whereas the other type has a conical neck (*Fig. 281* [*b*]) which fits into the countersink of the nail hole and provides a more secure hold.

The first type, which has a thin shank, is suitable only in emergencies. The heel nails are withdrawn and replaced by driving in a frost nail along the track of the old nail.

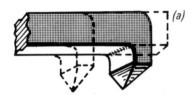 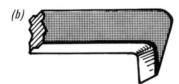

Fig. 280. (a) The heel of a front shoe turned down to form a "sharp"; (b) Calkin of a hind shoe converted to a wedge.

prevailing, the type of horse and the work required. But in each case the most economical, simple and efficient method is the one of choice.

ROUGHING OR SHARPING

This is an effective and convenient method as a temporary expedient. The heels of a front shoe are drawn out to provide enough iron to turn down and form a point, which is referred to as a "sharp" (*Fig. 280* [*a*]). This shortens the shoe and if repeated several times the bearing surface is reduced and the heel presses on the seat of corn. The calkins of the hind shoes are converted from square to a wedge shape with a sharp edge (*Fig. 280* [*b*]).

The disadvantage of this method is that the shoes have to be removed each time the projections require sharpening. This is time consum-

Fig. 281. Frost nails: (a) with flat undersurface of head; (b) with a conical neck.

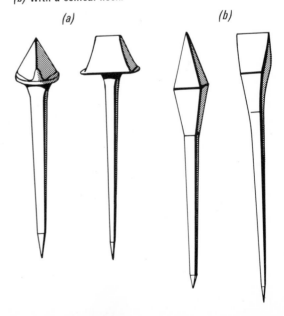

The second type is used with specially prepared nail-holes. At the onset of winter, in many commercial stables, it was a common practice to fit shoes a little wide at the heels and to stamp nail-holes at the heels to take frost nails. These nail-holes are stamped outwards so that the nail does not enter the hoof. This allows the point to be cut off and the cut end to be hammered tightly down on the foot surface of the shoe and firmly turned down over the edge to obtain a firm grip (*Fig. 282*).

It is the practice to insert a nail in each heel of both front and hind shoes. Nails with wedge shaped heads are inserted with the edge of the outside heel nail across the shoe and of the inside heel nail in line with the shoe.

Frost nails have the advantage that they are easily, safely and quickly inserted and can be renewed as necessary. But they soon work loose and wear out quickly. Therefore, they are only suitable in emergencies, during short spells of frost and for horses when not in constant use.

FROST STUDS

Fitting frost studs is the most satisfactory method of giving horses a secure foothold and preventing them from slipping on icy roads. At the commencement of winter horses are either shod with machine made shoes with holes prepared to take frost studs or their shoes are punched or tapped to take them.

The standard frost stud is the screw-in type (*Fig. 283* [a] *and* [b]). It is important for the shank to be equal in diameter to the head, if not the stud soon works loose and the head breaks off leaving the threaded shank in the shoe. The heads are made in a variety of patterns but the most useful, for all practical purposes, is either pointed or wedge shaped.

If a stud is not inserted when the shoe is fitted then as the heels gradually wear thinner a

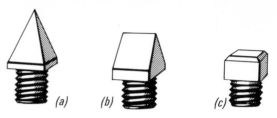

Fig. 283. Frost studs, screw-in types: *(a)* pointed; *(b)* wedge shaped; *(c)* a flat square stud or blank.

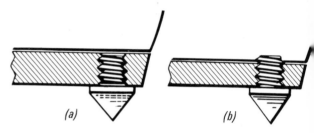

Fig. 284. Frost stud: *(a)* correct fit; *(b)* shoe has worn thin.

burr forms around the edge of the hole. Before a stud can be inserted the burr has to be removed with a tap and if the stud is screwed home, due to the thinness of the heels of the shoe, it will press on the bearing surface causing pain and lameness (*Fig. 284*). The easiest way of overcoming these problems is to insert a stud with a flat square head (*Fig. 283* [*c*]) called a blank, when the horse is shod. This prevents the heels from wearing down and when removed leaves a clean hole of the proper depth to take the stud.

Frost studs with either round or square shanks have the advantage of simplicity and economy. The shank of the stud and the punched out hole in the heel of the shoe are both slightly tapered. This ensures a good fit and in consequence they remain securely in position under all conditions of work. These studs are easily removed with either a special tool or by a sharp tap on one side with a hammer.

Wedge shaped frost studs are inserted in the outside heel with the sharp edge of the stud across the shoe and in the inside heel with the sharp edge in line with the shoe. In view of their size it is advisable to remove them when horses are stabled, to prevent tread and elbow injuries.

Fig. 282. Method of securing a frost nail.

Pads for horseshoes

A PAD may be described as a sheet of leather, rubber, plastic, felt, cork or some other material which is placed between the foot and the shoe and held securely with nails, to protect the foot, reduce concussion and prevent slipping.

Section I: PADS FOR PROTECTION

LEATHERS

This is the term used to describe fixing a sheet of leather, $\frac{3}{16}''$ to $\frac{5}{16}''$ thick, on the bearing surface of the foot. It is the simplest and most universal pad used to protect the sole.

A sheet of leather is cut out to exactly the same shape and size as the shoe and then fixed to it with two nails. The protruding points are cut off to leave the leather held in place with the two stubs. The shoe is then nailed on in the normal way when the stubs are removed and replaced with nails. Finally, any protruding edges of the pad are trimmed to produce a neat and accurate fit.

Leather pads are a useful protection against thin and bruised soles and for punctured and diseased feet, but they have their disadvantages. Dirt and grit accumulate in the space between the sole and the leather which leads to an unhygienic state and predisposes to thrush. In addition, pressure of the frog soon wears through the leather. These problems can be controlled by packing the cavity with tow and Stockholm tar to obliterate the space and provide a level surface on which the leather can rest.

Section II: PADS TO REDUCE CONCUSSION

It is a common practice to fit a ring of leather between the foot and the shoe with the idea of reducing jar. It has no significant effect in reducing concussion, serves no useful purpose and interferes with the fit of the shoe. When the foot takes weight the leather yields and the foot moves closer to the shoe and when it is raised the leather expands. This movement between foot and shoe loosens the nails and is followed by a loose shoe and displacement of the leather.

HOOF CUSHION (*Fig. 285*)

This is the name given to a special rubber pad which is moulded to fit exactly the individual foot. It is made from a rubber solution which, when mixed with a hardener, sets to a firm spongy rubber consistency. Pads made of this material reduce concussion and are a useful adjunct in the treatment of bruised sole and chronic laminitis.

Method of fitting a hoof cushion.

(i) The foot is dressed, the shoe fitted and a sheet of plastic, $1/6''$ thick, is cut out to exactly the same shape and size as the shoe.

(ii) The pad is attached to the shoe with two nails and then the pad and the shoe together are fixed to the foot by partly driving the two nails. The shoe, pad and nails are then removed as a single unit.

(iii) The hoof cushion solution is mixed with the liquid hardener and stirred until a dough-like consistency is obtained. The mixture is then applied to the foot, filling up the clefts of the frog and the concavity of the sole until an even spread is obtained.

(iv) The plastic pad and shoe unit is nailed to the foot with the two nails already in position. The foot is put down and the opposite foot picked up so that the horse takes full weight on the treated foot. This squeezes out any excess of the mixture

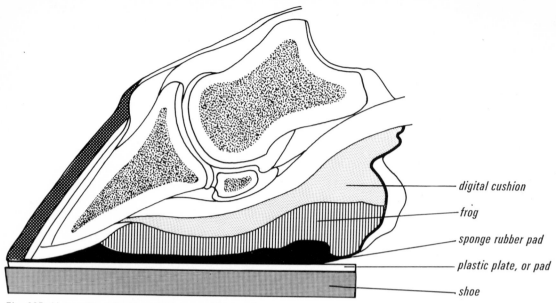

- digital cushion
- frog
- sponge rubber pad
- plastic plate, or pad
- shoe

Fig. 285. Aintree Hoof Cushion. A sponge rubber pad is moulded to the bearing surface of the foot and retained in position with a plastic plate or pad, placed between it and the shoe.

which then sets to form a perfectly moulded foot pad.

(v) After 5 to 7 minutes the shoe can be nailed on and any protruding hoof cushion trimmed off.

A satisfactory fit is obtained because any excess of the mixture is squeezed out and only a thin film remains between the sheet of plastic and the wall. In addition, the plastic sheet is rigid and not compressible and so no movement occurs between it and the shoe to loosen the nails.

Hoof cushions are very durable and can be expected to last two or three shoeings.

Section III: PADS TO PREVENT SLIPPING

Pads made of rubber, mounted on either a leather sheet or a synthetic material are used to prevent slipping and to reduce concussion.

FROG PAD (*Fig. 286*)

This was the first type to be introduced and is simply a leather sole to which an artificial rubber frog is attached. It provides a good foothold but has little else to commend it.

Unless precautions are taken grit and dirt accumulate under the leather base, with all the ensuing problems of an unhygienic state, which can lead to thrush.

SHEATHER'S PNEUMATIC PAD (*Fig. 287*)

This is a modification of the frog pad but with its solid rubber pad replaced by an air-cushion pad which is compressible at each step. The design is intended to enhance the anti-slipping properties of a frog pad, to relieve the natural frog of continual pressure and prevent the accumulation of dirt between the pad and the sole. These pads serve no real or practical purposes and are only of historical interest.

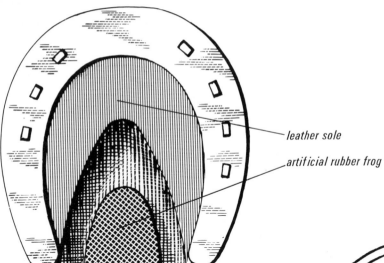

leather sole

artificial rubber frog

Fig. 286. Frog pad. A leather sole to which an artificial rubber frog is attached, and retained in position by the shoe.

Fig. 287. Sheather's Pneumatic Pad. A modification of the frog pad with the solid rubber pad replaced by an air-cushion pad.

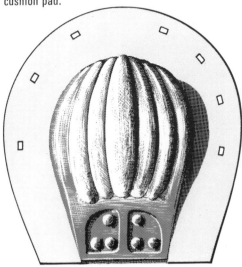

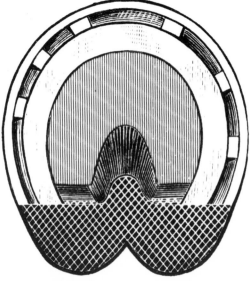

Fig. 288. Bar Pad. A rubber pad, attached to a sheet of leather or synthetic material which fits across the base of the frog and the heels, and is retained in position with a short shoe.

BAR PAD (*Fig. 288*)

This consists of a rubber pad, attached to a sheet of leather or synthetic material, which fits across the base of the frog and the heels and is retained in position with a short shoe. These pads are a satisfactory anti-slipping device, reduce concussion and in selected cases, may be useful in the treatment of corns and chronic laminitis.

GRAY'S FLEXIBLE BRIDGE
BAR PAD (*Fig. 289*)

This is a rubber pad, mounted on a flexible metal base, which fits across the base of the frog and the heels. Such pads vary in thickness from $\frac{1}{4}''$ to $\frac{5}{8}''$ and are fixed to the shoe before it is nailed on. They have the advantage over the standard bar pad that the anterior of the frog and the sole remain exposed. They prevent slipping and their flexibility reduces concussion.

satisfactorily. Presumably pads give them a feeling of insecurity, but this quickly wears off and their action improves.

It must not be overlooked that a normal healthy foot requires no protection against concussion. This is adequately met by the elasticity of the frog, expansion at the heels, descent of the sole and the slope of the pastern. In general it can be said that frog and bar pads, apart from preventing slipping for which more

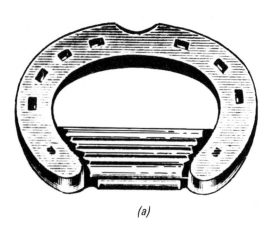
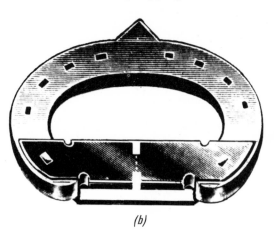

(a)   (b)

Fig. 289. Gray's Flexible Bridge Bar Pad. *(a)* a rubber pad, mounted on a flexible metal base; *(b)* foot surface of shoe illustrating the metal base of the bar pad, which is fixed to the shoe with a rivet.

Frog and bar pads were introduced primarily to prevent horses from slipping on the smooth surfaces of modern roads. They reduce concussion and bar pads can be said to have advantages over a bar shoe in that they are lighter. When some horses are fitted with pads they take time to become accustomed to them and to work

economical, practical and satisfactory methods are available, serve very little useful purpose.

If in suitable cases it is considered they will be of benefit in alleviating concussion they should only be used for a short time because continual pressure on the frog will cause it to atrophy.

CHAPTER TWELVE

Special horseshoes

FARRIERS are frequently called upon to make special shoes for defective feet, to prevent interferences, to protect the foot, and to alleviate lameness.

Section I: INJURIES CAUSED BY THE SHOE

TREADS

A tread is the name given to an injury of the coronet and as the name implies it is caused by the shoe. It is generally due to the shoe of the opposite foot when the horse is turning or, when horses are working in pairs, by one horse treading on its fellow. Another cause is "itchy legs". This is due to the parasite *Chorioptes equi* which causes the horse continually to stamp its feet and often rub one leg with the shoe of the opposite foot with resulting injuries to the coronet.

A tread can range from a simple bruise to an open wound. All treads must be treated as serious because not only is a deep wound of the coronet followed by a false quarter but also, if infection supervenes, it may result in necrosis of the lateral cartilage and the development of a quittor.

Shoeing. Treads occur most frequently when horses are shod with calkins and, especially during the winter months, if these are sharpened to prevent slipping. To reduce the incidence of treads, calkins should be low and square and the shoe fitted close at the heels. When frost studs are fitted they should be removed when the horse is stabled and cases of itchy legs must be treated.

CAPPED ELBOW

A capped elbow is the name given to any swelling at the point of the elbow. In many cases it is an acquired bursa due to the inner heel of the shoe striking the point of the elbow when the horse is lying down. It is associated also with hard and uneven stable floors which coupled with insufficient bedding can result in a horse bruising its elbows when getting up.

Shoeing. This is directed towards preventing the heel of the shoe from coming into contact with the point of the elbow, and is met by fitting a shoe with the inner heel shortened and fitted close.

Shoe for capped elbow (Fig. 290). This shoe has a short and narrow inner heel. The end of the heel is hot rasped off obliquely and rounded so as to resemble the back of the bowl of a spoon.

Fig. 290. Shoe for capped elbow.

Fig. 291. Three-quarter shoe. An ordinary shoe which has up to a half of one branch cut off.

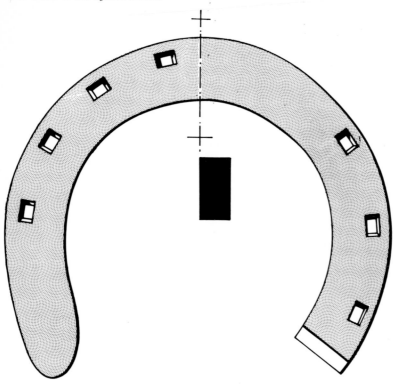

Three-quarter shoe (Fig. 291). This shoe has up to a half of one branch, usually the inner, cut off. It is either cut off square or with the half-round cutter and the end bevelled and filed smooth. As this shoe has no heel to strike the elbow it is often used in the treatment of capped elbow but has little to recommend it for this or any other purpose.

Valuable foot surface is lost, it unbalances the foot, and the end of the shortened branch produces an abnormal pressure point, causing the heel to sink, which is unphysiological and detrimental to the foot.

Many cases of capped elbow, due to the inner heel of the shoe striking the point of the elbow when the horse is lying down, can be prevented without recourse to altering the shoe by simply putting on a sausage boot when the horse is stabled.

Section II: SHOEING DEFECTIVE FEET

Defective feet are classified as feet which are misshapen or abnormal due to conformation of the foot or limb, or have become misshapen due to neglect or bad shoeing.

FLAT FOOT

A flat foot is one which is large in circumference, has an excessively sloping wall (*Fig. 182 [b]*) low heels, a prominent frog, and a sole which lacks the normal concavity. Care must be taken to differentiate flat front feet which are congenital in origin from those due to chronic laminitis.

Shoeing. Pressure on the sole can be alleviated by fitting a seated-out shoe. Under no circumstances should the sole be pared out to increase its concavity as this only reduces the bearing surface and protection to the underlying sensitive foot.

Seated-out shoe (Fig. 292). This is a most satisfactory shoe for flat feet as it relieves the sole of pressure at its junction with the wall. It has a wide web with the inner edge of the foot surface seated. The seating is carried back to the nail-holes and around the shoe except at the heels which are left flat to allow normal weight bearing.

The suction created by seated-out shoes in heavy going is a disadvantage as they may be pulled off and cause an accident.

Fig. 292. Seated-out shoe. The seating is carried back to the nail-holes and around the shoe except at the heels.

UPRIGHT FOOT

An upright foot is one which has a very upright wall (*Fig. 182 [c]*) a short toe, high heels and a small frog. It is often referred to as a mule or boxy foot and in extreme cases as a club foot (*Fig. 182 [d]*).

Upright feet do not require any special shoes but care must be taken to ensure that the feet are correctly dressed and the normal pastern foot axis maintained. If not, the foot gradually becomes more upright, which can lead to a knuckling over of the fetlock joint.

TWISTED FOOT

A twisted foot may be a congenital defect,

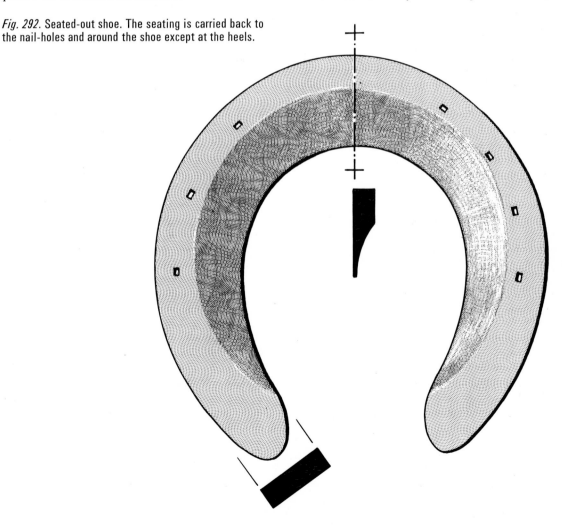

due to neglect or bad shoeing. If it is congenital in origin it cannot be remedied by corrective shoeing but can be prevented from getting worse by being properly dressed. On the other hand, if it is due to neglect or bad shoeing then attention to dressing the foot and to shoeing will result in a gradual return to its normal shape.

In the majority of cases irregular growth of the hoof is due to errors in dressing the foot. If the bearing surface is not kept level there is an uneven distribution of the body weight which results in the wall being deflected. Overgrowth of the inner wall, because it is more upright, results in the bearing surface turning in, whereas the outer wall which is more sloping bulges outwards (*Fig. 293*).

A twisted foot is corrected by gradually lowering, at 2 or 3 week intervals, the side of the wall which is too high until a level bearing surface is obtained. When this is attained the weight over the bearing surface is correctly distributed and normal frog and sole pressure are established.

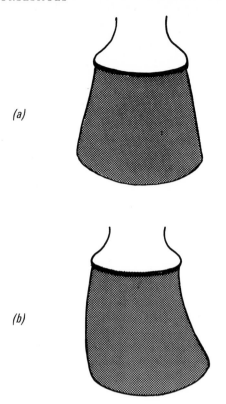

(a)

(b)

Fig. 293 (a). Normal foot; *(b)* twisted foot. Overgrowth of the inner wall results in the bearing surface turning-in whereas the more sloping outer wall bulges outwards.

Shoeing. A standard shoe is fitted but made to conform to the adjudged normal outline of the foot and not that of the twisted foot.

On the inside of the foot where the wall turns in the shoe is fitted wide, to conform with the adjudged normal outline of the bearing surface, and its sharp outer edge is bevelled off. On the outside of the foot where the wall bulges out the shoe is fitted as close as possible, consistent with being able to drive the nails safely, and the overhanging wall is rasped off flush with the shoe (*Fig. 294*).

This method of dealing with a twisted foot, due to neglect or bad shoeing, is most effective and it is only a matter of time before the twist is corrected and the foot restored to its normal shape.

Fig. 294. Method of fitting a shoe to a twisted foot. The shoe is fitted wide on the inside, close on the outside and the overhanging wall is rasped off flush with the shoe.

WEAK OR LOW HEELS
These terms are used to describe the condition of the wall at the heels when it curves inwards

Fig. 295. Bar shoe. An ordinary shoe which is joined at the heels by a bar that presses on the frog.

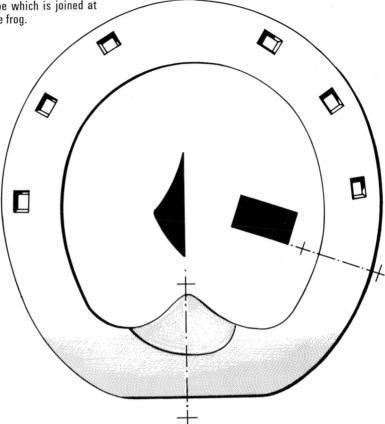

under the sole. The inturned wall provides a bearing surface and pressure on it by the shoe exacerbates the condition.

Weak heels are corrected by cutting down the curved-in portion of the wall until normal weight bearing is established anteriorly, and posteriorly to the angle of the heel.

Shoeing. A bar shoe is the most suitable shoe for treating weak heels as it relieves pressure on the curved in portion of the wall by transferring it to the frog.

Bar shoe (*Fig. 295*). A bar shoe is an ordinary shoe which is joined at the heels, by a bar that presses on the frog. The posterior edge of the ground surface of the bar is bevelled off to reduce concussion when the heels come to the ground and to reduce the chance of it being

struck by a hind shoe and pulled off.

The bar of the shoe subjects the frog to continuous pressure which is abnormal, and in time results in atrophy of the frog. Thus the commonly accepted view that a bar shoe stimulates growth of an atrophied frog is erroneous. The usefulness of a bar shoe is restricted solely to taking weight off areas of the wall by transferring it to the frog. For these reasons a bar shoe is suitable for treating weak heels and corns, but it must not be overlooked that there is a limit to the continuous pressure which the frog can sustain without commencing to atrophy.

A bar shoe has a number of disadvantages. It is heavier than an ordinary shoe and therefore requires more nails to secure it, provides a poor foothold, and can be used only for horses working at a slow pace.

CONTRACTED FOOT

A contracted foot is smaller than normal, narrower at the quarters and heels, has an excessively concave sole and an atrophied frog. It can result from prolonged disuse of the limb due to disability or pain, faulty dressing of the foot, and especially by opening up the heels and excessive paring of the sole. Methods of shoeing can also contribute. Calkins which are too high reduce normal frog pressure, and heel nails placed too far back prevent normal expansion of the foot.

The method of treatment employed to treat a contracted foot will depend on the cause. If it is associated with disease or injury which responds to treatment, then as normal function of the limb returns so gradually the foot will regain its normal shape. On the other hand if it is associated with an incurable condition no useful purpose will be served by instituting any measures to effect expansion.

Conditions due to faulty preparation of the foot or bad shoeing improve immediately these errors are corrected. For example, lowering calkins to obtain frog pressure or working the horse in tips to protect the toe whilst allowing the back of the foot to take weight and function normally. In addition to this and similar basic measures, grooving the heels to obtain expansion is helpful in selected cases.

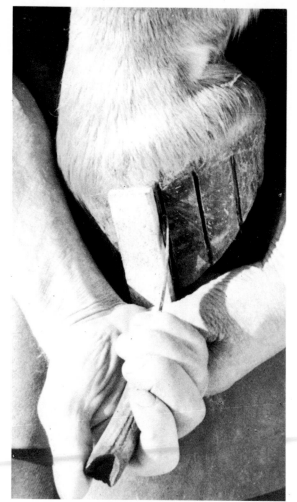

Fig. 296. Method of grooving the wall.

Grooving the wall (Fig. 296). A number of techniques are employed to obtain expansion at the heels. The following method is both simple and effective. The foot is brought forward and positioned either on the farrier's leg or on a tripod. Using a drawing knife, three or four parallel grooves are cut at intervals of $\frac{3}{4}''$ from the coronet to the bearing surface. The grooves are placed on both the lateral and medial aspects of the heels, extend down to the white line and each is $1/5''$ in width. If the wall is very hard it can be softened by cold water footbaths, 1 hour twice daily for 2 to 3 days.

Shoeing. Many ingenious designs of shoes have been used to treat contracted feet. They range from shoes with the foot surface sloped outwards to exert counter-pressure to mechanical devices designed to force the heels of shoes apart. The majority have been based on a misunderstanding of the anatomy and function of the foot which has led to unsound arguments in their support and few have met with any lasting success.

Slipper shoe (Fig. 73). The foot surface of this shoe is sloped outwards which allows the wall to expand under the pressure of weight bearing.

The slope must not be excessive and confined to the quarters and heels. If the outer edge of the foot surface is more than $1/12''$ to $\frac{1}{8}''$ lower than the inner edge it puts excessive strain on the white line which leads to separation and a loose wall. For this reason this shoe fell into disfavour but with due attention to the slope, which must be confined to the heels, the shoe is useful in the treatment of slight cases of contraction.

Shoe with bar-clips. This shoe has a flat foot surface with a clip at the inner margin of each heel. The clips lie in the clefts of the frog close up against the bars. To expand the foot, every 10 to 14 days the heels of the shoe are forced about an $\frac{1}{8}''$ apart with a special shoe spreader.

This method causes pain and lameness and serves no useful or practical purpose.

Smith's expanding shoe (Fig. 297). This is a shoe with both branches hinged, $1\frac{1}{2}''$ to $2''$ from the heels, and fitted with bar-clips. Across the heels is fitted a threaded bolt and nut arrangement which is tightened to force the heels apart. Adjustments are easily made and cases have been recorded in which the heels of the foot have been expanded by a $\frac{1}{4}''$ after a week's treatment.

Fig. 297. Smith's expanding shoe.

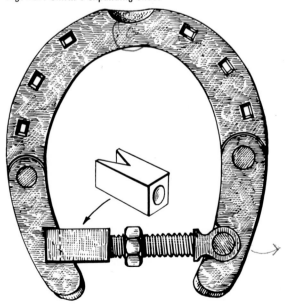

Section III: INJURIES CAUSED BY ABNORMALITIES OF GAIT

These injuries are frequently referred to as "interferences" and are caused by defective action and poor conformation. This results in a limb being struck by either the shoe of the opposite foot or of a hind foot and causing a contusion or wound. It may be due to working an unfit or tired horse, faulty dressing of the foot or bad shoeing. Such cases are easily dealt with by careful attention to dressing and balancing the feet and fitting the shoes. But cases due to defects of conformation such as toe-out, and abnormalities of gait can be alleviated only by corrective shoeing.

Before a horse is shod to prevent these injuries their cause must be sought and identified. The conformation of the horse's limbs and pastern foot axis must be examined and its action observed at all paces. Each horse has to be considered individually in order to select the most suitable shoe to prevent injury as all horses with the same abnormality of gait do not necessarily require the same shoe or to be shod in the same manner.

BRUSHING

Brushing is the term used to describe an injury caused by the horse striking the inside of one leg, generally in the region of the fetlock, with the shoe of the opposite foot.

The injury ranges from a slight contusion to an open wound and is particularly common in young and unfit horses. Cases due to faulty dressing of the foot by over lowering the inner half of the wall or by bad shoeing, such as fitting the shoe too wide on the inside, are easily dealt with as obvious faults. On the other hand in all cases due to an abnormality of gait, resulting from a defect of conformation, the actual cause of the injury has to be identified before the most suitable corrective shoe can be fitted.

It is not always easy to decide which part of the shoe is responsible for the injury because the leg may be struck by either the toe, quarter

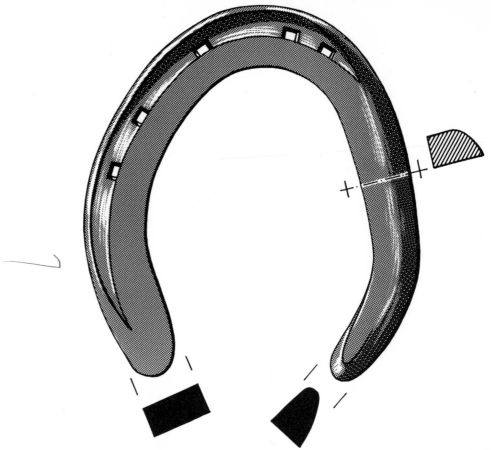

Fig. 298. Knocked-up shoe. The inner branch is narrow
with the ground surface sloped downwards and inwards
and rounded off.

or heel of the shoe. This can be detected by
chalking or greasing the wall or the shoe and
noting where it is rubbed off and at what pace.

The action taken to prevent brushing has to
be related to the cause, the frequency and the
severity of the injury. Many cases of slight
brushing in front can be overcome by simply
fitting a flat and lighter shoe, and if behind, by
shoeing without calkins or by replacing the
inside calkin with a wedge heel. If these simple
measures do not prevail then fit the inner branch
of the shoe close, and rasp off the overhanging
wall until it is flush with the shoe.

Shoeing. A variety of shoes are recommended
to prevent brushing injuries. Each shoe has its
special merit which has to be related to the
cause in each individual case.

Knocked-up shoe (*Fig. 298*). The inner branch
is narrow, thus reducing the bearing surface,
with the ground surface sloped downwards and
inwards and rounded off.

The outer branch is fitted to the outline of
the wall, has 3 or 4 nail holes and sometimes a
quarter clip. The inner branch is fitted close and
any projecting wall is rounded off. The branch

is blind except for 1 or 2 nail holes at the toe. Hind shoes have the inner calkin replaced by a wedge heel.

This shoe is recommended to prevent brushing injuries caused by the toe or mid-quarter of the shoe.

Feather-edged shoe. (Fig. 299). This is an exaggerated type of knocked-up shoe. The inner

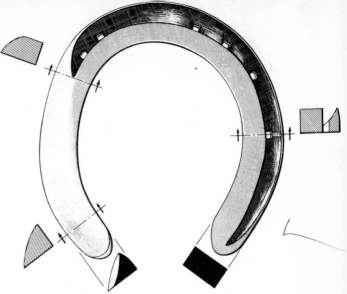

Fig. 300. Knocked-down shoe.

quarter clip and sometimes with 1 or 2 nails at the heel of the inner branch to prevent it from lifting and to keep the shoe in place.

This shoe is recommended for horses with a toe-out conformation and which brush with the posterior quarter and heel of the shoe.

The "G" shoe (Fig. 301). This is a bar shoe, with a calkin on the inside heel but the inside

Fig. 301. The "G"

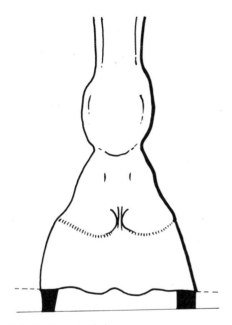

Fig. 299. Feather-edged shoe.

branch, which is blind, is very narrow and higher than the outer. It is claimed that this shoe by raising the medial side of the foot throws it outwards from its normal line of flight and thereby prevents brushing. In practice it wears very quickly at the toe and the results are disappointing.

Knocked-down shoe (Fig. 300). The foot surface of both branches are the same width but the edge of the inner branch where it strikes the opposite leg is knocked down and rounded off. The shoe is usually fitted with a toe and outside

toe is finished short with no branch. The shoe is fitted with a toe and outside quarter clip and the inside wall between the toe and the calkin is reduced and rounded off with a rasp.

The calkin tends to throw the foot outwards from the path of its normal flight, and as there is no part of the shoe on the inside of the foot a brushing injury can only be caused by the rounded off wall.

This shoe has the disadvantage of an uneven ground surface, it deprives the wall of a third of its bearing surface and can only be recommended when other shoes have failed to prevent brushing and then only for horses which work at a slow pace.

SPEEDY CUTTING

This is an injury which occurs on the medial aspect of the limb, in the region of the knee, when the horse is moving at speed. It ranges from a contusion to an open wound and is caused by the inner edge of the toe or branch of the shoe of the opposite foot. It is more liable to occur in horses that are base narrow, have turned-out toes and larger flat feet, and tends to happen when the horse is leading with the wrong leg or changing legs.

Shoe for speedy-cutting (Fig. 302). This shoe is suitable for both speedy-cutting and brushing. The inner branch is made straight from toe to quarter with the outer edge rounded off. The branch may be left blind but as speedy-cutting happens at speed it is advisable to secure the branch with 1 or 2 heel nails. After fitting the shoe the projecting wall is rounded off level with the straight edge.

There are a number of inherent disadvantages associated with fitting anti-brushing and cutting shoes. These include the difficulty of securing a blind branch, the close fitting of the inner branch which may result in pressure on the sole, reduction of the bearing surface which can lead to uneven distribution of weight, and, as the shoes do not provide a very secure foothold, they

Fig. 302. Shoe for speedy cutting. The inner branch is straight from toe to quarter with the outer edge rounded off.

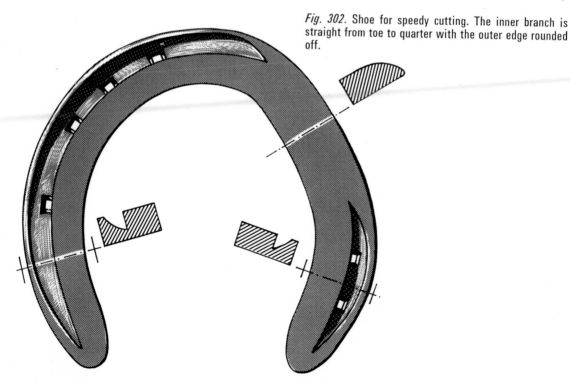

are conducive to slipping. Against these disadvantages must be weighed the advantages of the shoes preventing or alleviating the injuries, and keeping the horse in work. Furthermore with careful attention to dressing the foot and forging the shoe, the loss of bearing surface is minimal, a level bearing and ground surface can be maintained and with good nailing shoes can be adequately secured. But it cannot be over emphasised that the correct pattern of shoe has to be selected to meet the defects of conformation and gait for each individual case.

FORGING

Forging or clacking is due to faulty action and occurs at the trot when the horse strikes the heel or inside of the toe of a front shoe with the toe of the corresponding hind shoe (*Fig. 303*). Also, it can occur when the hind shoe is carried outside the front foot and the inside of the toe strikes the heel of the outside branch of the front shoe. Forging is an annoyance due to the noise made and a danger when the shoe is struck as it may be pulled off or bring the horse down.

Forging is met with in young horses and in horses that are tired or out of condition. In these cases it gradually disappears as the horse improves in condition and gets fit. It is particularly common in short bodied and long legged horses, horses that go wide behind and especially if their feet are overgrown.

Shoeing. The actual contact between the shoes takes place when the hind foot is reaching the end of its flight and as the front foot leaves the ground. Therefore, to prevent forging attention has to be given to fitting a shoe to hasten the break-over of the front feet and to delay that of the hind feet.

Many cases of forging can be prevented by fitting a concave shoe in front and increasing the break-over by rolling the toe and slightly raising the heels. If this does not prove satisfactory then fit a hind shoe with a well rounded square or dub toe (*Fig. 304*). The shoe should be set well back and the protruding wall rounded and rasped flush with the shoe. To delay break-over the heels should be lowered and left a little long so as to trail when the foot comes to the ground and act as a brake.

Diamond toed shoe (Fig. 305). This is a hind shoe with the ground surface, on both sides of the toe, bevelled downwards and backwards. The heels are about an $\frac{1}{8}''$ lower than the toe and the shoe is fitted with quarter clips.

This shoe is only suitable for horses which forge by carrying a hind foot outside a front foot. When this shoe is used the outside branch of the front shoe should be fitted close at the heels and in some cases it may be necessary to hasten break-over by rolling the toe and raising the heels.

A diamond toed shoe should not be used to combat simple forging as the point may strike and bruise the sole of the front foot.

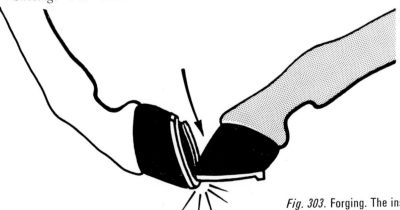

Fig. 303. Forging. The inside of the toe of a front shoe is struck with the toe of the corresponding hind shoe.

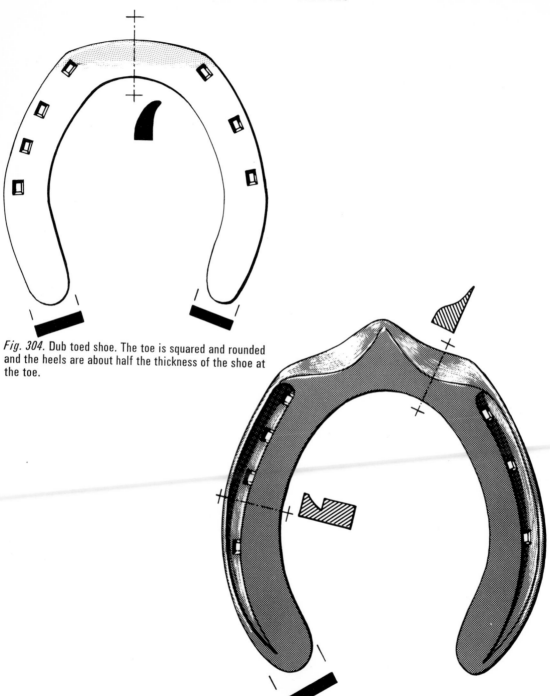

Fig. 304. Dub toed shoe. The toe is squared and rounded and the heels are about half the thickness of the shoe at the toe.

Fig. 305. Diamond toed shoe. A hind shoe with the ground surface, on both sides of the toe, bevelled downwards and backwards.

OVER-REACHING

An over-reach is the name given to an injury which occurs between the back of the knee and the bulbs of the heels. It is caused by the inner edge of the ground surface of a hind shoe striking the front leg when the horse is moving at a fast pace, and the front leg is not sufficiently extended or the hind leg is over extended (*Fig. 306*). As the hind leg moves backwards the inner edge of the shoe catches the back of the front leg and either bruises or cuts the skin, when it hangs downwards as a triangular flap. If the injury occurs above the fetlock joint it is called a "high over-reach", and if at the back or side of the heels, the most common site, a "low over-reach". If any of these areas is hit by the toe or outer edge of the shoe the injury is referred to as a "strike".

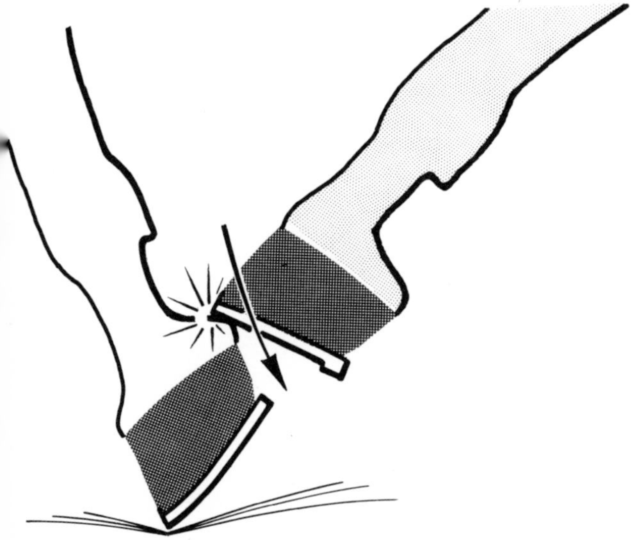

Horses with a short body and long legs, or with short front and long hind legs are reckoned to be most prone to over-reaches. These injuries occur most frequently at the gallop, although they are sometimes met with in trotters, and when a horse jumps on to rising ground.

Shoeing. To prevent these injuries the horse must be shod to hasten the break-over of the front feet so that the leg is not overtaken and struck by a hind foot. This is achieved by fitting front shoes with a rolled toe and raised heels, and with the heels a little short to prevent them being caught by a hind shoe.

The heels of the hind shoes should be about half the thickness of the shoe at the toe, and left a little long, up to $\frac{1}{2}''$ to delay breaking-over of the foot. In addition, to assist prevention further and reduce the severity of the injury the shoe should be set well back with the inner border of the toe concave or well rounded out (*Fig. 307*).

STUMBLING

Stumbling is due either to the horse catching its toe or digging in into the ground. It occurs when a horse is tired, has long overgrown feet or goes on its toe due to lameness or reduced flexion of its fetlock joint. A horse is always more liable to stumble when recently shod and before the shoe has worn to conform with the horse's action.

Fig. 307. Shoe for over-reaching. The inner border at the toe is well rounded out and the heels are about half the thickness of the shoe at the toe.

Fig. 306. Over-reaching. An over-reach occurs when a front leg is overtaken and struck by the inner edge of the hind shoe.

Shoeing. To prevent stumbling the toe must be prevented from coming into premature contact with the ground. This is attained by rasping the toe short and fitting a shoe with the toe "rolled" or "set-up" (*Fig. 308*) and with slightly raised heels to increase break-over.

A good indication of the extent to which the toe will require to be shortened and the toe of the shoe turned up to prevent stumbling, and for the horse to travel safely, can be gained by studying the worn shoe.

Section IV: SURGICAL SHOES

Surgical shoes are designed to assist in the treatment of diseases and injuries of the limb and foot by providing protection and relieving pressure.

CORNS

A corn is a bruise of the sole in the angle between the wall and the bar, the so-called "seat of corn". Corns occur most frequently in front feet, the inner angle being more often affected, are especially common in horses with wide flat feet and low heels. They are rarely seen in hind feet.

A corn is caused by pressure. It may be due to a stone under the heel of the shoe, leaving the shoes on too long so that the heels come to press on the seat of corn, and faults in shoeing such as fitting the heels too close or a shoe with heels too short or narrow. Upright pasterns predispose to concussion, and this, coupled with fast work on hard roads is a contributory factor.

Clinical features. A corn is recognised by the

Fig. 308. Rolled toe shoe. At the toe, half the width of the web is set up at an angle of 20° to 25°.

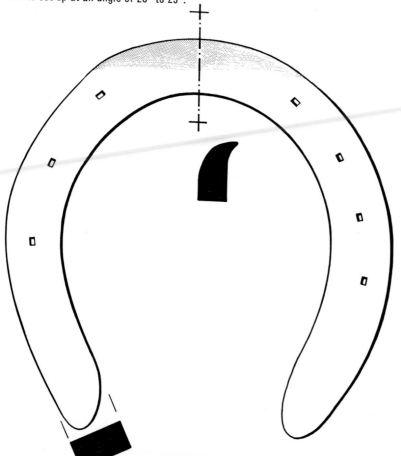

red discolouration of the horn due to the extravasation of blood. Corns are classified as *dry* when no inflammatory exudate is present, *moist* when it is present, and *suppurating* when complicated by infection.

Treatment. This comprises removing the cause, controlling the inflammation and relieving pressure. In the majority of cases all that is required is to pare down the discoloured horn to relieve tension, give the horse 2 to 3 days' rest, and fit an ordinary shoe, making sure the heel rests evenly on the wall and the bar. If infection has supervened then veterinary advice should be sought.

Shoeing. A shoe is required which will protect and relieve pressure on the seat of corn and thereby enable the horse to continue in work. A three-quarter shoe is often recommended for treating corns but it is not a suitable shoe as it provides no protection and has other inherent disadvantages (*Fig. 291*). A bar shoe (*Fig. 295*) which takes pressure off the heels by transferring it to the frog is useful for bilateral cases.

Three-quarter bar shoe (Fig. 309). This shoe has from 1″ to 1½″ cut off a heel. The bar rests on one heel, the base of the frog and the bar of the opposite heel. It is used for treating single corns as it has the advantage of supporting the heels whilst relieving the seat of corn of pressure but has the disadvantage that the corn is left unprotected.

Fig. 309. Three-quarter bar shoe. The shoe has 1″ to 1½″ cut off one heel.

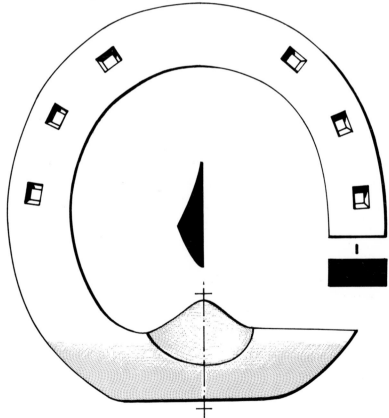

Shoe with "set" heel (*Fig. 310*). The ground surface of one heel of this shoe is lowered or set down about a $\frac{1}{4}''$ and so makes no contact with the ground. The foot surface of the shoe makes normal contact with the bearing surface of the foot and the heel is spread out a little to provide extra protection. This is a good shoe for treating corns as it protects and relieves pressure over the area. The three-quarter ground bearing surface is a technical disadvantage but in practice is of little practical significance.

Shoe with "dropped" heel (*Fig. 311*). This shoe is the opposite to a shoe with a set heel. The foot surface of the heel is lowered about $\frac{1}{8}''$ and therefore makes no contact with the bearing surface.

Although this shoe relieves a corn of pressure it is not satisfactory. It does not provide protection as the recess soon accumulates dirt and grit, and as the posterior part of the wall is not weight bearing an abnormal pressure point is present, which has the same unsatisfactory effects as "easing" the heels.

Fig. 311. Shoe with "dropped" heel. The foot surface of the heel is lowered by about $\frac{1}{8}''$.

Fig. 310. Shoe with "set" heel. The ground surface of the heel is lowered by a $\frac{1}{4}''$.

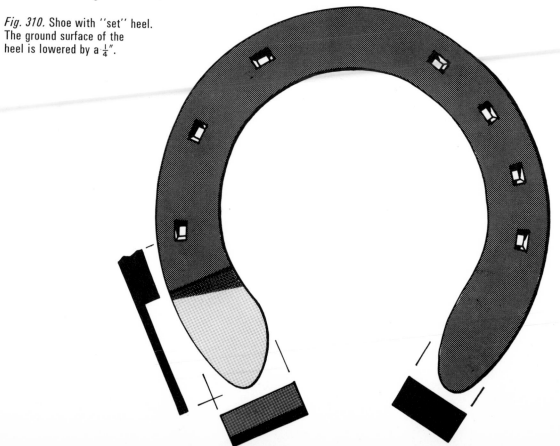

Fig. 312. Anchor or "T" shoe.

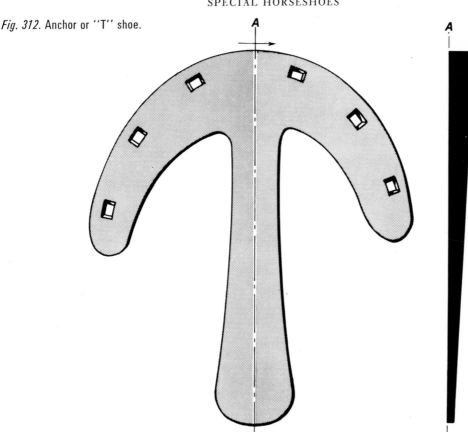

Anchor or "T" shoe (Fig. 312). This shoe can be described as a tip that is connected to a plate which covers the frog. It was introduced for the treatment of corns complicated by a contracted foot because all weight bearing on the back of the foot is taken by the frog and the seat of corn is relieved of pressure.

But this shoe has a number of disadvantages. It does not protect the seat of corn, is easily pulled off, can only be used for horses working on the land, and really it has no practical application.

FALSE QUARTER

A false quarter is a permanent defect of the wall. It is due to an injury of the coronary band which results in the secretion of abnormal horn.

Clinical features. A false quarter appears as a shallow fissure containing abnormal horn, and which extends, in the direction of the horn fibres, from the coronet to the bearing surface of the foot. The wall immediately on either side of the fissure is raised above the level of the surrounding horn. False quarters persist throughout life without causing any adverse effects unless they become infected.

Treatment. No treatment is required unless the fissure becomes infected when a veterinary surgeon should be consulted. Any excess of horn on either side of the fissure should be rasped down to maintain a smooth surface.

Shoeing. No special shoe is required. Fit a

shoe best suited for the horse and if considered necessary pressure on the extremity of the fissure can be relieved by easing the wall on either side (*Fig. 320 [b]*).

KERATOMA

A keratoma is a horn tumour which develops on the inner aspect of the wall.

Clinical features. The tumour is composed of hard glistening horn, cylindrical in shape, ranging from a $\frac{1}{4}''$ to $1\frac{1}{2}''$ in diameter and extending varying distances up the wall from the bearing surface towards the coronet. It is first detected at the bearing surface where it appears as a mass of hard horn, between the wall and the sole, which deflects the white line inwards. As the tumour increases in size lameness gradually develops with the horse going on its heels. A radiograph of the third phalanx at this stage will reveal a smooth groove in the bone caused by pressure of the keratoma (*Fig. 313*).

Treatment. In the early stages the extremity of the tumour is pared to relieve pressure by the shoe. This measure is only palliative and in no way checks the growth of the tumour which eventually has to be totally excised.

Shoeing. A plain flat shoe with plenty of cover, is called for to prevent excessive pressure on the toe, and low heels. Alternatively, pressure on the tumour can be relieved by easing the underlying foot surface of the shoe by $\frac{1}{8}''$. No nails should be driven near the tumour.

KNUCKLING

Knuckling or "over at the fetlock" is due to contraction of the tendons of the digital flexors which, by reducing extension of the fetlock joint, raises the heels. It may be congenital in origin, develop spontaneously in young stock and in adult life follow tendon injuries or chronic arthritic lesions which inhibit normal joint movements.

Clinical features. The degree of knuckling

Fig. 313. Radiograph of a third phalanx showing the groove caused by the pressure of a keratoma.

varies considerably. In slight cases the foot is kept flat on the ground with a straight fetlock joint, in more advanced cases the heels are raised with the fetlock joint knuckled forward, and in severe cases the front of the fetlock joint may touch the ground. The animal goes on its toe, is unable to get its heels to the ground and stumbles.

Treatment. In foals and young stock it is essential to keep the tendons of the digital flexors under constant tension to prevent permanent shortening. This is attained by keeping the fetlock joint extended by having the heels rasped down and the animal exercised. If in spite of these measures the condition gets progressively worse, it may be necessary to fit a shoe with an extended toe-piece, about $1''$ in width and some $1''$ to $1\frac{1}{2}''$ in length (*Fig. 314*). This acts as a point of leverage and maintains

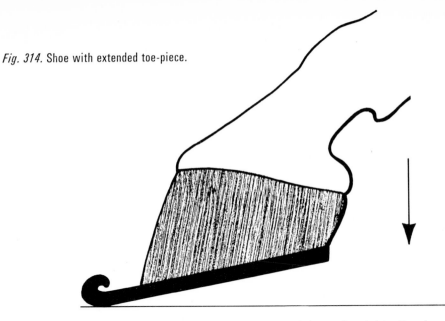

Fig. 314. Shoe with extended toe-piece.

continual tension on the contracted tendons.

In adult horses it is essential that the tendons play their full part and that contraction is not enhanced by reduced function. To this end the horse should be fitted with a shoe that has a thick toe and thin heels, and kept at work.

LAMINITIS

This disease is generally accepted as being an aseptic inflammation of the sensitive laminae and invariably both front feet are affected. A number of causes are recognised and include errors in feeding, metritis following foaling, allergies and concussion.

Fig. 315. Acute laminitis. Due to pressure of the inflammatory exudate, the horse's weight, and the pull of the deep digital flexor tendon, the pedal bones have rotated and perforated the sole.

Acute Laminitis. In these cases the horse's feet are hot and painful. It adopts a stance to relieve weight on its affected feet, is disinclined to move, and when it lies down is reluctant to rise. When it does move it lifts its feet quickly with each stride and goes on its heels. The inflammation of the sensitive laminae is accompanied by marked exudation. The pressure of this exudation coupled with the horse's weight and the pull of the deep digital flexor tendon is accompanied by a rotation of the third phalanx. In consequence its antero-inferior border presses on the sole which becomes flat or even convex (*Fig. 315*).

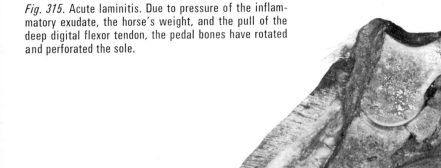

Chronic Laminitis. This is a sequel to an acute attack and is characterised by changes in the shape of the foot and the type of lameness.

Clinical features. The foot becomes elongated from front to rear and narrower transversely. The wall may be almost vertical at the heels but becomes flattened towards the toe. The wall is characterised by the so-called "laminitic rings" which appear as waves or rings of horn, and are due to irregular growth. These rings are widely spaced posteriorly, but as they pass forward they converge to meet on the anterior and flattened portion of the wall (*Fig. 316*). The sole is either flat or convex due to pressure from the rotated third phalanx and the space between it and the wall is filled with a pumice-like horn. The horn at the white line is dry, crumbly and easily breaks down. At the walk the horse's gait is quite typical; it goes distinctly on its heels and in a stiff and shuffling manner.

Shoeing. The disease process cannot be influenced by shoeing but special shoes can be

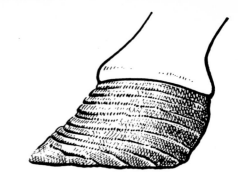

Fig. 316. Chronic laminitis.

fitted to relieve pain, and improve the horse's action. Before fitting a shoe a more normal shaped foot should be fashioned by reducing the prominent bulging toe and lowering the heels. The shoe fitted must take pressure off the dropped sole and assist the horse's action. Each case must be carefully assessed in relation to the severity of the changes in the foot and the work required of the horse.

A seated-out shoe (*Fig. 292*), which is modified by slightly rolling the toe and thinning

Fig. 317. Rocker-bar shoe. A wide webbed bar shoe

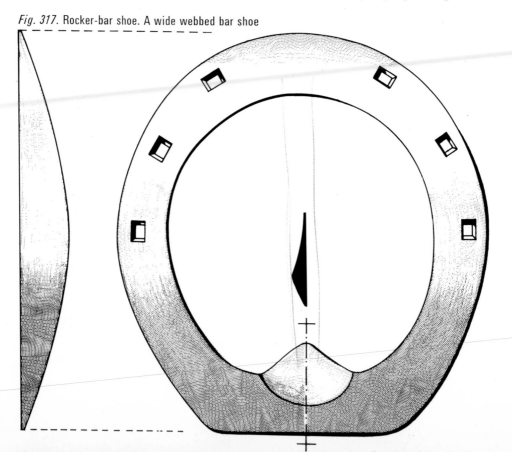

the heels, will assist the horse's action and is very satisfactory for slight cases.

Rocker-bar shoe (*Fig. 317*). This is a wide webbed bar shoe. The web is twice the thickness of a standard shoe at the quarters and gets gradually thinner towards the toe and the heels. Some shoes are made thinner at the heel than at the toe, others have the toe slightly rolled, but all require to be seated-out to take pressure off the sole.

A horse with chronic laminitis lands on its heels and then rolls its foot over on to its toe. The rocker-bar shoe has a place in the treatment of these cases by minimising, to some extent, the effects of concussion and assisting the action of the foot, but it is suitable only for horses working at a slow pace.

The action of many horses suffering from chronic laminitis can be improved still further by fitting a hoof cushion with either a modified seated-out shoe or rocker-bar shoe.

Fig. 318. Radiograph of a classical case of navicular disease. The dark shadow at the centre of the bone indicates rarefaction and cavitation of the underlying bone.

NAVICULAR DISEASE

Navicular disease is the name given to pathological changes affecting the navicular or distal sesamoid bone of the horse and is characterised by erosion of the fibro-cartilage on the tendinous surface with destruction and cavitation of the underlying bone (*Fig. 318*).

The disease may be uni- or bi-lateral, is most frequently encountered in hunters and hacks, is rarely seen in ponies, and all too often affects horses in their prime of life, between 7 and 9 years of age.

Clinical features. To alleviate pain in the posterior part of its foot the horse rests its foot with the heels raised, and points its toe. Lameness is insidious in onset. At first it wears off with exercise but gradually becomes permanent. The horse goes on its toe and this leads to stumbling. With the passage of time the shape of the foot changes, the heels contract, the frog atrophies and the sole becomes vaulted.

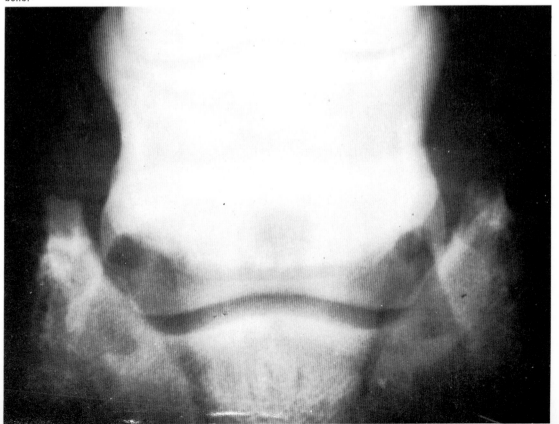

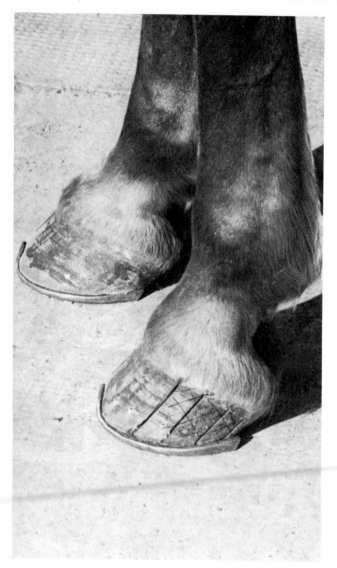

Fig. 319. A case of navicular disease treated by grooving the heels and fitting a rolled toe shoe with raised heels.

Shoeing. Navicular disease is incurable, but in an early case the pain can be alleviated, stumbling prevented and the usefulness of the horse prolonged by attention to its shoeing. The horse's action is assisted and much improved by fitting a rolled toe shoe with raised or wedge heels (*Fig. 319*), which conforms in shape to the worn shoe.

SANDCRACK

A sandcrack is a fissure of the wall which commences at the coronet and extends a variable distance down the hoof. Sandcracks are classified by their position, toe or quarter sandcracks; by by their length, as complete or incomplete, depending on the distance they extend from the coronet towards the bearing surface; and by their severity, as simple if only the horn is involved, complicated if the sensitive structures are affected, and suppurating if infected.

Cases occur most frequently when the horn is dry and brittle such as during hot weather, or when the periople has been destroyed by excessive rasping of the wall. They develop spontaneously and especially when the horse is moving at a fast pace on a hard surface and sustains a sudden abnormal distribution of its weight by treading on an uneven surface.

Clinical features. As a rule the crack is obvious and if the sensitive foot is involved the horse is acutely lame.

Treatment. This is directed to removing pressure from the free extremity of the crack and to immobilising its edges. With a *superficial sandcrack* these objects can be attained by cutting two grooves to isolate it. If it is incomplete the two grooves should be cut, in the form of a V, from the coronet to the extremity of the crack (*Fig. 320* [*a*]), but if it is complete then two parallel grooves are cut, one on each side of the crack from the coronet to the bearing surface (*Fig. 320* [*b*]).

To relieve pressure on and effectively immobilise the edges of a sandcrack the grooves must be about 1/5″ wide and cut to the depth of the white line. Also, the bearing surface at the extremity of a complete crack is eased to prevent any pressure from the shoe at this point.

A *complicated sandcrack* requires its edges to be held together by some mechanical method of fixation to obtain their immobilisation. This is attained by either applying special sandcrack clips, or by driving a horse shoe nail across the crack.

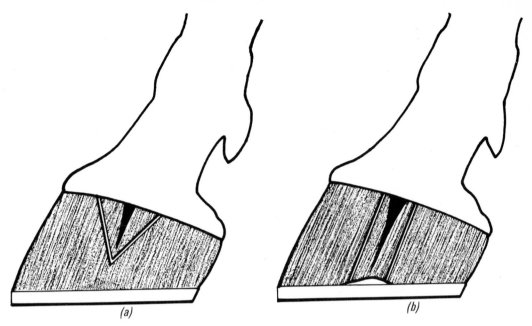

(a)   *(b)*

Fig. 320. (a) Superficial sandcrack, incomplete. Two grooves are cut from the coronet in the form of a V to meet at the lower limit of the crack; *(b)* Superficial sandcrack, complete. Two parallel grooves are cut, one on each side of the crack, from the coronet to the bearing surface.

Immobilising the edges of a complicated sand-crack using a standard horseshoe nail.

(*Fig. 321*). A typical complicated sandcrack extending from the coronet to the bearing surface of the foot.

(*Fig. 322*). After cleaning out, and paring the edges of the sandcrack the special tool, heated to a dull red heat, is used to fashion a bed for the nail on each side of the sandcrack. If only one nail is to be used the beds are fashioned just above the centre of the sandcrack with the inner edge of the bed about a $\frac{1}{4}$" from the edge of the sandcrack. If two nails are used then the proximal nail is inserted $\frac{1}{2}$" below the coronet and the other nail $\frac{3}{4}$" below it.

(*Fig. 323*). A horseshoe nail, slightly bent on flat, is driven across the sandcrack.

(*Fig. 324*). The nail is driven home using the point of a buffer as a punch.

(*Fig. 325*). The point of the nail is turned over and cut off with pincers.

(*Fig. 326*). The end of the nail is turned over and tapped into position whilst the head of the nail is retained in position with the end of a handle of the pincers.

(*Fig. 327*). Procedure completed. The edges of a complicated sandcrack immobilised with a horseshoe nail.

Shoeing. When the foot takes weight the sandcrack opens; therefore, a shoe which puts extra weight on any part of the bearing surface, such as one with thickened heels or calkins, is contraindicated. In most cases all that is

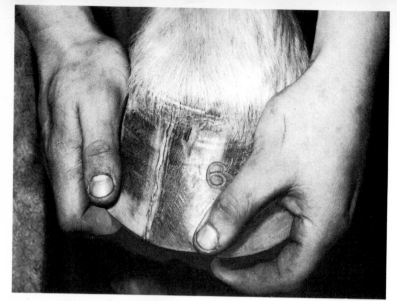

Fig. 321. A typical complicated sandcrack extending from the coronet to the bearing surface of the foot.

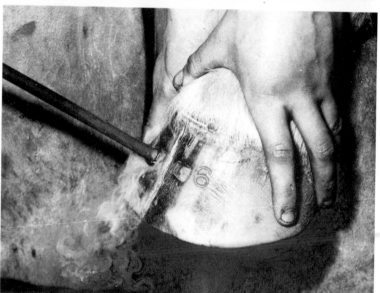

Fig. 322. After paring the edges of the sandcrack a special tool, heated to a dull red heat, is used to fashion a bed for the nail on each side of the sandcrack. If only one nail is to be used the beds are fashioned just above the centre of the sandcrack with the inner edge of the bed about a $\frac{1}{4}''$ from the edge of the sandcrack. If two nails are used then the proximal nail is inserted $\frac{1}{2}''$ below the coronet and the other nail $\frac{3}{4}''$ below it.

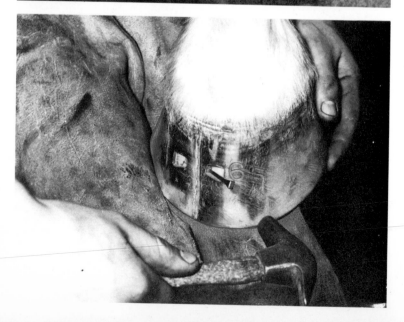

Fig. 323. A horseshoe nail, slightly bent on flat, is driven across the sandcrack.

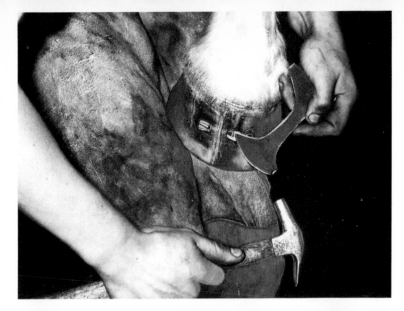

Fig. 324. The nail is driven home using the point of a buffer as a punch.

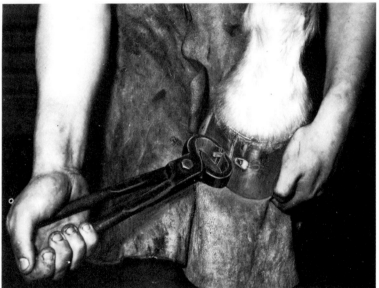

Fig. 325. The point of the nail is turned over and cut off with pincers.

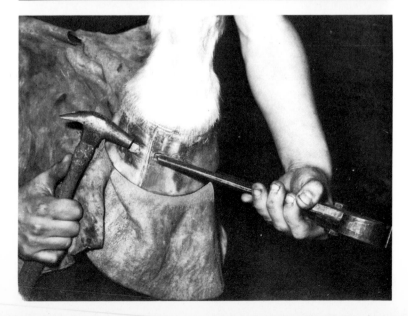

Fig. 326. The end of the nail is turned over and tapped into position whilst the head of the nail is retained in position with the end of a handle of the pincers.

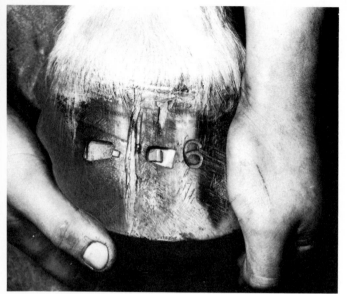

Fig. 327. Procedure completed, the edges of a complicated sandcrack immobilised with a horseshoe nail.

required is a plain flat shoe with toe or quarter clips. Easing the shoe immediately under the sandcrack is often practised, but the cavity soon fills with dirt and grit which increases pressure and can lead to infection.

For draught horses a bar shoe, with $\frac{1}{2}''$ to $\frac{3}{4}''$ of the branch cut out immediately under the crack, is popular. The gap prevents any direct pressure on the crack and as horses with sand-cracks, especially at the toe, go on their heels the bar assists their action.

False sandcrack (*Fig. 328*). A false sandcrack is a single simple crack in the wall which commences at the bearing surface and extends a variable distance up the hoof. It is most liable to occur in dry and brittle hooves, and especially if the shoe has been left on for too long or has been fitted too close, and in consequence the wall protrudes over the edge of the shoe.

All that is required in these cases to prevent the crack from extending is to cut a horizontal groove across its apex, $\frac{1}{2}''$ to $\frac{3}{4}''$ in length and down to the white line and relieve pressure on its extremity by either easing the bearing surface of the wall or the foot surface of the shoe.

SEEDY TOE

A seedy toe results from the separation of the horny and sensitive laminae at the toe to form a cavity which is filled with a crumbling and mealy type of horn (*Fig. 329*).

Clinical features. It is generally first discovered by the farrier when the foot is being dressed. In simple cases the cavity is about $1''$ deep and lameness is not present unless complicated by infection, or by an accumulation of dirt and grit pressing on the sensitive foot.

Treatment. In simple cases this consists of scooping out the degenerate horn and packing the cavity with tow and Stockholm tar. In more extensive cases the wall over the whole of the cavity has to be removed, the dressing being kept in place either by fixing a plate of metal to the wall or by filling the cavity with plastic horn.

Shoeing. Fit a plain shoe with a wide web at the toe to protect the bearing surface and to retain the dressing. If it is considered necessary to take weight off the seedy toe then seat out the

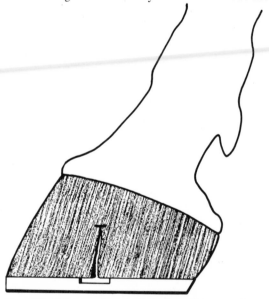

Fig. 328. False sandcrack. A horizontal groove is cut across the apex to prevent it extending and the base is relieved of pressure either by easing the foot surface of the shoe or the bearing surface of the wall, Fig. 320 (b).

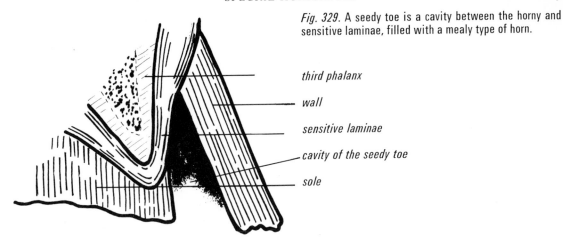

Fig. 329. A seedy toe is a cavity between the horny and sensitive laminae, filled with a mealy type of horn.

third phalanx

wall

sensitive laminae

cavity of the seedy toe

sole

shoe over that area. No clips should be placed or nails driven near the cavity. In extensive cases it may be necessary to provide extra protection by fitting a leather pad or a hoof cushion.

SIDEBONE DISEASE

Sidebone disease is an ossification of the lateral cartilages (*Fig. 330*). It is very common in

draught horses and the external cartilage of their front feet is most frequently affected.

The actual cause of sidebone formation is not clear. It is recognised as an hereditary disease, and a direct blow and concussion are accepted causes. There is a natural tendency for cartilage contiguous with bone to become ossified and this may account for many cases.

Fig. 330. Sidebone disease. Ossification commences at the attachment of the lateral cartilage to the wing of the third phalanx and gradually extends to involve the whole of the cartilage.

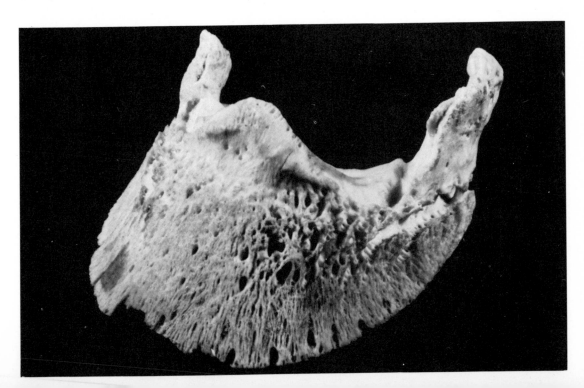

Clinical features. As the cartilage ossifies it gradually loses its elasticity, becomes progressively more rigid and sometimes assumes an enormous size. In these cases it projects above the coronet which overhangs the wall.

Lameness is not a feature of sidebone disease, although it sometimes occurs during the formation of sidebones, and especially in cases with contracted feet which prevent normal expansion of the posterior part of the foot. In these cases the branch of the shoe on the affected side wears progressively thinner from the quarter to the heel.

Treatment. Unless lameness is present no treatment is indicated. When lameness is present which is due to compression between the ossifying cartilage and the non-yielding wall,

especially when complicated by a contracted foot, then relief may be obtained by grooving the heels (*Fig. 296*) which by allowing expansion, reduces pressure and relieves pain.

Shoeing. The best shoe to fit is one which corresponds to the worn shoe (*Fig. 331*). In a unilateral case the branch of the shoe on the affected side requires to be gradually thinned down from the nail hole at the toe to the end of the heel and the width of the web gradually increased so that its outer edge corresponds with the outline of the overhanging coronet. This branch extends a little beyond the heel and to allow for expansion it is left blind.

Horses with bilateral sidebone disease wear the toe of the shoe and their action is improved by fitting a rolled toe shoe with raised heels.

Fig. 331. A shoe for sidebone disease. The branch is thinned down and gradually increased in width from the toe to the heel and is blind except for the two nail-holes at the toe.

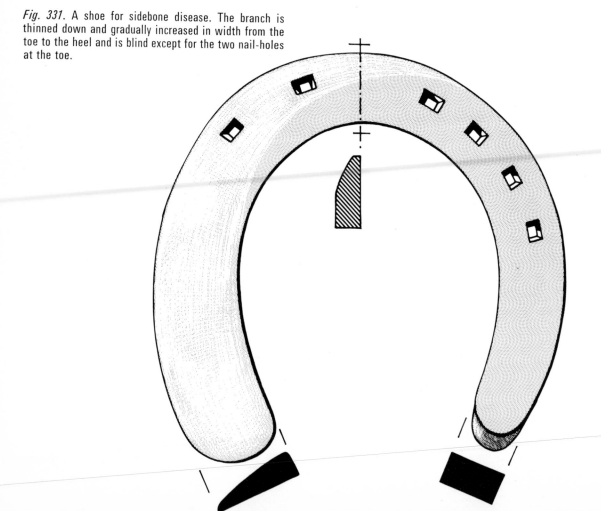

BONE SPAVIN DISEASE

Bone spavin disease is an osteoarthritis involving the medial aspects of the intertarsal and tarso-metatarsal joints, and is characterised by new bone formation at the margins (*Fig. 332*).

Clinical features. These comprise local signs and the type of lameness. The most pertinent local sign is a distortion of the outline of the medial and the lower aspect of the hock by the new bone formation at the so-called "seat of spavin". The lameness is distinguished by imperfect flexion of the hock and is due to the pain caused by compression. In consequence the horse goes on and drags its toe which results in abnormal wear of the shoe at the toe.

Shoeing. To overcome the horse dragging its toe and to facilitate its action, the toe is shortened and a shoe fitted with a rolled toe and raised heels. As calkins are inclined to catch in the ground it is recommended they are replaced by sloping wedge heels (*Fig. 333*). These measures certainly improve the horse's action but do not allay the gradual development of chronic contraction of the flexor tendons.

SPRAINED JOINT

A sprained joint occurs when a joint, as a result of an accident, passes beyond its normal range of movement and stretches or tears the joint capsule and periarticular structures.

Healing is by fibrous tissue laid down in the structures damaged and is followed by a reduction in the normal range of joint movement.

The fetlock joint is most commonly affected and is characterised by enlargement and restriction of normal movements, particularly flexion, which leads to stumbling.

In these cases the horse's action varies considerably. Some wear only the toe of the shoe whilst others wear both the toe and the heel. The new shoe should be made to conform with the wear of the old shoe, which always requires the toe to be rolled and in some cases has to be combined with lowering the heels.

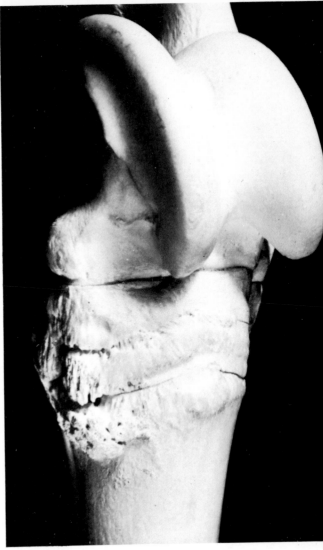

Fig. 332. Bone spavin disease. A bone spavin is an osteoarthritis which involves the medial aspect of the intertarsal and tarso-metatarsal joints.

Fig. 333. Shoe for bone spavin disease. The toe of the foot is shortened and a shoe is fitted with a rolled toe and sloping wedge heels which do not catch and allow the foot to slide.

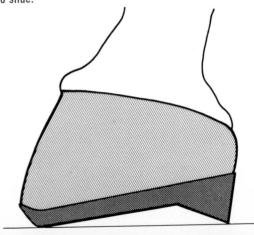

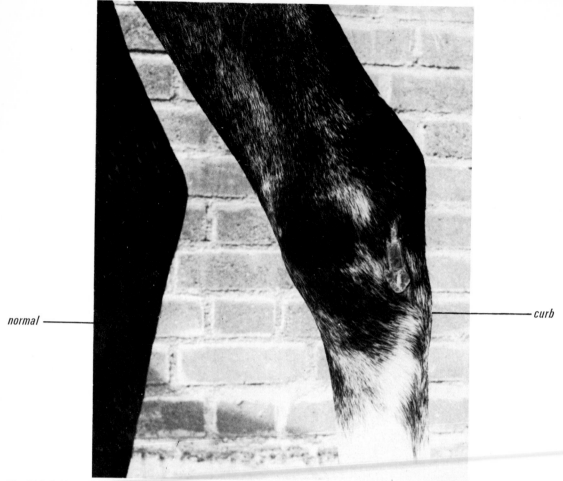

normal ———   ——— curb

Fig. 334. A ''curb'' is a sprain of the plantar ligament.

SPRAINED LIGAMENT

A sprain of the plantar ligament is called a "curb" and is recognised as a localised swelling on the postero-inferior aspect of the horse's hock (*Fig. 334*).

The condition is most frequently seen in riding horses and occurs either as a result of hyperflexion of the hock when a horse is pulled up sharply and thrown back on its hocks, or when jumping when violent attempts are made to extend the hock.

To relieve tension on the sprained ligament the horse stands with its heels raised, and goes markedly on its toe.

Shoeing. To relieve tension on the plantar ligament the horse should have the heels of the shoe raised. Calkins are contra-indicated as they cause too much resistance and therefore a shoe with a sloping wedge heel that does not catch and allows the foot to slide is recommended.

SPLINTS

A splint is an exostosis which develops upon a small metacarpal or metatarsal bone. It is most frequently encountered in young horses, up to 6 years of age, doing fast work on hard surfaces. Splints are classified according to their size, position and shape (*Fig. 335*). A small, well defined exostosis is simply termed "a splint", if it encroaches on the knee joint, a "knee" splint, and a number of splints along the edge of the bone is referred to as a "chain" splint.

The cause of a splint is concussion which results in a sprain of the interosseous ligament and a tearing of the adjacent periostium. The inner splint bone is more commonly affected and this may be accounted for by direct weight bearing between it and the second carpal bone, whereas on the lateral aspect the fourth carpal bone articulates with both the large and small metacarpal bones.

Clinical features. The local signs are pain and swelling. The degree of lameness is directly related to concussion. Lameness increases with exercise, is more severe on hard than on soft ground and a horse which walks almost sound will be very lame at the trot. But once the inflammatory symptons have subsided and the splint is no longer active the horse will go sound provided the splint does not interfere with the action of the knee, the suspensory ligament or the flexor tendons.

Shoeing. Treatment is based on limiting concussion which can be achieved by complete rest in a loose box. A variety of shoes both with and without foot pads have been used to reduce concussion and thereby relieve splint lameness. The results have been disappointing. All that can be done, or indeed is required, is to ensure an even distribution of concussion by a level bearing surface and a well fitted shoe.

In severe cases a hoof cushion to reduce concussion, and a rolled toe shoe with raised heels to assist breaking-over of the foot, may be helpful.

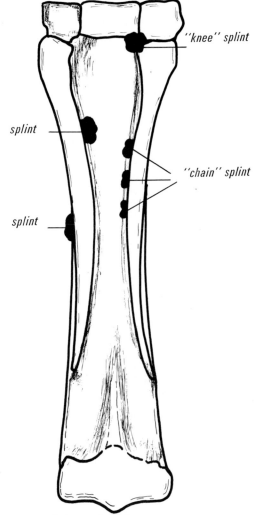

Fig. 335. Types of splint.

STRAINED TENDON

A strained tendon is the term used to describe an aseptic inflammation of a tendon following severe stress, and when applied to horses generally refers to a strain of the superficial and deep flexors of the legs.

It is invariably due to some incoordinate movement, which results in the tendon fibres being torn and is accompanied by heat, pain and swelling.

Shoeing. In an acute case the horse is severely lame and pain can be relieved by raising the heels to reduce tension on the tendons. This may be accomplished by raising the heels with a Patten shoe (*Fig. 336*). The height of the heels will range from 1" to 3" depending on the severity of the injury and the type of horse.

Fig. 336. Patten shoe. Basically this is a shoe with the calkins joined by a bar which is set on obliquely to rest flat on the ground.

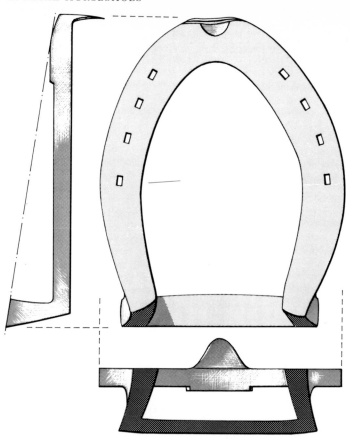

Fig. 337. Swan-necked shoe. The heels of the shoe are continued upwards to the height of the ventral surface of the normal fetlock, and bent at right angles for 2 inches. The branches are then continued downwards and backwards to the ground level of the shoe. The top of the two branches is joined by a bar, which is padded, to form a platform on which the fetlock rests.

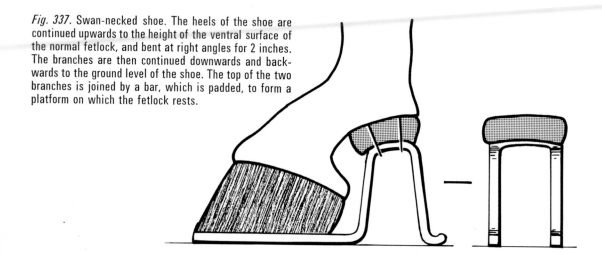

Marmaduke Loves Tasty, Chewable Filaribits®

(diethylcarbamazine citrate)

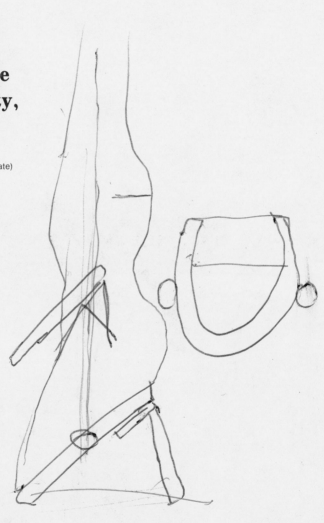

Strained tendons heal by fibrosis which is accompanied by contraction. Therefore, as healing progresses the height of the heels must be gradually reduced; if not, chronic contraction and shortening of the tendon will result and the horse will be unable to get its heels to the ground. It is doubtful if a Patten shoe has a place in the treatment of strained tendons. Pressure bandaging or a plaster of Paris cast provide the necessary support to reduce tension and as pain is relieved and healing takes place the horse is not prevented from taking normal weight. This gradual and increasing tension on the injured tendon during healing prevents its excessive contraction and shortening.

RUPTURED TENDON

When the deep digital flexor is ruptured the fetlock sinks and the toe turns up. If the suspensory ligament is also ruptured then the fetlock and pastern rest on the ground.

Shoeing. To assist healing the ends of the ruptured tendon must be retained in close apposition and this can be attained by supporting the lowered fetlock with a swan-necked shoe (*Fig. 337*).

This is a most useful shoe which has a very definite place in the treatment of rupture of the tendon of the deep digital flexor and suspensory ligament.

It is surprising how quickly horses adapt to this shoe and how soon they move freely around, but care must be taken not to bed them on straw as they can get easily tangled up, fall and injure themselves.

Glossary

A

ABAXIAL — not situated in the axis of the body, away from the centre line.

ABSCESS — a localised collection of pus.

ACUTE — sharp, having severe symptoms persisting for a short time.

ADHESION — abnormal joining of parts to each other.

AFFERENT — conducting towards a centre.

ALLOY — a mixture of metals.

ANASTOMOSIS — a communication between two tubular organs or a connection between two normally distinct organs.

ANATOMY — the science dealing with the form and structure of living organisms.

ANNEAL — to soften metal by controlled heating and cooling to make its manipulation easier.

ANTERIOR — situated at or directed towards the front, the opposite of posterior.

ANTISEPTIC — a substance which inhibits the growth of micro-organisms.

ANKYLOSIS — abnormal immobility and consolidation of a joint.

ARTERY — a vessel in which oxygenated blood flows away from the heart.

ARTICULATION — the place of union or junction between two or more bones of the skeleton, a joint.

ATROPHY — decrease in size of a normally developed organ, or tissue, wasting.

AXIS — straight line through a centre, centre line of the body or any part of it.

B

BASILAR — pertaining to the base.

BEARING SURFACE — of foot, surface in contact with the ground.

BORIUM — trade name for tungsten carbide, a very hard material.

BREAK-OVER — point in the stride at which the foot leaves the ground.

BROKEN-IN — of foot, when the medial aspect of the wall is lower than the lateral side.

BROKEN-OUT — of foot, when lateral aspect of the wall is lower than the medial side.

BURR — small piece of metal in or over a nail-hole.

BURSA — a sac containing synovia interposed at points of pressure between a tendon and bone or between tendons.

BURSITIS — inflammation of a bursa.

C

CALKIN — projection on the ground surface of the heel of a horseshoe.

CANCELLOUS BONE — the lattice-like structure in bone.

CAPILLARY — hair-like extremity of an artery or vein.

CARBOHYDRATE — an organic compound of carbon and water.

CARPUS — the bones comprising the articulation between the radius and metacarpal bones, in the horse the knee joint.

CARTILAGE — the gristle or white elastic substance attached to the articular surface of a bone.

CAUDAL — pertaining to the posterior or distal ends, nearest the tail.

CHAMFERED	–	surface sloped or bevelled off.
CHRONIC	–	persisting for a long time, the opposite of acute.
CLENCH	–	stub of shank of horseshoe nail that is bent over where it emerges from the hoof.
CLIP	–	a small projection anywhere along the outside or inside edge of the foot surface of a horseshoe.
COLLATERAL	–	being by the side, subsidiary.
CONDYLE	–	rounded eminence at articular end of a bone.
CONGENITAL	–	present at and existing from the time of birth.
CORIUM	–	fibrous inner layer of skin which is well supplied with blood vessels and nerves and contains the hair roots, sebacious and sweat glands.
CRANIAL	–	pertaining to the cranium, surface of limb or organ towards the head.
CREASE	–	depression on the ground surface of a shoe in which the nail-holes are located, the fullering-groove.
CRUCIATE	–	shaped like a cross.
CYST	–	a cavity lined by epithelium and containing fluid or semi-solid material.

D

DEGENERATION	–	alteration to a lower or to a less healthy state.
DIAPHYSIS	–	the shaft of a long bone between the epiphyses.
DIGIT	–	toe, portion of leg below the fetlock joint.
DISINFECTANT	–	an agent which destroys infection-producing organisms.
DISTAL	–	farthest from a point of reference, as from a centre, median line.
DORSAL	–	directed toward or situated on the back surface, opposite to ventral.
DUMPED	–	hoof rasped away at toe to make a shoe fit which does not conform to the outline of the foot.

E

EFFERENT	–	conducting or progressing away from a centre.
ENDOSTIUM	–	the lining membrane of a hollow bone.
EPIDERMIS	–	the outermost, non-vascular layer of the skin.
EPIPHYIS	–	portion of a bone which in early life is distinct from the shaft, the ends of a long bone.
EPITHELIUM	–	the cellular layer lining the alimentary tract, the outer layer of mucous membranes and the skin.
EXOSTOSIS	–	a new growth of bone protruding from the outer surface of a bone.
EXTENSION	–	an increase in the angle of a joint, straightening a flexed limb.

F

FLEXION	–	the act of bending, a decrease in the angle of a joint.
FOOT	–	hoof and all the structures contained therein.
FOOT POUND	–	the amount of energy necessary to raise one pound of mass a distance of one foot.
FOOT SURFACE	–	surface of shoe in contact with the hoof.
FORAMEN	–	an opening in various tissues of the body for the passage of other structures, such as blood vessels and nerves.

G

GANGRENE — death of tissue, associated with loss of blood supply, followed by invasion of bacteria and putrefaction.

GELATIN — a transparent substance forming a jelly in water derived from skin and bones.

GROUND SURFACE — surface of horseshoe in contact with the ground.

H

HYPERTROPHY — increase in volume of a tissue or organ produced entirely by enlargement of existing cells.

I

INFERIOR — below or lower.

INFLAMMATION — a protective tissue response to injury or destruction of the cells characterised by heat, pain and swelling, and loss of function.

INORGANIC — not having the organs or instruments of life, not having organic structure such as metals, rocks etc.

INTRA- — word element, inside of, within.

INTER- — word element, between.

L

LAMINA — a thin, flat plate or layer.

LAMINITIS — inflammation of the sensitive laminae of the horse's foot.

LATERAL — pertaining to or situated at the side.

LEG — lower extremity of limb distal to knee or hock joint.

LESION — site of structural or functional change in body tissues produced by disease or injury.

LIMB — leg and all the component parts which join it to the body.

M

MALIGNANT — progressing in virulence.

MARROW — soft inorganic material filling the cavities of bones.

MEDIAL — pertaining to or situated towards the midline.

MEDULLA — the middle, applied to the marrow cavity of bones.

METAPHYSIS — the wider part at the end of the shaft of a long bone, adjacent to the epiphysis.

MUCOUS MEMBRANE — membrane covered with epithelium which secretes mucus, and lines canals and cavities.

O

OEDEMA — an abnormal accumulation of fluid in intercellular spaces of the body.

ORGANIC — pertaining to or having organs and pertaining to carbon compounds produced by living animals or plants.

OSSIFICATION — formation of or conversion into bone.

OSTEOARTHRITIS — hypertrophic degenerative joint disease.

OSTEOBLAST — an immature bone producing cell.

P

PAPILLA	–	a small projection or elevation, nipple-shaped.
PATHOLOGY	–	the scientific study of the alterations produced by disease.
PATELLA	–	a short bone which articulates with the distal end of the femur to form the femoro-patella articulation of the stifle joint, the knee-cap of man.
PECTORAL	–	pertaining to the chest.
PERIARTICULAR	–	situated around a joint.
PERICHONDRIUM	–	the membrane covering the surface of a cartilage.
PERIOSTEUM	–	a specialised connective tissue covering bones and having bone-forming properties.
PHALANX	–	any bone of a digit or toe.
PHYSIOLOGY	–	the science dealing with the function of various parts and organs of living organisms.
PLEXUS	–	network of blood vessels or nerves.
POSTERIOR	–	directed towards or situated at the back, opposite of anterior.
PROPHYLACTIC	–	tending to ward off disease.
PROTEIN	–	a compound containing carbon, hydrogen, oxygen, nitrogen and usually sulphur and phosphorus.
PROXIMAL	–	nearest to a point of reference, as to a centre or median line, or to the point of attachment or origin.
PUS	–	a thick fluid composed of living and dead white blood cells with partially liquified necrotic tissue debris.
PYRAMIDAL	–	pointed or cone-shaped structure or part.
PLANTAR	–	pertaining to the sole of the foot.

R

RAMIFY	–	to branch, to diverge in different directions.
RAREFACTION	–	condition of being or becoming less dense.
REFLEX	–	directed backwards, an automatic response to a given stimulus.
RHOMBOID	–	shaped like a kite.

S

SEATING OUT	–	hammering down and bevelling the inside of the foot surface of a shoe.
SEMILUNAR	–	shaped like a half-moon.
SESAMOID	–	shaped like a sesame seed, nodular.
SHAFT	–	the mass of a simple elongate structure, as a long bone, between the extremities.
SINUS	–	an abnormal channel permitting the escape of pus.
SUPERIOR	–	above or upper.
SUPERFICIAL	–	situated on or near the surface.
SYNOVIA	–	a transparent, viscid fluid secreted by synovial membranes and found in joint cavities, bursae and tendon sheaths.

T

TARSUS	–	the bones comprising the articulation between the tibia and the metatarsal bones, in the horse the hock joint.
TENDINITIS	–	inflammation of a tendon.

TENOSYNOVITIS   –   inflammation of a tendon sheath.
TRAUMATIC   –   pertaining to external force which damages the organism.
TUBEROSITY   –   an elevation or protuberance.

V

VENTRAL   –   directed towards or situated on the belly surface, opposite of dorsal.
VEIN   –   a vessel in which blood flows towards the heart, carrying blood that has
                           given up most of its oxygen.
VOLAR   –   pertaining to sole or palm, posterior surface of a horse's leg.

Bibliography

ADAMS, O. R. *Lameness in horses*, 3rd edition. Lea and Febiger, Philadelphia (1974).

BLUNDEVILLE,* Thomas *The Fower chiefyst offices belongyng to Horsemanshippe*. Wyllyam Seres, London (1565).

BRIDGES,* Jeremiah *No foot, no horse; an essay on the anatomy of the foot of that noble and useful animal a horse*. J. Brindlay and R. Baldwin, London (1752).

BOURGELAT, Claude *Essai théorique et pratique sur la ferrure*, 3rd edition. Huzard, Paris (1813).

BUTLER, D. *The Principles of horseshoeing*. Doug Butler, Ithaca, New York 14850 (1974).

CLARK, Bracy *A series of original experiments on the foot of the living horse, exhibiting the changes produced by shoeing, and the causes of the apparent mystery of this art*. B. Clark, London (1809).

CLARK, James *Observations on the shoeing of horses: together with a new inquiry into the causes of diseases in the feet of horses*. 3rd edition. William Creech, Edinburgh; T. Cadell and T. Longman, London (1782).

COLEMAN, Edward *Observations on the structure, economy and diseases of the foot of the horse, and on the principles and practice of shoeing*. Edward Coleman, London (1798–1802).

CRANFIELD, D. M. *Elements of farrier science*, 2nd edition. Albert Lea, Enderes Tool Company, Minnesota 56007 (1968).

DOLLAR, J. A. W. and WHEATLEY, A. *A handbook of horseshoeing, with introductory chapters on the anatomy and physiology of the horse's foot*. David Douglas, Edinburgh (1898).

FIASCHI,* Caesar. *Traité de le manière de bien emboucher, manier, et ferrer les chevaux*. Dédié au Roi Henri II, C. Perrier, Paris (1564).

FITZWYGRAM, Lieut. Col, F. *Notes on Shoeing Horses*, 2nd edition. Smith, Elder & Company, London (1863).

FITZWYGRAM, Lieut. Gen, Sir Frederick *Horses and Stables*, 5th edition. Longmans, Green & Company, London (1903).

*As quoted by Fleming in *Horse-shoes and horse-shoeing*.

FLEMING, George *Horse-shoes and horse-shoeing*. Chapman and Hall, London (1869).

FLEMING, George *Practical horse-shoeing*, 3rd edition. Chapman and Hall, London (1878).

GAMGEE, Joseph *A treatise on horse-shoeing and lameness*, Longmans, Green & Company, London (1871).

GOODWIN, Joseph *A new system of shoeing horses: with an account of the various modes practiced by different nations*. Longman, Hurst, Rus, Orme and Brown, London (1820).

HOLMES, C. M. *The principles and practice of horse-shoeing*. The Farrier's Journal Publishing Company, Leeds (1949).

HUNTING, William *The art of horse-shoeing*, 4th edition. Revised and edited by A. B. Mattinson, Bailliere, Tindall & Cox, London (1922).

LAFOSSE, Etienne Guillaume *Observations et découvertes faites sur des chevaux, avec une nouvelle pratique sur la ferrure*. Hochereau le jeune, Paris (1754).

LUNGWITZ, A. and ADAMS, J. W. *A textbook of horseshoeing for horseshoers and veterinarians*, 11th edition. 1913. Reprinted Oregon State University Press (1966).

MACQUEEN, J. *Fleming's practical horse-shoeing*, 11th edition. Bailliere, Tindall & Cox, London (1921).

MEGNIN, J. P. *De l'origine de la ferrure du cheval*. P. Asselin, Paris (1865).

MOORCROFT, W. *Cursory account of the various methods of shoeing horses, hitherto practised, with incidental observations*. W. Moorcroft, London (1800).

MILLER, W. C. and ROBERTSON, E. D. S. *Practical animal husbandry*, 5th edition. Oliver and Boyd, Edinburgh (1947).

OSMER, William *A treatise on the diseases and lameness of horses, in which is laid down a proper method of shoeing*. Wilson and Whitehouse, Dublin (1746).

REEKS, H. Caulton *Diseases of the horse's foot*. Bailliere, Tindall & Cox, London (1906).

RUINI,* Carlo *Dell' anatomia e dell' infermita dell cavallo*. Heredi di G. Roffi, Bologna (1598).

SIMONS, M. A. P. *The future of farriery*, Veterinary Record, 98, 4 (1976).

SISSON, S. and GROSSMAN, J. D. *The anatomy of the domestic animals*, 4th edition. Saunders, Philadelphia (1953).

SMITH, F. *A manual of veterinary physiology*, 3rd edition. Bailliere, Tindall and Cox, London (1907).

SMITH, Maj. Gen, Sir Frederick *A History of the Royal Army Veterinary Corps 1796–1919*. Bailliere, Tindall and Cox, London (1927).

SNAPE,* Andrew *The anatomy of the horse*, T. Flesher, London (1683).

SOLLEYSEL, Jacques Labessie, de *The complete horseman or, perfect farrier*. Translated into English by Sir William Hope. 2nd edition R. Bonwicke, T. Goodwin, London (1706).

SPRINGHALL, J. A. *Elements of horseshoeing*. University of Queensland Press, Brisbane (1964).

WALKER, R. E. *Bulletin of the Veterinary History Society*. No. 1 (1972).

WISEMAN, R. F. *The complete horseshoeing guide*, 2nd edition. University of Oklahoma Press (1974).

YOUATT,* William *The Horse*. Baldwin and Cradock, London (1846).

*As quoted by Fleming in *Horse-shoes and horse-shoeing*.

Index